The Easier Way to Sew for Your Family

Books by Mary Johnson

SEWING THE EASY WAY

SEW FOR YOUR CHILDREN

MARY JOHNSON'S GUIDE TO ALTERING
AND RESTYLING READY-MADE CLOTHES

THE EASIER WAY TO SEW FOR YOUR FAMILY

The Easier Way to Sew for Your Family

BY MARY JOHNSON

E. P. DUTTON & CO., INC. | New York | 1972

Published simultaneously in Canada
by Clarke, Irwin & Company Limited, Toronto and Vancouver

Library of Congress Catalog Card Number: 70–189131
SBN 0–525–096620

Portions of this book are taken from
SEW FOR YOUR CHILDREN by Mary Johnson.

To Tom, Gail, Laura and Carol

Contents

1. Sew for Your Family   11

2. Clothes for the Teen-age Girl and You   33

3. The Glamorous Evening Dress (with Underlining)   66

4. Making Separate Skirts, Pants, and Shorts   83

5. Tailoring Coats and Jackets   102

6. Little Girls' Dresses for All Occasions   151

7. All About Shirts   162

8. Putting New Life into Outgrown Clothes   171

9. How to Handle Various Fabrics   180

10. Bound Buttonholes and All Types of Pockets   193

11. Fashion Detailing   213

    Index   237

The Easier Way to Sew for Your Family

1

Sew for Your Family

Why sew?

Every woman likes to see her family attractively dressed. Her pleasure is even greater when she sees them dressed in clothing she herself has made. The fun of choosing fabrics, colors, and styles to suit each individual member is doubly gratifying: it gives her an outlet for her own good taste, and does so at a price she can well afford.

True, a flair for choosing nice things can be equally well expressed in ready-made clothing. But the woman with discriminating taste can't always afford to buy the things she likes, especially if she must dress several children on a limited budget. She can exercise her sense of style to her heart's content, with no financial pressure, when she sews for her growing family.

What about the beginner?

The ability to make handsome wearing apparel is not limited to the woman with extensive sewing experience and plenty of spare time. It is within the reach of every woman who likes good quality. Following the infallible modern sewing methods and short-cut techniques that are outlined in this book, anyone can turn out nicely fitting, well-made clothing with her very first attempt. The work will be easy and her progress smooth. She will do things correctly the very first time.

Even the woman who has just learned how to thread her sewing machine can make clothes comparable to those made by her experienced friends. When you stop to think about it, this is not surprising. It is a known fact that when a beginner decides to follow exactly a set of instructions which she is convinced are foolproof, she is apt to turn out better-finished results than those of an experienced sewer. Her desire to do a good job compels her to pursue instructions faithfully and completely, and because she has never sewed before, she wouldn't know how to deviate from them if she wanted to. Her very ignorance is a safeguard, for she has no previously learned bad sewing habits to unlearn! Thus, with ease and accuracy, she produces praiseworthy results in her very first sewing project.

On the other hand, an experienced sewer may become so engrossed in mastering some tricky detail that challenges her sewing ability that she fails to do full justice to the more basic and simple steps involved in her project. Just a matter of pressing darts in the wrong direction or trimming a seam improperly may cause disappointment. Good-looking clothes are not always those designed with intricate lines and details. A style involving simple construction steps can be equally lovely, if the work is properly handled and the garment is fitted to perfection.

Don't feel concerned if the order of the steps for assembling garments, as well as the actual construction of the individual parts, is different from the system described in the guide sheet that comes with your pattern. The simplified steps and short-cut techniques in this book are aimed to take the struggle out of sewing, and to make it the fun it should be. All unnecessary steps have been eliminated. In their stead are simple, logical, easy-to-understand instructions to give you confidence in your own ability. Even the experienced seamstress will find help here.

With this modern approach sewing time is cut to a minimum, so that even the busiest mother can make the important garments for her family and still have time to do her share of community service and family chauffeuring.

Many an indulgent mother has been known to do without something she would have liked for herself just to see that the children are well dressed. This need not be, once she learns to sew. Everyone in the family benefits from her accomplishments. Lovely things can be made at home for one third the cost of comparable ready-mades, so dressing three children for the price of one is no great feat. The trick is to analyze what to make yourself, and what should be purchased ready-made. Make only the items that will save you money. In this way the clothing dollar will stretch further, and you will not wear yourself out uselessly at the sewing machine.

Sew what?

It is not practical to sew everything either for yourself or for family members. You can purchase some things ready-made for the same money, or even less than what you would spend for the material, pattern, and notions such as thread, zipper, buttons, and seam binding needed to complete the item at home.

A perfect example is sleep-wear for children. In considering the eventual cost, you should add up the price of the material needed, plus the pattern, the buttonholes that you may have to have commercially made, unless you own a machine that makes them at home, and the buttons and elastic. In addition you should consider that such garments have to be made with a special kind of seam, called flat-fell seaming, or French seams, which require two separate operations. These take twice the time of simple seams and are not as easy to sew. Instead of making a pair of pajama pants, you could in less time be running up a pair of pants for a girl or boy to wear to school. In less than the time it takes to make the pajama top, you can make an extra special blouse or shirt to go with the pants.

The same considerations apply to making such garments for grown-ups, unless for some reason or other, they cannot be fitted in ready-mades. Sleep-wear manufacturers do a tremendous job of taking care of the whole family and they sell their wares at prices most of us can afford. Where you save money, and yourself, is in making the major items of apparel, so here is where it is best to spend your time and talent, as well as your energy.

Sewing for teen-agers

Nothing brings mother and daughters closer together than planning new sewing projects, whether the item is to be an addition to the school wardrobe, a dress for some special occasion, or a gown for the prom. This makes for a fine relationship and, once developed, it continues even when the young lady starts to sew for herself. Every now and then she'll consult her mother if she hits a snag, knowing that she'll get the help she needs. The girl who grows up in a home where sewing is one of the "performing arts" will continue to be interested in sewing when she has her own home, and eventually she will pass the interest on to her own girls, especially if sewing is associated with fun, delightful results, and financial gain, all at once.

Boys take just as much pride in the things their mothers make for them as their sisters do. Mention that you have seen some fabric that would make your growing son a great-looking sport jacket, and see him do a double take. He's likely not to leave you alone until you put the job in the works, and as you sit at the sewing machine he may hang over your shoulder, supervising the project, ready to try the jacket on at the drop of a pin! Is there anything wrong with such "togetherness"? Not on your sweet life, so encourage it.

Those "blessed" fads

Don't expect to agree with teen-aged offspring on all their choices of wearing apparel. Fads come and go and wearing them when they are "the thing" is part of the fun of being that age. Their choices, boys' as well as girls', will now and then cause you to gasp, but try to look at these decisions from their angle, and if the investment in money and time is not too great, they'll love you just that much more for going along on the joy ride of making them outfits in patterns and combinations of colors, textures, and prints you never thought possible. You'll get a kick out of seeing them enjoy wearing the garment or outfit you mentally threw up your hands at! This is how you let them get fads out of their system. Eventually their good taste will come to the fore and they'll enjoy it that much more. Give in sometimes. You liked fads yourself when you were their age.

Sewing for the smaller kids

As already mentioned, it is not practical to sew everything, especially for preschoolers. Play clothing—such as dungarees, shorts for the summer, cotton T shirts, overalls—can be purchased reasonably enough ready-made, especially by the mother who watches the newspapers for seasonal sales. She can buy such items at prices she couldn't possibly match if she were to make them herself. Preschool children are happiest when they are dressed in clothes they can play in freely, and not worry about. So the most profitable clothes to make for them at home are their dress-up things—coats, snow pants, Easter outfits, and such.

About sewing for twins

Dressing two girls alike is fun and much easier when the clothes are home-sewn. It is not always possible to buy two identical articles in the same size ready-made. The same is true when the twins are boys. You'll dress them both for about the same price or less than you would spend on ready-mades for just one.

While quite young, and before boy-and-girl twins start school, they can be dressed in brother-and-sister outfits. Choosing materials that are neither too girlish or boyish in appearance will make them right for both. Their winter outfits could be identical, except with the girl buttoning her coat from right to left, and her brother buttoning his from left to right. For spring and fall, their blazers could be of the same material, buttoning them correctly in boy and girl directions, with the boy having trousers to wear with his blazer and his sister wearing a tiny skirt of the same material as the trousers. How difficult it would be to find such matchmates for your twins if you had to go out to buy them!

A word about Sunday clothes for children

If the "best" things are planned carefully, in styles that are not too fussy, and colors that are not too delicate, the garments will be easier to convert into everyday school wear after they have been replaced by newer things. It is wise to keep this in mind when choosing the fabrics and styles for best clothes, particularly when there is only one child in the family, or no younger one of the same sex.

If there are other children in the family, greater liberties can be taken in selecting styles and fabrics for the dressier things, as there will be somebody waiting to inherit them and put them to use while they still look new.

Making clothes that fit while new

The common theory that children's clothing should be oversized while new so that the poor children may grow into them is certainly not a very practical one. The garment may be worn out long before the wearer has caught up to it in size, and meanwhile the newest and prettiest time of the garment's life is being wasted.

Children vary so greatly in size per age group that it is often a problem to know how to choose the correct pattern size, one that will fit nicely from the start without giving you the frustration of endless adjustments. Here is the rule to follow: just as for adults, children's patterns should fit perfectly in the shoulders, upper chest, and neckline.

The shoulders, upper chest area, and neck of a child do not change nearly so rapidly in size as do lengths of waist, arms, and legs. Although it seems logical to think that when an article is cut too large, it can easily be reduced in size by fitting and refitting, this practice in sewing clothes will lead only to failure. It is impossible to reduce a neckline that is too big, an armhole that is too deep, a chest area that is too wide, without running into a chain of adjustments which eventually hopelessly distort the style of the garment and result in a product with no resemblance to the original idea.

The way the shoulders fit governs the way the rest of the garment will fit. When the shoulders fit well, you need only concern yourself with the length at the bottom of the garment and the end of the sleeves. There is no limit to the amount of extra length that can be included in a garment without affecting its styling.

There is no necessity to disturb the original styling of a pattern by folding it here and there vertically or horizontally to make it fit the body. This practice is pure guesswork and is not recommended. There are infallible ways to arrive at perfect fit without guesswork or hardship.

Whatever type of figure your child may have, the clothes you make at home will compare in appearance with ready-mades of good quality if you determine accurately the pattern size needed, use modern construction methods and short cuts, and simplified techniques to avoid overhandling.

Sewing for the man of the house — the boss

Here is the person who would definitely be the biggest booster of your talents, if you would once in a while make something for him. A sport jacket in his size is no more work than making one for the little fellow, except that the seams are longer.

Perhaps he's had a secret yen to own a really loud vest with brass buttons, but didn't want to spend the money for such an extravagance. Can you imagine his delight at finding one under the Christmas tree? Can you also imagine his pleasure when you tell him that you were able to make it for only about one third the cost of those expensive ones in the stores? He'll sing your praise to any willing ear.

How to measure yourself and the girls of the family

You should check your measurements if you have not been sewing for yourself for any length of time, or if you have gained or lost noticeable weight, or changed the style of your foundation garments. Foundation garments do make a difference in body measurements, and the same goes for brassieres. Here is where the body measurements are taken:

Measuring little girls	*Measuring full-grown girls*
Chest (not bust yet)	Bust
Waist	Waist
Hips or Tummy	Hips
Length of Waist	Length of Waist
Length of Skirt	Length of Skirt
Length of Sleeves	Length of Sleeves

Measurements are taken on small girls the same way as on grown ones. Place the tape measure over the fullest part of the bust line, or over the middle of the growing girl's breast, and hold it there firmly so it will not slip off, but don't draw it too tightly. Around the waistline pull the tape measure to the tightness that feels most comfortable, just as if it were a belt or waistband. Hips are measured where the lower body is largest. Some people are longer than others from the waist to the hips, so measure a few places below the waist until you come up with the largest measurement, and use that one for the hip dimension. Do this for yourself as well as for your girls.

The waist length is measured from the collarbone down to where a belt would be worn at the natural waistline location. Skirt lengths fluctuate greatly and are influenced by fashion, so measure from the waist down to the most becoming length and be sure to leave enough for a hem to turn up. Tiny girls wear their skirts considerably shorter than do bigger girls, while bigger girls wear theirs shorter than teen-agers, and teen-agers usually wear theirs shorter than their mothers do. The style of a dress or a skirt has a bearing on what the length should be. Experiment with the length by pinning the garment first to one length and then another before you make the final decision. You do this, of course, after the garment has been completed to the stage of deciding the length.

Full-length sleeves are measured from the armpit down to the wrist, adding enough material for turning up. If the sleeves are to be short, no measurement is needed.

How to measure men and boys

The measurements needed for sewing for the boys and men of the family are as follows:

Neck
Chest
Waist
Hips or seat
Trouser length
Sleeve length

The neck size will be needed for shirts, and the ready-made shirt size is a very good and accurate guide here, for both boys and men. The chest measurement is taken over the largest area of the chest. Waist measurement is taken at the normal waistline over a shirt even if the pants are to be hip-huggers. For the length of the trousers hold the pattern up to the waist and if any addition is needed, add it to the bottom of the legs. Shirt-sleeve lengths are measured from the center back of the neckline, at the collarbone, with the tape measure extended out to the wrist and the arm held out horizontally. If extra length is needed, add to the bottoms of sleeves, not to the bottoms of the cuffs. Nothing special has to be measured when the sleeves are short because this kind of length does not have to reach down to any specific part of the arm.

Extra length is added at the bottoms of jackets and shirts if the individual is taller than average, whether adult or otherwise.

What you should know about patterns

American patterns are incomparably superior to those made in other countries. They are graded in a full range of sizes in most designs. All the pattern sizes of all the patternmakers are cut in accordance with government standards, making it possible for you to choose whatever design suits your fancy from any catalogue and still be sure of buying exactly the same size each time. The consistency in pattern sizing makes it simple to achieve a good fit, once the important matter of correct size has been determined.

Whether a garment is to be for an adult or a child, the shoulders, upper chest areas, and neckline must fit well to start with; therefore the pattern size that will furnish the correct fit in those areas is the size to use. A well-fitting ready-made garment is about the best guide in judging the pattern size to use.

It is impossible to reduce necklines that have been cut too large or to pull up shoulders that droop. A pattern that is too large in the neck and shoulders will yield a poor-fitting garment. Folding a pattern to shorten it, or to narrow it down, or slashing it here and there to widen or lengthen it, is definitely not the way to achieve successful results in sewing. The clothes you make at home will compare in appearance with good ready-mades only if you follow the steps presented here.

What you should know about pattern sizes

The measurements that are printed on pattern envelopes are actual body measurements and not the amount of space there is in the garment itself. In addition to the body measurements, each pattern piece contains a certain amount of "ease" that makes the design what it is—form-fitted, boxy, gathered, or whatever. The amount of ease that is allowed in each pattern piece of a design makes the finished product an exact duplicate of the designer's creation, with just the right amount of space needed for the garment to look as it should and to be comfortable at the same time. When the person's body measurements are the same as those given on the pattern, and you know the shoulders and neckline will also fit correctly, so that no drastic alterations will be needed in those areas, the garment will end up as it should, with the proper amount of ease built into it.

When the body measurements are larger than those printed on the pattern envelope, the amount meant for built-in ease is used up and the styling of the garment is often distorted. The only way to be sure that this does not happen is to add on to the pattern pieces involved in order to preserve the amount of ease the garment is meant to have. Otherwise you may be disappointed.

How to determine the right pattern size

Disappointment in sewing is often due to the fear of cutting things too small. Some areas of a garment must fit well to start with so that no alterations are needed there. To repeat, it is how the shoulders, neckline, and upper chest areas of the garment fit that are important. The pattern size must provide you with a correct fit in those areas before anything else.

If in previous experience in sewing for yourself or your family you ran into the problem of having to adjust the shoulders or neckline of a garment, either before or after cutting it, then the pattern size used was wrong. You should choose either the next smaller or next larger pattern size, depending upon past experience, so that a good fit can be achieved without altering either the pattern or the garment in the upper section of the body.

When sewing for teen-agers, continue to use the same pattern size until it is obvious by last season's things that the size has been outgrown. Then purchase the next larger size for future sewing for that individual. Then take new measurements and also check lengths to be sure that the garment will come out the right size everywhere when completed.

Pattern size is determined for an adult in the same way. If weight gain has caused clothing made from one pattern size to become uncomfortable and outgrown looking, and ready-made garments have also become too small, you should use the next larger pattern size.

If the adult has lost enough weight to be obvious in the fit of last season's clothing, you should purchase the next smaller size in patterns for his or her wearing apparel.

The pattern size if you are a tiny woman

Patterns for women are now being made in smaller sizes than in the past, but there are some very tiny women who complain that the patterns are still not small enough for them. If you have this problem, you should choose the style you like from the pattern catalogues and buy it in the smallest size available in that style. Cut the garment like the pattern, even if you measure smaller here and there, and then at the time of the fitting, take the garments in more generously at the side seams. It is fatal to try reducing the pattern pieces, so don't try it.

It is also advisable to stay away from patterns where the smallest size available is a size twelve. This would be too large a pattern size for the tiny woman to work with. Look further for a style that does come in a smaller size. You'll find it.

Pattern problems of the larger woman

Fortunately there are more pattern fashions designed now for the larger-sized woman than in the past. However, they are not as plentiful as they should be, and the larger woman must, therefore, satisfy herself by choosing the style she likes and then buying the pattern in the largest size in which that particular pattern is made. If the pattern does not come in a size for a 40-inch bust, she must look further; if it does, she can add whatever she has to at the side seams to make it large enough for her own measurements, as long as they do not exceed 6 inches beyond the pattern measurements. As much as that can very easily be added to the sides of the garments without causing any distortion to the style of the garment.

The pattern size and its influence on style

Do keep in mind that it is how the pattern fits the upper part of the body, the shoulders, and neckline that determines the proper placement of the styling seams, the fitting darts, panel widths, and other details featured in the "styling areas" of the front and back units of the garment. The designer has placed these details where they will create the most pleasing effect and where they will do the best job of camouflaging whatever figure problems you wish to hide. If the neck and shoulders are misfits from the start, the important parts of the design will not come where they belong and trying to shift them to where they should be is not easy.

By using the pattern size that needs no alterations in neck and shoulders the true style of the pattern will be preserved in the front and back units of the garment. In the area where the personal measurements exceed those printed on the pattern envelope additions will be made in the "hidden areas," the direct side edges, to compensate for whatever difference there is so that the ease in the garment is preserved. Only in this way can the lines of the pattern design be truly reproduced in fabric. If the neck and shoulders of the pattern are right, but the personal measurements happen to be smaller than those of the pattern, the cloth is cut exactly like the pattern pieces. The garment will be reduced to the correct size of the individual later when the parts have been assembled to the right stage for fitting, and changes will be made at the sides, the "hidden areas."

Here's some extra help in determining which pattern size to use for sewing for the children:

The average size

If the youngster is average-sized for his or her age, weighs about what he should, and is about the right height, use the same pattern size as the age. Then hold the pattern up to the child and if you wish, add to the bottoms of sleeve, pants, and skirt pieces so that there will be enough to let down later.

Petite children

The pattern size next smaller than the age is better for the smallish child so that the shoulders and neckline will fit well. You may have to add length to hems and sleeves and also at the waistline of a girl's dress if it is styled with bodice and skirt joined together at the waist. Hold the pattern up to the girl or boy to make sure you add to bottoms wherever the pattern is not quite long enough. This means adding to bottoms of boys' sport jackets and shirts as well.

The bigger than average

Use the pattern size next larger than the child's age. Measure the chest, waist, and hips to see what difference there is between the child's measurements and those of the pattern, and add on to side seams of the garment to make up this difference. If the measurements of the individual and the pattern are alike, you will still have to check the length. Extra may be needed, so play safe.

The chubby type

Use the pattern size next larger than the age of the child. The pattern pieces may be too long here and there, but they can be shortened before placing them on the fabric, allowing generously for hems and growth. Sleeves should be checked and increased in width if necessary, although the larger-than-age-sized pattern may be sufficiently full. The length of sleeves should be generous for letting down and hemming.

The tall slender type

The slim child, narrow in the shoulders but tall in height, should have clothes cut from the pattern size that is comparable to age, so that the shoulders fit closely enough. To use the pattern size right for the height would result in failure. The shoulders and neck would be too wide, and would exaggerate thinness. Extra length will have to be added to the bottoms of the garment, including sleeves. For girls, it is absolutely necessary to add extra length to the dress bodice for a longer waistline. This figure type will surely need it.

The difference between toddlers' and children's patterns

Toddlers' patterns are for the wee people who, although they have outgrown infant sizes, have not quite grown high enough to be eligible for children's pattern sizes. These patterns have the same chest and tummy measurements as the children's patterns in the same sizes, but are 2 inches shorter in length and ½ inch narrower in the shoulders. They come in sizes from six months to about four years, and are aimed for the tots who still have their baby fat.

Children's sizes are for those who have already lost their baby fat and have grown taller. Although their weight may be the same as the toddlers', it is distributed differently.

Girls' patterns

Girls' patterns are designed for the growing youngster whose figure is still immature. Fitting darts are not as important in her styles as they will be later on. Shallow darts are featured on the bodice more for detailing than for fit. These patterns come in sizes from seven to fourteen.

Sub-teen patterns for girls

Sub-teen patterns are for the young shape that is still growing, but one that has started to round out and show signs of curves. The patterns are more shapely than those for girls, but not quite so much as the teen patterns. The more developed upper area of her figure entitles her to new words when measuring—it now being "bust measurement" instead of "chest measurement."

Teen patterns

These patterns are designed for the young ladies whose figures have developed a bit more and who have grown a little taller than the sub-teen. They are not quite tall enough to use Junior Miss patterns yet.

Junior Miss patterns

These patterns are designed for the young teen-ager whose figure has developed to the stage where the bust line is more pronounced, although her full height has not yet been reached.

About patterns for boys

The same principles apply to buying patterns for boys as for girls. Buy jacket patterns in the size comparable to age for the average boy, or the next smaller or larger if they are above or below average in size for their ages. For sport-shirt patterns use the same size as they wear in ready-made shirts. For trouser patterns, go according to waistline measurement and then hold the pattern up to the waist to check the length. Be sure to allow for growth and cuffs.

Changing to another size

It is only necessary to change to the next larger pattern size when the child's shoulders and chest have broadened. You will know the right time to change by the fit of the shoulders in the garments that the child has been wearing. The rule is simple: when you have to change to a larger size in ready-mades, do the same with patterns.

Fabrics for children's wear

Fabrics for children's wear do not have to be expensive, but they should be good and durable—the kind that will stand up to hard wear and many trips to the cleaner's or the washing machine. For this reason, tweeds are particularly desirable for children's coats and suits. The wide range of colors, mixtures, and weights in which they are woven makes them equally suitable for girls and boys, for Sunday best and everyday wear, for the warmest winter things as well as for lighter wear for fall and spring. Materials that will not show the crease and discoloration when an old hem is let down are also recommended. Some fabrics shed such creases more easily than others.

The remnant tables in fabric departments are "naturals" for the makings of children's wear. Girls' blouses, skirts, shorts, as well as boys' sport shirts, can be made from the small remnant pieces that are available in good quality—and at fine discounts. Some of the pieces are large enough for more important items for the tiny tots.

Many interesting combinations can be achieved when using remnants, when a piece of fabric is large enough only for one item of an ensemble. For example, if there is only enough tweed for a winter coat, the pants can be made from another harmonizing or contrasting remnant, in an entirely different weave, texture, or color from the coat fabric. Velveteen, corduroy, flannel, or twill—lined with cotton flannel —would make nice-looking leggings.

There are so many ways to use remnants that the woman with imagination can be in her glory planning ways to combine fabrics for interesting effects. The coat collar, trimmed with the pants material, and both fabrics combined in a matching hat, would complete a very smart ensemble for a little girl. One piece of material would make a pair of pants for a little boy, while another harmonizing piece would make a sport jacket to go with them. Just draw on your imagination— the list goes on forever.

The story about plaids

Plaids and children belong together. The vast variety of plaids and the many textures in which they are woven from the different fibers make them ideal for children's wear. They are worn in classrooms with equal aplomb by boys and girls, from nursery school onward. No young person's wardrobe is quite complete unless it includes a number of articles made of gay, exciting plaids.

Plaids are just as smart for Sundays as for everyday wear. Besides their versatility, plaids are popular because they do not show the rugged wear that young folks give them. This is particularly true when hems and sleeves must be let down. Creases and other markings that are so obvious and objectionable on many fabrics are hardly noticeable on plaid garments, because the old hemline blends in and disappears among the horizontal lines of the plaid design. These are only a few of the many reasons for the popularity of plaids with growing youngsters and their mothers. And so the little extra time involved in the all-important exact matching of the horizontal lines of the plaid in every seam of the garment is surely time well spent.

Choice of style for plaid

The fewer the pieces in a plaid garment, the more pleasing the finished product. The material itself is the major factor in creating the attractiveness of the total effect. Too many seams will only tend to produce a confusion of unrelated lines. For example, in a plaid material, a style featuring a curved yoke would not be as smart as a garment with a straight-line yoke. The curves would conflict with the straight lines of the plaid. Simple styling avoids chopping up the lines of the plaid design.

When in doubt about the suitability of the cloth to the style, be guided by the illustrations on the pattern envelope. These usually show how different effects are created by the choice of fabrics. The thing to do is to choose from the pattern catalogue a style that is shown in an illustration using cloth similar to your fabric. In this way you will know exactly what the garment will look like when finished. There will be no disappointments in store for you.

There is much information on the pattern envelope to make your sewing ventures successful. Not all materials make up to advantage in all styles, so the pattern envelope lists suitable materials under the heading of "fabric suggestions." Consult this list to see whether or not the weight, texture, and type of fabric you prefer are appropriate to your pattern style.

Materials with nap and how they are used

Some materials have a definite one-way directional surface finish which is known as "nap." This nap is easily recognized when the hand is rubbed up and down on the right side of the cloth, parallel with the selvage edges. The surface of the cloth will feel rough to the touch when stroked one way, and smooth when stroked in the opposite direction.

In using materials with nap it is important that the pattern pieces be laid on the cloth with the nap running in only one direction on each part of the garment. The pattern pieces cannot be staggered or dove-tailed for the purpose of saving yardage, since disregarding the direction of the nap would lead to disaster. The parts of the garment that were cut with the nap going downward would be considerably lighter in tone than the parts that were cut with the nap going in an upward direction. In fact, the parts would look so different that it would be hard to believe that the complete garment had been cut from the same bolt of cloth.

When materials with nap are recommended as suitable for pattern designs, the work sheet that comes in the pattern envelope will feature special layout diagrams showing how to place the pattern pieces properly on the napped fabrics so that the garment will be all one tone of color when completed. It would be wise to circle this diagram with a pencil to make it stand out from the other diagrams, so that you don't use any other diagram by mistake.

When the nap is handled properly, the material will wear better, staying smooth and pretty for the lifetime of the garment. With nap running opposed to its natural direction, the cloth is very apt to become shaggy.

The fibers from which the cloth is made determine the direction in which the nap must run in the garment. Woolens, as well as other napped materials made from animal fibers, such as camel's-hair cloth, cashmere, and vicuna, should be cut with the nap directed smoothly downward, exactly as the fur grew on the living animal, or as hair grows on a person's head or body. The reflection of light on the downward nap produces a sheen that gives the fabric a luxurious appearance.

Velveteen and corduroy also have a directional nap. The fibers of these materials are cotton. Because cotton is a plant, which grows up from the ground and gets nourishment from the sun, the nap should go upward when such material is used for garments. The colors will then be rich, more attractive, and somewhat darker than when the nap is run downward, and the garments will not show wear as quickly.

Associating the nap of the fabric with animal or plant life will help to remind you which way is correct for the nap to run. Here is a piece of good advice: In case you have started to cut the garment, and then find that the first piece has been cut with the nap going in the wrong direction, continue cutting *all* the pieces that way. The garment will at least be wearable, because each piece will be of the same tone of color. If you corrected the position of the other pieces after making your mistake, the colors would be so different in the switched sections that the garment would be a sad sight.

Occasionally manufacturers of ready-made clothes cut light-colored velveteens and corduroys with the nap going in a downward direction to give the light colors a silvery hue. This is done purposely. With the darker tones the nap is always upward to get the richness of the jewel tones and to prevent a dusty appearance.

No such liberties are taken with woolen materials. The only sections in which the nap may run in opposite directions are collars and cuffs or pocket welts. Even these parts are more commonly seen with the nap running the same way as in the rest of the garment.

Napped "miracle fabrics," woven of synthetic yarns, should be handled the same as fabrics made of the natural fibers they resemble.

About synthetic fabrics

Modern synthetic fabrics are excellent for both boys' and girls' wear. They are a real blessing to mothers. Most of these fabrics do not need pressing after laundering, or if any ironing is needed at all, a light touch-up on hems and collars is sufficient. Synthetics come in every imaginable texture, from the heaviest coatings to the sheerest organzas, in perfect imitations of their natural cousins, the wools, cottons, and silks. In working with them, handle them as you would their natural counterparts.

Yardage requirements and fabric width

The yardage requirements specified on the pattern envelopes are based on the average widths in which the suggested fabrics are woven. Domestic woolens are woven approximately 54 inches wide, but it's not unusual to find some as narrow as 50 inches and others as wide as 60 inches.

Cotton materials are woven approximately 35 and 36 inches wide. Silks and rayons come about 39 inches wide, and the modern synthetics can be anywhere from 35 to 60 inches wide, depending on whether they are of dress weight or are of coating and suiting textures. The synthetic fabrics resembling cottons or rayons may be in widths from 35 to 45 inches wide; the suit and coat weights for these synthetics come in widths similar to those of wool, from 50 to 60 inches wide. Naturally, with such variations, you'll want to check the width of synthetic material before deciding upon the necessary yardage. The clerk in the yard goods department will be very willing to help you in this matter.

Pattern companies always make allowances for the slight differences that may exist between the fabrics recommended and others that can be used. If your cloth is an inch or two different from the specified width, the yardage would still be the same as called for on the pattern envelope. Only when there is a great deal of difference, such as 36-inch material applied to a pattern specifying 45-inch fabric, would there be a problem.

When sewing for children, it's a good idea to buy a bit more fabric than called for on the pattern chart, so that extra length can be added on at the bottom for growth. This is especially important when sewing for children who are taller than average for their age, since they need the extra length to start with. The extra amount needed depends upon the width of fabric used: ⅛ yard of 54-inch material, ¼ or even ½ yard if the cloth is narrower.

Extra yardage should also be purchased when working with plaids, especially large ones. It is of utmost importance to match accurately the horizontal lines of plaid designs in all of the joining seams. This matching almost always requires a little more yardage than that needed for styles using small checks, over-all designs, or plain materials that do not involve any such matching. When uneven plaids are purchased, extra yardage is required because the patterns, in addition to matching the horizontal lines of the plaid design, will have to be placed on the fabric a certain way.

Extra yardage may also be required when you are working with fabrics that have a one-way direction: those with the surface nap (of camel's hair, fleecy coatings, velvet, velveteen, and corduroy); the printed fabrics which feature flowers, birds, or other one-way designs that must be cut specially to be right side up on the finished garment. Many plaids, too, have a one-way direction in their weave. This is true of woolens as well as of other plaid materials.

It is quite possible that an occasional pattern will not have the information on the yardage requirement for fabrics that have a directional nap or design, in which case there won't be a diagram showing how to place the pattern on the cloth. You'll have to do a little planning on your own before buying the material to find out the amount you will need to lay the pattern pieces on such fabric to best advantage. Usually extra material is required when it has to be used a special way, and when the pattern specifies the yardage only for nondirectional fabric.

Here's what you do: Fold a bed sheet lengthwise to represent the width of the fabric you intend to buy. Proceed to pin the pattern pieces on it with all the bottom parts of the pieces aiming toward *only* one end of the sheet, and all the tops in the opposite direction. When all the pieces have been placed in the right cutting position, merely measure the sheet to see how much of its length has been used. This then will be the yardage to buy of the napped or one-way design cloth.

With so many new synthetic materials on the market, it is not always possible to keep up with the many different widths in which they are manufactured. If a fabric you like comes in an odd width, buy your pattern first and pin it to a bed sheet, after folding the sheet to represent this new width, and that way you can determine how much yardage will be required. Some of the new knits come 60 inches or even wider, and not all patterns give the amount needed of such new widths.

When the material is of an unusual width, plus having a surface finish that has a nap, or a one-way design, you will have two reasons to check the yardage requirement with a bed sheet. It's worth the time it takes to do this because you may have a real problem if you run short.

How to shrink fabric if necessary

Today most of the woolen and cotton mills that produce good quality fabrics preshrink their products before they distribute them. There are several different trade names for this shrinking process, but they all mean pretty much the same thing. These fabrics can be used with utmost confidence, without any fear of shrinkage after the garment is made up. Some materials have a printed guarantee either on the bolt or on a tag, stating that they have been shrunk at the mill and are ready to be sewed. Trust these labels.

It is wise, though, to remember that not all fabrics have been preshrunk. If you are using material that you have had for some time, and are not sure whether or not it has been preshrunk, shrink it before starting to work with it. Some of the fabrics that come from foreign countries may not be shrunk, and unless they are actually labeled "preshrunk," take the proper precautions or you may regret it. Fabrics can be shrunk at home very easily, or sent to the neighborhood tailor who will do it for a very reasonable price.

There are different ways of shrinking woolens, but the following is the easiest: Moisten a crash or linen dish towel thoroughly and wring out the excess moisture. Place the wet towel on the wrong side of the cloth, which is left folded lengthwise, just as it was when purchased. Woolens come folded wrong side out, you know. Set the dial on your iron to "wool" and steam the cloth by running the iron back and forth on the cloth, slowly and lightly, until all the towel has been covered by the iron. Keep the iron flat on the towel and move it back and forth slowly. If the iron hops up and down on the wet towel, some areas in the material underneath remain dry and unshrunk. If the material doesn't look even and flat when you remove the towel, repeat the process until the surface of the wool is perfectly smooth. Do this to the full length of the fabric. When one side of the folded cloth has been shrunk, turn it over so that the underpart can be shrunk also. Steam does not penetrate through to the under layer of folded wool, so repeating is necessary.

A special word of advice: It is necessary to use a wet cloth even though you have a perfectly good steam iron. The steam iron will work beautifully on seams and darts, but doesn't have enough steam pressure to do an adequate shrinking job.

Up-to-date cotton fabrics of good quality can be depended upon to have been shrunk before they left the mills so take the manufacturer's word for it. If you are not sure whether your cotton has been shrunk, however, dunk it in lukewarm water, wring it out, and hang it out to dry or put it into your drier. Press out the wrinkles and it will be ready for use.

In cottons that are not permanently finished, or disciplined, some of the original dressing which makes them crisp is lost during shrinking. Replace this dressing by adding a bit of starch to the lukewarm water when dunking, and don't allow the cloth to dry thoroughly. If it is only partly dry, it will easily press into shape. You'll see that it has retained its original crispness through this small operation.

Shrinking polyester

Polyester materials, both knits and weaves, should also be dunked in lukewarm water, along with the zippers you plan to use, and then allowed to dry in a drier or to drip-dry before using them, just in case they do shrink a bit. You'll be playing safe. These do not require pressing after they have dried if they are removed from the automatic drier immediately.

About sewing equipment

Although you need only a few items of equipment to do a good sewing job, your tools should be in fine working order. Mechanical trouble in your sewing machine can certainly damage your enthusiasm, if not your project. Keep your machine in good condition. An ironing board, an iron, and a pressing cloth should be close at hand at all times when you sew. Even though you use a steam iron it may be necessary to use a press cloth too, since the steam from the iron doesn't always do a good-enough job on certain hard-finished fabrics such as serge or heavy coating. Old linen or crash dish towels make fine press cloths because they retain moisture long enough to produce steam. If the cloth is nonabsorbent and thin it dries too quickly, and the pressing job isn't adequate.

A good sharp pair of scissors about 7 or 8 inches long will serve for general cutting purposes. The points should be long and very sharp, rather than round and blunt. No special scissors will be needed for cutting through buttonholes and set-in pockets.

When buying a pair of scissors, it is advisable to have with you a piece of the softest and most difficult kind of fabric to cut, so that the scissors can be tried out. Voile, chiffon, or very lightweight nylon make ideal testing pieces. If these can be cut without any trouble, the scissors will work even better on other firmer materials. Fit the scissor handles to your own hands, so that they do not cause discomfort when they are used constantly. Be sure that the blades operate freely without binding or stiffness, as they don't always loosen up with use.

You will also need some fine dressmaker pins, a tape measure, and a couple of pieces of blackboard chalk: white chalk for marking dark fabrics and a pale pastel chalk for marking the lighter colors on which the white chalk could not be seen.

As time goes on and you gain more sewing experience, you will buy additional sewing gadgets. By then you will be a better judge of what you will find most useful. In the meantime, these few essentials will carry you through.

What you need to know about your sewing machines

You should know how to thread your sewing machine correctly, how to wind and insert the bobbin, and how to replace the needle, because they do break now and then. The instruction book that comes with your machine will show you exactly how to do all these things. You do not need to know what is happening inside of the machine, any more than you have to know what happens inside the automatic transmission of your automobile. In sewing as in driving, just observe a few simple rules and when trouble arises with your equipment, call on a good mechanic or let him call on you to see what the trouble is.

If your sewing machine has not been used for a long time, it may need cleaning and lubricating. Lint and dust settle in the working parts of the machine and cause loss of power and speed. The man of the house can easily clean and lubricate it for you if he is so inclined. Every sewing machine department or store carries the special grease for electric motors, and the oil for the parts. Buy the special kind made for sewing machines only, as others may be too heavy and clog up the works even more. Machines are precision built and must be treated with care and respect. They'll then give you lifetime service.

Mothers take warning: Children are fascinated by the levers, dials, and knobs of sewing machines. You are not always around the machine when they are, and the stitching on many a machine has misbehaved because of some young "fixer." If rearranging the dials, knobs, and levers to where you left them doesn't correct the situation. you'd better cart the head of the machine to the nearest mechanic to have it readjusted. Then deliver a few stirring words of advice on what will happen the next time your young ones "make like mechanics."

If you are troubled constantly by thread-breaking while sewing, it may be that the shaft of the needle is not inserted deeply enough into the needle holder. Loosen up the turnscrew and move the needle up as far as it will go; this ought to correct the situation. Thread-breaking is also caused by inserting the needle into the holder with the flat side of the needle shaft in the wrong direction. Some needles have a rounded shaft, while others are only half round. Investigate to see if you have the needle in correctly. If you're not sure, reverse the needle, with the flat side of the shaft on the opposite side from where it was, and see if that helps.

Threads and needles

Mercerized thread is the best for machine sewing woven materials made from natural fibers, like cotton, wool, and linen. The newer polyester threads are best for all stretch-type fabrics and knits, regardless of what their fiber content happens to be. This thread has a certain amount of stretchability and "gives" without the stitches breaking in the seams when strain is put upon the garment in wearing. The seams and the threads snap right back to their natural flatness when the strain is removed from the knit.

There is also a new kind of sewing-machine needle with a "ballpoint" end instead of the usual sharp end. The rounded point goes in between the yarns of the knit when stitching garment parts together instead of penetrating through them, so the yarns do not become broken or weakened. The round point of this needle also prevents the machine from skipping stitches here and there when working with lightweight and thin jersey type knits. This has always been a problem in the past when only the pointed needle was available for sewing machines, particularly with jerseys made of synthetic fibers.

Sewing-machine needles come in different sizes, from the heavy to the fine, and a medium-sized one is good for general sewing. The same applies to ball-point needles. The average number of machine stitches used for clothing is about 12 to 14 to the inch. Mark off an inch of space with a pencil on a scrap piece of cloth and stitch from one mark to the next to see how many stitches there are in the space. With the regulator—either a lever, a dial, or a knob—located near the wheel on the right-hand front of the machine, keep adjusting until you get the right number of stitches into the 1-inch space.

If your machine functions properly and the stitches look good on both sides of the seam, don't tamper with it. It is not necessary to reset it every time you sit down to sew. If the cloth is too heavy or too thin for the setting you have, you'll know soon enough by the work the machine produces in these textures, and it is then that you ma[?] whatever mechanical adjustments are necessary, following the man[?] that comes with your machine.

Full-time use from automatic machines

Besides plain sewing, an automatic machine has many [...] er faculties just waiting to be put to use. You can have the time of your life trimming your children's or grandchildren's wearing apparel with the different fancy stitches the machine does by merely flipping a lever or changing a cam. The mock smocking made by the automatic machine looks almost real. Machine-made embroidered buttonholes are very easy to do and they will last as long as the garment will. Clothing that regularly ends up in the family laundry will last much longer if you use the zigzag stitch to finish the inside seams, because then they will not fray. So get familiar with your sewing machine and put it to full-time use and it will pay for itself in no time at all.

̣ ̣hes for the Teen-age Girl and ̣ou

Every girl or woman wants to be attractive. To be born pretty is not enough. Even the most beautiful face may go unnoticed unless a person makes her figure attractive as well. Attractiveness is within the reach of all of us, regardless of age or figure type, if we wear clothes that flatter in every way. That is what clothes should do. They do not have to be bizarre in style or expensively priced, but they should be suited to one's type, pleasing in fit, flattering in color, and made from material that is suited to the design. Only then will the true personality be reflected; the clothes will look as though they were made for the individual and for no one else in the world.

All girls have their figure problems, just as adults do. These problems are easily solved with the right kind of clothing. The figure will take on a slimmer appearance if the style is chosen for that purpose, and if a few principles of line are observed. When styles are chosen haphazardly, the figure fault may be exaggerated instead of minimized. The fact that a girl is not as tall as she'd like to be, or as slim, is not really important. What is more important than actual size is a well-proportioned look, so that one part of the figure compares pleasingly in size with other parts. Fashions are constantly changing, but the principles remain the same.

The average type

If a girl is considered fairly average in size for her age, being neither too thin or too plump, neither too tall or too short, she can wear almost any style she wishes, and by choosing the right colors she will have a fine wardrobe. The best way to choose color is to hold the cloth right up to the face, so that whatever color is being worn will be completely covered up, and at a single glance it will be possible to judge whether the fabric color is becoming or not. One tone of color may be more flattering than another, so don't automatically rule out all reds, or greens, or yellows, or whatever without trying them in this fashion.

Fashions for the very thin type

To camouflage thinness and to produce dainty slimness instead, choose styles with round necklines and collars. Dresses should be styled with soft fullness rather than in straight lines. Princess styles with flared fullness and a semi-fitted midsection are flattering. Shirt-waist designs with gathered or pleated skirts are also good dress choices and these will do a terrific camouflaging job. Stripes running crosswise will also give the figure a fuller and more rounded appearance. Double-breasted styles in coats and jackets, as well as dresses, are also good choices. Soft-textured materials rather than mannish hard weaves for coats and suits are best.

Styles for the not-so-slim type

No matter what figure type a girl happens to be, she can be made to look slimmer if the styles of her garments feature vertical lines, like princess styles, and if the interesting details of the design are placed where the figure is most pleasingly proportioned. For example, wearing pockets above the waistline instead of on the lower part of the dress will make her look slimmer in the hips and tummy areas. If she is overdeveloped above the waistline, simple styling above the waist with interest placed below the waist is best.

Streamlined fashions that do not define the waistline too noticeably are good choices to camouflage the midriff. Tight fitting at the waist should be avoided. Bulky fabrics and large prints and plaids will make the body look larger than it actually is, but small prints and checks are good.

How to dress and stay "ageless"

How old you are is not really a matter of great importance, but how you look for your age is. Many women believe that they will stay young-looking forever if they just continue wearing fashions that are aimed toward the junior miss. Unfortunately this is not so, even if you have successfully retained your girlish figure. Clothes that are too young only tend to call attention to your maturity, as the contrast between juvenile clothing and the skin, the eyes, and the hair of the matured woman is too great for a pleasing effect.

The young miss can wear anything she wants to, even the sophisticated things that her older friends look so smart in, but the fortyish woman must be much more analytical in her choice of wearing

34

apparel. If the styles are too young, she gives the impression that she is trying to hide her age and isn't really getting away with it. However, the transition from girlhood to a perennial age of smartness need not cause her to change her mode of dress too drastically.

The styles chosen should be neither too young nor too old, as long as they are "ageless" looking—that is, sophisticated enough to separate them from junior fashions, but far removed from the dowdy fashions associated with "sensible matronly" things. "Ageless" styles are up to the minute in design, color, and fabric and are of good quality material and fine workmanship. They fit superbly because they are suited to the type of figure the person has.

To judge the ageless quality of a garment, whether it is being made at home or purchased ready-made, try to picture in your mind how a person ten or twelve years younger than yourself would look in the garment in question. If she would look well dressed in it, and not appear as if she were wearing something too old for her, fine! Now you go a bit further in your analysis: Picture how somebody ten or twelve years older than yourself would look in the same garment. Would she look smart and up to the minute? That's great! If both of the mental pictures are pleasing, you can be sure that the garment will have that important "ageless" look that will reflect your good taste and styling sense, and nobody will care how old you are. You'll look both stylish and ageless.

As already stated, it is not how large or small you are, how tall or short that matters, but how well you can dress the figure you have and make it look as well proportioned as possible regardless of what figure problems you are trying to hide.

Introducing fabric and pattern to each other

Again, the pattern chosen should be in the size that will fit the shoulders and upper chest area without alterations, one comparable to the size worn in ready-made clothes. It is true that some things are purchased in one size and others in another, but the pattern size should be the same as that of the more important ready-made apparel, the clothes that fit best in the shoulders and chest.

No drastic pattern alterations needed

As you can readily see, no drastic pattern alterations are recommended here, only simple additions to be made where they will not affect the style in any way. Reducing size by folding pattern pieces this way and that, or increasing size by slashing them in different places and inserting tissue strips between the slashes is taboo. Such steps are purely guesswork and can very easily distort the pattern design.

The methods recommended here for cutting the garment to size, and then fitting it correctly and simply are infallible, and will produce the best results possible.

On one side of the pattern instruction sheet you will find layout diagrams that illustrate how to place the pattern pieces on cloth of varying widths. Since these diagrams look very much alike at a quick glance, it would be wise to circle the one that represents the width of your cloth and your pattern size, so that you can recognize it immediately each time you refer to it. If there is a slight difference between the width of your cloth and the widths shown in the diagrams, follow the one closest to the width of your fabric. An inch or two won't matter.

I should mention here that, although I recommend that you follow the instruction-sheet diagram for placing the pattern on the cloth, the simplified techniques I use for constructing the garment are considerably different from those the pattern instructions give. Simply ignore the pattern instructions and follow the easier methods given here.

Pattern pieces are generally pinned to the wrong side of the cloth, so that the markings for darts and other fitting devices can be accurately transferred from the pattern pieces to the wrong side of the cloth for stitching.

Coatings and suitings made of wool, or in imitations of wool, are usually folded wrong side out before they leave the mill, so they will stay clean and lint-free. They should be left folded that way when pattern pieces are pinned to them. Cottons, on the other hand, are usually folded with the right side out and must be reversed before

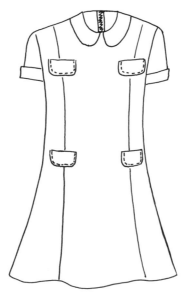

Figure 1

36

starting to place the pattern, so the marking and stitching can be properly done on the wrong side. This, of course, is necessary only if the cloth has a definite right and wrong side, as in a print, sateen, or piqué. If the cloth is reversible, as in the case of ginghams or chambrays, either side can be used as the right side.

Each pattern piece bears a symbol signifying the "straight of the goods," the indicator that will guide you in placing the pattern pieces accurately on the fabric weave. These indicators should be placed in a position parallel with the threads that run the length of the material, or to be technical, on the warp. Occasionally pattern pieces are placed on the horizontal weave of the cloth, or the woof, when an interesting effect is desired such as when using striped or bordered materials.

I have chosen a classic princess style dress to get you acquainted with the best way to cut, mark, assemble and fit a dress so it will be smart, comfortable, and something to be proud of. (Fig. 1.)

Laying the pattern

The work of pinning the pattern to the cloth should be done on a solid surface. Use your kitchen table, two card tables put together, or get yourself a cutting board the next time you're at a notion counter. They are relatively inexpensive and handy to use. Lay the board on your bed or dining-room table and do your cutting on it.

Follow the layout diagram on your pattern sheet for the width of the material you will be using and the pattern size you have purchased, the one you have circled with pencil, and then proceed with the pinning, imitating that diagram as closely as possible.

Our Fig. 2 shows a typical layout. There is no special way to insert pins into the work, but if you insert them parallel with the edges to be cut, you'll find it quite easy. A pin inserted into each corner of the small pieces will be enough, and putting the pins about 12 inches apart in the larger pieces will be sufficient to hold the cloth and pattern together for cutting. Insert the pins inside of the printed line that surrounds each piece; otherwise the pattern pieces will fall off the cloth after the cutting has been done and before you have had the chance to transfer the important symbols from the pattern to the material.

Smooth the fabric with your hands after you have spread it on the flat surface and before you start pinning; then get all the pieces pinned into position before you begin cutting, just in case you have to shift a piece or two to make everything fit on the yardage. You might have to move a piece of the pattern here or there to allow for increases that you might need at the sides, or at the bottom, to make the finished garment fit the personal measurements.

Before cutting, check to be sure that the straight of the goods symbol on each pattern piece is correctly aligned with the true grain of the cloth on each part of the garment. If the fabric has a printed design, does it have a one-way direction? Or if there is a nap, are all the pattern pieces correctly pinned on the cloth?

Let us assume that a young lady wears a size nine in ready-mades and that this size fits her shoulders and neckline well and does not require alterations. This would then be her pattern size also. The standard pattern specifications for this size are 32-inch bust and 34-inch hips. (We are purposely ignoring the waist measurement in this particular style because it is not defined enough to be important now, and this matter will be covered fully later.)

The girl's own body measurements are 35-inch bust (a difference of 3 inches), and her hips are 36 inches (a difference here of 2 inches). Purchasing the pattern in the next larger size would not be the answer because the neck and shoulders of the garment would end up the wrong size, with a gaping neckline and droopy shoulders. It is important to bear in mind, however, that although we are using the best-fitting ready-made size for our guide in choosing pattern size, the ready-made garment, as a general rule, is cut more generously throughout the body areas than the pattern of the same size. It is only in the upper parts, the ones that govern the placement of the styling lines in the rest of the garment, that the two are alike. In the cutting of the garment we must provide the extra body space that the individual requires, so that the whole garment will be pleasing in looks and comfort.

If the differences between the standard measurements of the pattern and those of the individual are not properly taken care of, the garment will suffer in appearance as well as in fit. The larger body measurements will use up the "ease" that the style requires, and the results will definitely be disappointing. The same is true if you use a pattern that is too wide in the shoulders and too broad in the neckline, but in this case alterations cannot be made without distorting the design. Avoid this problem by using a pattern that fits in the right places to start with, and then go on from there. The work will progress smoothly and rapidly and you'll gain confidence in yourself as you proceed, knowing you are doing the right things at the right time.

Where and how to increase garments

You provide for the difference between the person's measurements and those of the pattern at the direct side edges of the front and back garment units, the "hidden areas." Divide the difference by four and add the resulting amount to the left and right edges of the front and back by drawing it on the wrong side of the cloth with blackboard chalk that has been sharpened to a point. Use white chalk on dark materials and a light pastel chalk on fabrics on which the white would not show up. Do the side edges of the front and back units alike.

In our example (where the girl's bust measurement is 3 inches larger than the pattern measurement and the hips are 2 inches more), draw a chalk line ¾ inch away from the cutting line of the pattern, starting at the top of the side seams of the front of the garment and proceeding downward until the waistline area has been passed. Then gradually, and in a very subtle way, start tapering the chalk line to bring it closer to the pattern so that the addition made at the hip area will be only ½ inch. The line is then continued down to the bottom of the pattern piece, ending ½ inch away from the cutting line, so that the silhouette of the design remains intact.

Do the same chalking to the side edges of the back of the garment, starting with the ¾-inch increase at the top of the side edge and tapering it so you end up with ½ inch at the hip and hem. You have now provided the needed 3 inches in the bust and 2 inches at the hips without any distortion of the "styling areas" of either the front or back of the garment. Since only the side panels of both units had been added to, the centers are left in their original shape and size, as you will note in Fig. 2.

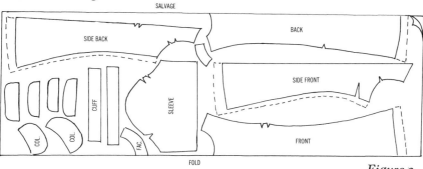

Figure 2

This method of reaching a good fit is foolproof. Garments handled in this way will always end up with the right amount of "ease" that each particular style requires. The amount of extra space included in a garment differs with the garment's styling, some having more space than others. Here the form-fitted design I have chosen has just enough ease in it to make the garment conform becomingly to the body with just enough space in addition to allow for comfortable movement. But where personal measurements exceed those given with the pattern, the garment without the additions would end up being too snug.

As there is no satisfactory way of measuring to see how much ease there is in a particular style of garment, you must trust that if you follow the rules of "adding-to" that I have given, you'll preserve the

39

design in its original state and will end up with the amount of ease the style of the garment is meant to have.

What? No side seams!

There are many patterns that do not have direct side seams. They have side panels instead, and to make alterations providing extra space in such garments it is necessary to split the side panel in the area of the underarm, separating the panel pieces and pinning them to the cloth with a space between them that will represent the needed amount. The panels will end up the same shape on the outer edges, but they will be somewhat wider. There is no other satisfactory way of coping with such designs when they require enlarging.

The direct underarm area of the pattern is marked with a symbol of some kind, and it is here that the splitting is done from top to bottom. If the amounts needed for increasing the garment in the bust and hip area are alike, the pattern is separated evenly from top to bottom, as illustrated in Fig. 3. When more is needed in one area than in another, as in our case here, the panels are spread farther apart where the increase is larger. For the 3-inch additional bust measurement and a 2-inch additional hip measurement, widen the space 1½ inches at the bustline of each panel and end up with 1 inch at the bottom. You use one half the total amount needed when you add to panels instead of the one fourth used on seam edges.

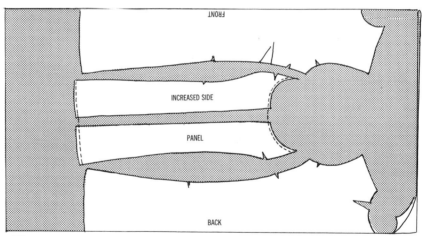

Figure 3

Quite often a long vertical dart is shown on the panel piece to give the design more shaping at the sides. You split the panel as already explained and after cutting the cloth the pattern is taped together again and the dart is traced from the pattern piece to the cloth so it is the shape and size it should be.

It is a very good idea on this type of design to pin the panels together and try them on first before stitching them together. If any taking in is necessary, do it on the edges of the altered panels, not on the ones that are located in the direct front and back of the style. You then do the stitching.

Cutting kimono styles to fit

When additions need to be made to styles featuring kimono-style sleeves, draw them on the fabric with chalk before cutting, the same as you do for set-in-sleeve styles, starting at the base of the sleeves at the top of the side seams. (Fig. 4a.) If the sleeves need to be wider, carry the addition around the lower edges of the sleeves.

Some designs with kimono sleeves are cut to fit closer to the body than others. The close-fitting designs have a diamond-shaped piece, called a "gusset," inserted into the underarm section of the garment. The gusset provides comfort and freedom of movement. A printed line on the front and back pattern pieces for the garment shows where the material must be cut so that the gusset fits in properly, and a pattern piece for the gusset is also provided.

When the sides of the garment must be increased for measurements that exceed those of the pattern, only the length of the slashes at the underarms must be taken into consideration. Make the slashes from the increased side edges inward, but only to the depth of the original printing on the pattern pieces. (Fig. 4b.) In this way the gussets will fit properly into the spaces provided for them.

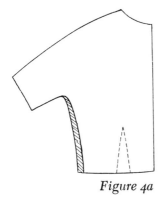

Figure 4a

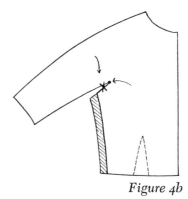

Figure 4b

How to widen the shoulder-blade area

If your sleeves tighten uncomfortably when reaching forward, or if the circulation threatens to stop when you wear sleeveless things and want to reach forward in them, you need to draw a crescent-shaped addition around the back armhole of any style with set-in sleeves. Don't think that the next larger size will solve your problem; it won't. Start the line at the top of the back armhole, right on the pattern cutting line, and gradually taper away as you proceed to draw downward so you are ½ inch or ⅝ inch away from the pattern when you reach the center of the armhole. Then start tapering inward gradually so the chalk line meets the pattern at the base of the armhole, carrying the crescent line to include any adjustment you had to make at the sides. The crescent will provide the extra room without changing the appearance of the garment in any way. The notches are clipped into the edge of the altered armhole ¼ inch deep where they are originally shown on the pattern. (Fig. 5.) Sleeves are cut like the pattern.

Figure 5

Adding on for extra length

To preserve the styling lines of a design in a streamlined way, it is best to add to bottoms of the garment parts for those individuals who are taller than average, or for those who like to wear their skirts somewhat longer than the pattern length provides. Those whose arms are long and who find full-length sleeves too short in ready-made clothing need to have extra length provided at the bottoms of the sleeves. To add length any other way could easily distort the design of the garment. This way is easier and the results are always pleasing.

How to shorten patterns

If the pattern needs to be shortened, take off the extra length at the bottom instead of folding the pattern pieces here and there. Folding distorts the design of the garment and takes away its proportioned appearance because it causes too abrupt a change in the shaping of the garment parts. It is true that some skirt fullness will be lost by altering the pattern in the way I recommend; but if the individual is that short, she shouldn't wear too much fullness. The limited amount of fullness will be more becoming to her in every way.

Nothing special has to be done to the sleeves if the arms are average in size, but if the sleeves of ready-made clothes bind in any area of the arms, provisions have to be made at the two side edges of the sleeve pieces so that they are about an inch or so wider than the arm measurements at their largest dimension. Additions do not have to be made in sleeves to compensate for increasing the armholes when the sides of the garment were increased. The sleeves will go in without any problem when the right time comes, just by following the simple directions.

Marking and cutting the garment parts

Even though you are anxious to give your pinking shears a workout, use straight-edged scissors to cut the garment parts for greater accuracy. All the pattern companies offer ⅝-inch seam allowance on all the pattern edges and unless the edges are joined together with this precise amount of seaming, the garment will end up a misfit even though you have taken the precaution of cutting it to the right size. If the seam is wider than ⅝ inch, the garment will end up too small. If the seams are too narrow, the garment will be too big. To avoid disappointments, be sure to observe the correct seam allowance when the parts are stitched together. The zigzag or scalloped edges produced by pinking shears make it difficult to judge the width of a seam edge accurately, especially on small pieces, like the tab trimmings featured on the front of our dress here, or the collar and facing pieces. Pinking shears should be used solely to trim away seam edges after joining parts of the garment together and before these parts are pressed open. In certain types of fabrics, pinking will prevent seam edges from becoming frayed. Pinking shears eventually become dull from use, and they must be returned to the manufacturer for sharpening. So to save time and effort, as well as your pinkers, use them only when absolutely necessary.

The cutting is done through the darkest lines that border the pattern pieces, with the exception of the edges where chalk lines have been drawn to provide larger personal measurements. Here the cutting is done through the chalk lines.

Cut with long even strokes, with one hand kept on the cloth while the other hand does the cutting. Walk around the table when cutting large pieces so that they can be left in their original place for the complete cutting operation. If you draw the material over to you, the shape of the pieces may be distorted. Keep the work flat on the cutting table; do not raise it.

There are notches on the pattern pieces every here and there to make assembling the different parts of the garment easy. The notches are in the form of diamonds and triangles. Do not overlook these notches, especially in the armhole and sleeve edges, as they help to accomplish a perfect job when they are matched with their mates. All you do to them is clip inward ¼ inch deep wherever they are, without cutting out any of the cloth, and don't snip deeper than ¼ inch either. The notches may be clipped in after each pattern piece has been cut, or you can save the clipping job and do it all at once when everything for the garment has been cut. Just don't forget to clip each piece.

There is a symbol at the top of all sleeve caps which needs to be identified with a clipping, although the symbol is not always a clipping mark but sometimes a dot or an arrow, or some other kind of marking. It is very important to identify this symbol, whatever it happens to be, because it will have to be matched accurately to the end of the shoulder seam when the sleeve is inserted.

Marking darts and understanding their purpose

You will find darts in different areas of most garments. They help to give the fabric the right shape to conform to the body contours most becomingly. Certain styles have darts at the shoulders, elbows, and waistline, and darts very often are used solely for the purpose of decorating the garment. If the darts are meant only to shape the garment to the body in a special way, they must be transferred accurately from where they are printed on the pattern to the wrong side of the garment. On the other hand, if the darts are shown on the outside of the garment, the pattern must be removed from the wrong side of the material after the garment piece has been cut and replaced on the outside of the material for marking so that the right shaping can be done on the side of the garment where the dart will show.

To transfer the darts to the cloth you use the point of a scissors to puncture holes in the pattern pieces about an inch or so apart, following the line of the darts. Using chalk with a sharpened point, make dots through the holes. After the top layer has been marked with chalk, do the same to the under layer also. Or you may stick pins through the dots on the top layer and then chalk where the pins come through on the under layer, or remove the pattern and place it on the under layer, using the same holes as you used in marking the top layer.

For the placement of pockets or decorations, like flaps or welts, there is usually a printed line on the pattern piece showing where these details should be attached. Mark these placements with chalk by puncturing the pattern first and when the pattern piece is removed, run a line of bright-colored hand basting through the marks through both layers so that the hand stitching will be visible on both sides of the garment parts. Just marking with chalk would not be enough, since the chalking does not stay on the cloth long enough to be useful. The stitching will be there when needed.

When working with certain types of materials, it is almost impossible to distinguish the right and wrong side of the cloth, once the pattern parts have been removed and the cut pieces have been separated from each other. It is a good idea to choose one side to be the right one, to avoid ending up with two right sleeves, or two left front pieces. Chalk some large crosses on the wrong side before separating cut pieces and you'll avoid having to rip and do things over.

It is a proven fact that overhandling a garment while making it is the most common reason for a homemade look. If you choose a style similar to the one described here, and each of the steps are carried out according to the instructions presented, the finished results will be gratifying in every way, in appearance and in the fitting as well. Doing first things first and doing each step in the simplest possible way makes the work pleasant and speeds progress at the same time.

Basting the garment pieces together first and then doing the machine work is very time-consuming and unnecessary. It also shows lack of confidence in yourself and in the pattern you are using. Do some positive thinking about your ability and you'll make clothing that fits and looks great at the same time.

Vertical seams, such as the panels of the princess dress, are pinned with the material right sides together. Start the pinning at the top of the shoulders and proceed downward. Insert the pins at right angles to the seam line and about 1½ inches apart. (Fig. 6.) Do the same thing to the back panels, including the center back seam, even though eventually there will be a long zipper inserted into that seam for an opening. The V-shaped darts located at the side seams of the front unit are also pinned through the markings with pins inserted at right angles to the seamline and about an inch apart.

All sewing machines, whether they are brand-new or not, will stitch over pins. Just try it! Place the seam underneath the presser foot with the bulk of the material on the left side so that the raw edges of the seam are at the right and the pinheads are off the seam edge with the points aiming from right to left. Although the pinning is always started

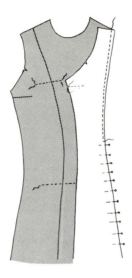

Figure 6

at the top of an article, it really doesn't matter whether the stitching is done from the top downward, or in the opposite direction, as long as you start with the bulk of the material placed at the left-hand side of the machine.

If you are uneasy about sewing over the pins without wearing a welder's mask, sew right up to the pin and then slow down a little so that you can withdraw it with the fingers of your right hand. Then proceed until you reach the end of the seam. Do this to each seam until the front and back units are completed. Keep the front and back units separate until after you have done the initial pressing.

The darts on each side of the front unit of the dress are stitched from the wide end toward the point, and as the point is approached, it is very important that the stitching be gradually tapered toward a sharp point and the stitches angled so they run right off the cloth, ending with two or three stitches without any cloth to sew through. The thread is then cut off to about an inch in length and left there. It will curl itself right up and thus reinforce the end of the line of stitching without the need of tying knots. If the material on the outside of the garment puckers at the end of a dart, it is because the stitching has not been tapered sharply enough.

Let me stress here that seams must be absolutely even throughout the construction of the garment. Seams that are joined together with wavy stitching will pucker and ripple the outer part of the garment and spoil its good looks. Use a seam guide if you have to. A strip of adhesive tape placed ⅜ inch to the right of the needle hole on the plate of your machine will do the trick nicely. Even the experienced person will find such a simple guide useful and of great visual aid. As a matter of fact, women owning brand-new machines with all kinds of

46

etched lines showing different seam widths on the machine plates have used the adhesive tape placed where the ⅝-inch line is so that they can do regular seams without any eyestrain. Putting the edge of the seam against the tape edge is a lot easier than looking for the correct line etched on the plate.

The more accurately you stitch the joining seams the more professional your finished product will look. Expect good results from yourself and don't hesitate as you go along to re-do something that does not please you. If you wait till later you may regret not doing the part over at an earlier stage when the job would have been easier. To rip out something that does not please you is a good sign. It indicates that you know the difference between what is good work and what isn't.

Press as you sew

I cannot overstress how necessary it is to press the seams and darts as you proceed from one unit to another. It is very important to know how, when, and where to press, whether you are making an intricate creation from some fabulous fabric or a lovely simple dress which entails only basic sewing ability. The finest workmanship and the best fabric will end up looking homemade unless the pressing has been done as completely as possible during the construction of the garment.

Always press on the wrong side of the cloth, using a light touch and gliding the iron slowly on the seams, with long movements back and forth instead of short jerky motions which would cause the edges of the seams to fold into pleats here and there. A steam iron is almost a "must" when sewing. It does a fine job on all types of fabrics without the need for a press cloth, and with the temperature set at the right heat for whatever type of material you are using, you are able to avoid scorching.

Press seams from the bottoms upward so that a certain amount of fraying of the seam edges is prevented. This also produces a smooth surface because it eliminates stretching in the seams if they happen to be cut on odd angles of the weave or knit. The correct pressing of darts is another thing that adds the professional touch to a finished garment, since the direction in which the dart is pressed affects the draping of the cloth. Front darts that run in a horizontal direction, like the ones at the sides of our princess dress, are pressed with the fold downward. If the darts ran in a vertical direction on any part of the front, these would be pressed with the fold directed toward the center of the front. Vertical darts on any part of the back are pressed with the fold directed toward the center back, no matter what section of the back they happen to be on. Elbow darts on long sleeves are pressed with the fold downward.

47

The long zipper in the center back opening

Now that you have stitched the center back seam together and pressed it open, rip it down to where the end of the zipper will come. The creases produced by the pressing will be very good aids for inserting the zipper easily—that is why the center seam was stitched up in the first place. Lap the left fold of the opening over the zipper teeth, overlapping just a trifle more than enough to cover the teeth. Insert the pins diagonally, pointing them up, and pin about 1 inch apart until the bottom of the opening is reached. Next, place the opposite fold right up against the zipper teeth and pin from the bottom of the opening toward the top, inserting the pins diagonally, still pointing up and 1 inch apart. (Fig. 7.)

Figure 7

Keep the zipper closed while sewing it into the garment, except at the very beginning—unless the zipper is left open about 1½ inches from the top of the neckline, it will be impossible to sew a straight line because of the bulk of the zipper tab. Start sewing at the top of the opening ¼ inch away from the left fold, and withdraw the pins when you get to them. The cloth crawls a little as it is being stitched and puckers would form between the stitches if the pins were not withdrawn.

When you have proceeded about 1½ inches down with the stitching, leave the needle in the work while you raise the presser foot and push the zipper tab up to the top of the opening so that it will be out of the way. Then lower the presser foot again and continue sewing to the bottom of the opening. Place your hands flat at each side of the work

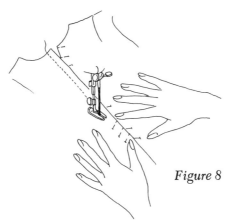

Figure 8

as you sew to prevent the presser foot from pushing the cloth. (Fig.
8.) At the bottom of the opening, leave the needle plunged into the
work and raise the presser foot to allow the work to be swung into
position for stitching across the bottom of the opening. Now lower the
presser foot and sew straight across, turning the wheel by hand for this
short length of stitching to prevent breaking the machine needle just in
case some part of the zipper happens to be underneath the line of
stitching. If the needle does not go down, it is because the opening is
not long enough for the zipper length to fit into, and the line of
stitching must be continued farther down on the first side of the
opening. You might have to break your thread here and do part of the
stitching over again at the bottom of the left side, continuing the
stitching a bit farther down to prevent the stitches from going between
the zipper teeth as you cross over from the left to the right side of the
opening.

Once the needle is on the opposite side of the opening, leave it
inserted in the work, lift the presser foot, and pivot the work again to
place it in position to sew upward on the closing. Hold the top fold out
of the way to stitch on the extreme edge of the right fold directly
against the zipper teeth. When you get near the top of the opening,
you will have to move the zipper tab again in order to continue a
straight line of stitching. This time, however, you must not only lift the
presser but also withdraw the needle and pull the work away from the
machine a little to the right in order to be able to get the zipper tab
moved down and out of the way. Then continue stitching in a straight
line to the top of the opening. (Fig. 9a.)

In garments with plenty of ease in their styling the long zipper is
often inserted with the folds evenly stitched at each side of the
opening and meeting directly over the center of the teeth. The one-fold
method, however, is the most practical to use when the style of the
garment is meant to follow the contours of the body closely or in a

Figure 9a   *Figure 9b*

semi-fitted manner. When folds meet in the middle of a zipper, the least amount of strain on the opening pulls the folds apart and the zipper is exposed, so even in easy-fitting garments the one-way lap can be used if preferred.

To insert the zipper with two equal folds, you follow the same method as for the one-way lap—you sew the seam first, then press it open and rip it down to the length desired. Lap the first fold just a little way beyond the middle of the zipper teeth, pinning in the manner already described; then do the opposite fold in the same way so that the two folds almost overlap each other in the center. This slight overlapping is needed in the pinning process because of the slipping of the folds during the stitching. If the folds just meet, the zipper will show when finished. (Fig. 9b.)

The hand-stitched zipper

On elegant dresses and gowns the zippers are often stitched into the openings by hand instead of by machine, thus imitating the finish used by the couturiers on their expensive creations. The preparation for doing the zipper by hand is the same as that used in preparing the opening for the machine stitching. The seam is stitched together first, then pressed with the edges apart, and the stitches are then ripped down to where the zipper will end.

The zipper is pinned into the opening either with a one-direction lap or with the folds meeting in the middle, and the handwork is done using a small backstitch. Start with a knot in your thread and bring the needle up to the right side of the opening through the zipper tape and the fold on the top, sewing the same distance away from the fold as you would if the work was to be done by machine. With the thread now on the outside of the garment, insert the needle about ¼ inch to the right of the emerging thread and then bring it to the surface again ½ inch to the left of the emerging thread, stitching through all the layers. The next stitch is taken with the needle inserted down into the work ¼ inch to the right of the thread on the outside, then brought out to the surface ½ inch to the left of the emerging thread. This places the stitches ¼ inch apart and the stitches themselves are ¼ inch long. Pull the stitches flat against the cloth, but not so tightly as to cause the cloth to pucker. They should not be too loose either. Use double strands of matching thread for a good firm job. (Fig. 10.)

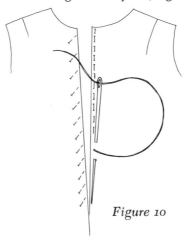

Figure 10

It is easier to do the hand stitching if the zipper is left open after having pinned it into the opening. Press the opening after the zipper is in, using a press cloth on the wrong side if the zipper is made of synthetic material, either nylon or polyester, but the metal zipper can be pressed without a press cloth, as long as the pressing is done on the inside of the garment.

Invisible zippers are very easy to use in garments of all kinds. They come in metal for the heavier fabrics and in synthetic for lighter weights. The procedure for inserting them is somewhat different than for inserting regular zippers but the instructions that come with them are very easy to follow. You must use a special kind of foot on your machine for the job, and the work is done by machine only, not by hand. The seam into which an invisible zipper is inserted is not stitched up first and pressed. Instead, it is left completely open from top to bottom; the zipper goes in first and the seam is afterward stitched from the zipper down. The finished closing looks like a plain seam with no part of the zipper or any stitching showing.

Joining the shoulders; making and attaching the collar

Join the front and back of the garment together at the shoulders and press the seams open; then proceed with the collar pieces. Collars are usually interfaced with a supporting material to keep them in shape. The interfacing material should be compatible with the outer fabric. For instance, if you are using drip-dry fabric that will not have to be ironed when the dress is laundered, the interfacing should also have this quality. If you want to be sure of getting the right kind of interfacing, take a piece of the dress material with you when shopping for it, or buy the interfacing at the same time you purchase the dress fabric, and the best kind will then be sold to you.

The collar pieces are cut double and the interfacing material is used single. Place the collar materials with right sides together and place the interfacing cloth against the wrong side of one of them. Pin all three layers together, then stitch around the outer edges with ⅝-inch seams, leaving the neck edge open. Trim off the seam edges in a layered manner to reduce bulk. This is done by cutting off the interfacing edge almost to the line of stitching. The layer beneath the interfacing is then trimmed down to ¼-inch width, but the third layer is left with its entire seam width to provide support to the finished collar. If the collar is pointed, cut the corners off diagonally close to the line of stitching at the points. Otherwise the ends will be lumpy when turned over. The rounded ends of collars are clipped inward at ⅜-inch intervals almost to the line of stitching after the edges have been layered. This will prevent the remaining seam edges from folding over here and there inside of the curves and causing ripples around collar edges when finished.

This dress has a two-piece collar and both pieces are treated alike, then turned right side out. The outer edges are shaped with the fingers, basted flat, and then pressed. As you baste, roll one collar edge so the seam is slightly on the underside of the collar, instead of lining up both collar edges evenly. The side of the collar that does not show a seam is the one used for the outside part of the collar. After pressing the collar pieces, trim away any material that extends beyond the neck edge of the collar so the top and bottom layers are even at that edge. If there is to be any detailing on the collar, such as top stitching, now is the time to do it, before attaching the collar to the neckline of the garment.

Because this happens to be a two-piece collar which meets in the middle of the front, put the two collar pieces close together and run a line of machine stitching ⅜ inch down from the raw edges just across the front to hold them together; otherwise they may separate while you are attaching them. Now pin the collar pieces to the neckline of the dress with the under-collar down against the right side of the dress, and pin the ends to the back opening evenly. Then pin 1 inch apart with the pins inserted at right angles to the seam. (Fig. 11.)

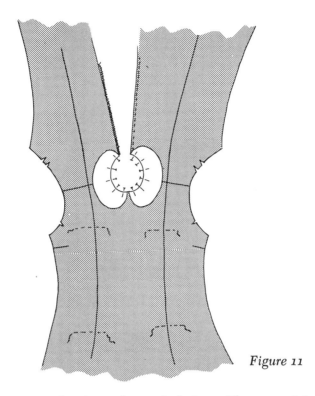

Figure 11

Most patterns provide pieces for neck facings. These are joined together at the shoulders and after pressing the seams open, the outer edges of the facing are finished off either with a tiny hem turned just once, or merely by running a line of machine stitching through the single layer about ¼ inch in from the edge, trimming off the raw edge with pinking shears close to the line of stitching. How to finish the facing is a matter of fabric thickness. If the material is lightweight, the hem edge will not show through on the outside of the garment as a ridge; but in heavy materials a turned-up hem will show; in that case pinking would be best.

Pin the facing against the collar with right sides together, withdrawing the pins partially from the collar and then reinserting them to include the layer of the facing. Be sure to match the centers and shoulders of the facing to those of the collar and garment as you pin all the layers together; otherwise the collar will not set well on the finished garment. If the parts that are going to be joined together are properly matched, there will be a ⅝-inch seam allowance extending beyond the back zipper closing, so be sure to check this before stitching, as those seam ends will be needed for finishing the facing properly after the stitching has been done.

Stitch the collar and facing to the neckline of the dress with ⅝-inch seams, with the dress underneath and the facing on top, and the collar between them, and be sure to run the stitching right out to the ends of the projecting facing. The seam is now trimmed off to a scant ¼-inch width all around the neck, and the facing is turned to the inside of the dress. The ends of the facings are tucked under at the back opening and hand stitched to the tapes of the zipper. The shoulders of the facing are matched to those of the garment and they are stitched together loosely by hand so that the outer side of the garment does not dimple where the stitching has been done. When the zipper has been inserted with a one-lap finish, it is necessary to fold the facing raw edge at an angle to prevent it from interfering with the workings of the zipper teeth.

A very common mistake made by many women who sew is tacking the outer edges of facings too firmly and closely to the garment itself. The tacking then becomes very obvious and the result is an unprofessional look. The least little strain of hand stitching is apt to show up on some materials, so inspect a good-looking ready-made dress that has a facing similar to the one just described, and you'll see how sparsely the neck facing is tacked—usually only to parts of the garment where there is a dart or a seam. The rest of the facing is left free, pressed neatly into place, and the pressing holds it where it belongs.

You will note on Fig. 5 that the placement of the flaps has been marked with hand basting. If the person happens to be of average height, the trimmings can be permanently attached to the markings before the garment is fitted, but if the individual is shorter or taller than average, it is better to wait until the fitting has been done, just in case the flaps have to be moved up or down to look better. If the tabs are made up ahead of time, they can be pinned wherever they would look best on the person, and the original basting would still be an accurate guide for judging the distance from where they were meant to be to where they will actually be stitched, either above or below the basted line.

Fitting the dress

When the garment has been cut from the correct pattern size and the personal differences have been taken care of at the "hidden areas" of the design where body measurements of the individual were more generous than the ones of the pattern, chances of a garment ending up a misfit are definitely eliminated. Some slight adjustments will be required here and there perhaps, but these will be minor ones and nothing that cannot be handled with ease and accuracy. Sometimes the texture of the material being used makes slight changes necessary, as each cloth has its own natural way of draping itself on the body. This also goes for the dress that has been cut from the smallest available size in some particular design for the tiny girl or woman who just

54

can't find the styles she likes in sizes small enough for her. She has had to settle for that smallest size, cutting the dress like the pattern pieces. The reductions she requires will be made when all the important work has been done on the front and back units of the dress with the exception of the neckline. This person might have to do minor adjusting on her neckline, but the extent of the adjustment will be judged after the fitting of the sides has taken place.

Garments should always be tried on with the right side of the material outward, never inside out. Only in this way can a perfect fit be achieved because you can see exactly where the garment has to be taken in or let out, and contours are not always alike on both sides even on the young. It can be readily understood that only by fitting a garment in this way can figure irregularities be carefully camouflaged and the style of the garment produced in its true and original lines.

The sides of the front and back units are now pinned with the wrong sides together so that the seams are on the outside of the garment. Insert the pins vertically, ⅝ inch away from the raw edges and about 1½ inch apart. When both sides have been pinned, the garment is slipped on and zipped closed. (Fig. 12.)

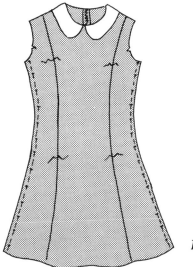

Figure 12

When fitting somebody else, move the pins closer or farther from the body after careful inspection to make the garment fit as it should. Unless one side of the body is quite different from the other, the pins are moved alike on both sides, but if there is a difference, the seams will have to be different widths so that the lines of the design remain alike on each side of the front and back units of the dress. When you are fitting the garment to yourself, you'll have to remove it to change the pins. Doing the fitting on the "hidden areas" of the garment will keep the style intact, but there is a limit to the amount that can be taken in successfully. When you're over the limit, the "styling area" of the front and back begins to wrinkle; you'll know then that the limit has been reached.

If and when wrinkling does occur in the direct front and back of the garment and the garment still needs further fitting, make adjustments by taking in a little on the styling seams or the darts that give the dress the shape it is meant to have. This is sometimes necessary for the waistline area of the person blessed with a tiny waist. An equal amount is taken in on each side of the seams or darts that are located toward the center of the front and back units.

The same principles apply in reverse when the space in the garment is somewhat limited because not enough was added to the side edges when cutting the garment. The side seams will now have to be made narrower in width, and if this doesn't take care of the problem, the styling seams or darts will have to be let out as a last resort. When such alterations are necessary, do remember that the answer does not lie in working with the next-larger pattern size. It means that in the future you must be sure to give full measure to the side seams to compensate for the existing difference between the body measurements of the individual and those of the pattern size. You'll always turn out a fine-fitting garment this way.

How to mark the inside of the garment for stitching

To make it possible to stitch the garment exactly as it was fitted, turn it inside out after removing it and rub blackboard chalk wherever a pin holds two edges together. You will produce a chalk mark on both parts at once, whether it is a side seam holding the back and front edges together, or an inside seam or dart where further adjustments had to be made for the reasons given above. You then remove the pins and allow the garment to remain flat until everything, including the collar or neckline, is taken care of in both the front and back. The chalk lines will remain on the wrong side of the cloth without rubbing off if the garment is handled carefully.

Neckline adjustments on collarless styles

If during the fitting the neckline was found to be a little too snug, and the facing has already been attached, it can be enlarged very easily by untacking the facing at the shoulders and turning it over to the outside of the garment. Then stitch a crescent-shaped line from shoulder to shoulder across the front with the deepest part of the crescent in the middle of the front. (Fig. 13.) The seam in the center

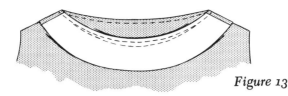

Figure 13

front could be ½ inch below the original one, then trimmed off to match the rest of the seam width. The facing is then turned to the inside of the garment, pressed, and retacked.

It is best to make this type of alteration with narrow crescents rather than to take a chance on enlarging the neck too much. A second crescent would start where the first one did, but it would go slightly deeper in the middle and then the seam would have to be trimmed off more before turning the facing into the garment.

The person with the thin neck, who always ends up with necklines that gap whether the clothing is made at home or purchased ready-made, will have her problem solved if a line of large machine stitching is made through the seamline of the neck edge. The stitching is then pulled up on the bobbin thread from both ends of the neckline opening, moving the fullness toward the center front. Easing the neck edge in this way will not cause the fabric to pucker or gather; it will just tighten up the flexible curved edge of the neckline and make it fit more closely. The garment should be tried on after the neck has been pulled up to be sure that it fits the way it should. The shoulders should be aligned with each other after the neck has been adjusted, and before the ends of the thread have been tied together, to hold the size until the facings have been attached.

The facings should be reduced through their centers so that they will fit the adjusted neckline. Fold back a part of the facing pattern in the center for this reduction, then cut the fabric pieces of the front and back facings. Then attach the facings to the neckline in the usual way.

Adjusting necklines featuring collars

As already mentioned, necklines are very flexible because of their rounded shape. By the right handling they can be increased or decreased without distorting the garment in any way. If the individual neck is thicker than is considered average for the size of the pattern used—and this happens to be a common problem even when buying clothes—the collar itself will have to be cut longer so it will surround the neck comfortably. Additions are made in the middle of the back of a one-piece collar for a garment that is styled without a back opening—on a shirtwaist dress, for example. This keeps the front ends of

57

the collar in their original shape. If there is an opening in the back and the collar is in one piece without a separation in the middle of the front—like a bias-cut rolled collar, for example—the addition is made in the center front. On the other hand if the collar is made of two pieces, one for the left and one for the right side of the neckline and they meet in the middle front and in the center back, the pattern piece must be slashed at the location of the shoulder and separated to allow the additional length needed in each piece without distorting the shape of either end.

You might find this hard to believe, but although the collar neck edges have been increased, the neckline of the garment is not enlarged at all. The flexible edge of the garment neck will conform and stretch willingly to the length of the increased collar without a problem, no matter what the material happens to be. If, however, the cloth is stubborn and simply refuses to go along with the stretching, you need only to clip inward less than ¼ inch at 1-inch intervals and the curved seam will expand willingly to fit the dominating edge of the collar line. It is the neckline edge of the collar that is important. If that fits, so will the neck of the garment fit eventually. Trimming down the seam edge to ¼-inch width when the collar has been attached will do this trick neatly.

Collars must be reduced in length for the girl with the thin neck, and the reducing is done by folding the center of the pattern piece at the shoulder location if the collar is styled in two parts. The job is just the reverse of the method of enlarging—instead of slashing and adding, you fold and reduce. The neckline of the garment is not disturbed at all. When the collar is ready to attach to the garment, it is pinned to the center of the neckline and the ends are matched to the areas where they belong. The curved line of the garment will fit well

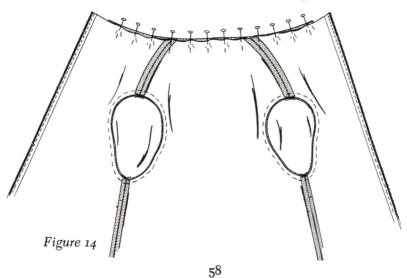

Figure 14

without puckering or wrinkling. It is the length of the collar edge that controls the fit of the garment neckline here, and the flexible edge will ease to it. (Fig. 14.)

The alterations described for dresses with collars will produce good results whether the neckline of the garment is finished with a shaped facing or with a narrow bias strip that covers the seam edges. It is not a bad idea to experiment first with a scrap piece of cloth to determine how much longer or shorter the collar should be cut than the pattern length. You'll have no guessing to do that way and you will tackle the work with confidence.

Sewing the sides of the garment

Now pin the dress at the sides with the right sides of the material facing each other and the pins inserted at right angles to the seam line. Start to pin at the top of the side seams and proceed downward, then sew through the chalk lines in either direction. Press the seams apart from the bottom toward the top to prevent fraying the cloth.

Sew the sleeves into their tubular shape and if the sleeves are short ones, finish the bottoms with hems or cuffs, or whatever finish the style of the pattern indicates. The completed sleeves will then be ready to insert into their respective armholes. If the sleeves are meant to reach down to the wrist, it is best to insert the sleeves into the armholes first, taking care of the length and hems or cuffs afterward so that the accurate length can be judged. Before going any further with the sleeves, check to be sure that you have not forgotten to make notches at the two sides of the cap and at the peak, so that the sleeves will match properly with the armholes and at the shoulders.

"Magic stitching" in the sleeve caps

The first step toward inserting sleeves perfectly into armholes of a garment is to sew a line of large machine stitching around the caps of the sleeves between the front and back notches. This line of stitching will not only be a guide in getting the sleeves sewn accurately into the armholes, but will also make it possible to place the fullness, or ease, in the caps where it will provide both comfort and good looks. With this stitching the job of getting that fullness inserted smoothly into the armhole is a breeze. No wonder we refer to it as "magic stitching"!

Adjust the machine to make the largest stitches; then place the right side of a sleeve under the presser foot exactly ⅝ inch in from the raw edge, starting right at the notches on either the front or back of the sleeve, but be sure that the "magic stitching" goes right down to the lowest double notch. (Fig. 15.)

Pin the notch at the peak of the sleeve cap to the end of the shoulder

59

seam with right sides together, and be sure you're starting with the right sleeve in the right armhole, or the left to the left so that the single and double notches match on sleeve and armhole. Now take hold of the work so that the inside of the garment is facing you and with your hands on each side of the armhole, as if you were holding the wheel of your car, steer the armhole to the left notch and insert a pin on the inside of the sleeve to hold it against the armhole there. Then steer to the right notch and do the same thing there. The inside of the sleeve resembles a dark tunnel looming ahead of you. Hold the "steering wheel" position throughout the complete pinning process. You'll note a tremendous amount of fullness in the sleeve cap between the shoulder and each of the pinned side notches.

To get this fullness worked in accurately on these areas, the bobbin thread is pulled so that the edge of the sleeve is reduced in length to compare with the amount of armhole edge into which it will have to be fitted and pinned. You first pull one end of the bobbin thread and distribute the fullness between the shoulder pin and the one at the left notch so that the fullness is even in this part of the sleeve. Then to hold the fullness in place you insert additional pins about an inch apart, with pins at right angles to the seamline. The same procedure is followed on the opposite side of the cap. (Fig. 16.) The underarm section is done next, stretching the edges a little if one happens to be a bit shorter in length than the other, which is quite possible, due to the fact that the armhole may have been increased for a person who has a larger bust measurement than the pattern, or decreased where the sides were taken in for the thinner-than-average girl.

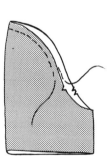

Figure 15

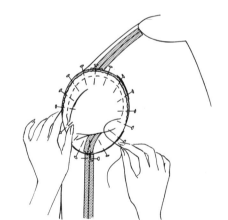

As already mentioned, it is not necessary to increase or decrease the width of the sleeves when changes are made in the side edges of a garment. However, if you wish to reduce or increase the width of the sleeves because a person's arms are larger or thinner than average, you can, of course, make a change in the size of the sleeves. The armhole and sleeve edges will conform to each other readily when the work is correctly held and when it is put under the presser foot the right way.

Sew the sleeves into the armholes with an exact ⅝-inch seam allowance. If the seams are narrower, the garment ends up being too broad across the shoulders and chest; and if the seams are too wide, the garment ends up too tight. Do the sewing inside of the sleeves, inside of the "tunnel," starting at the underarm section and continuing right over the "magic stitching" when you get to it. The fullness of the sleeve cap will flatten right down without a sign of gathering if the fingers of both hands are placed on each side of the large stitching as you sew through it. (Fig. 17.) It is usually a good idea to stitch the sleeves twice for extra reinforcement, doing the second line of stitching through the first stitching and in the same way you did the first.

When using bulky materials, a permanent smoothness is produced around the upper part of the shoulders and sleeves if the gathered fullness in the seam allowance beyond the "magic stitching" is trimmed off to ¼ inch. The rippling would eventually cause the top of the sleeves to become uneven where the fullness folded over underneath. Trimming off the ripples and leaving only ¼ inch prevents this from happening. Trim only the sleeve edge, not the armhole edge, and do the trimming only where the "magic stitching" is, not all around the whole sleeve edge. (Fig. 18.)

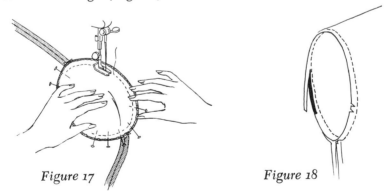

Figure 17　　　　　　　　　　*Figure 18*

Another very important bit of advice is this: Don't ever press the armhole seams after the sleeves have been inserted or you'll stretch them out of shape. True, they will get plenty of ironing when the garment is laundered or dry cleaned, but that kind of handling will not distort the shaping of the joining seam. It is in the process of constructing the garment that women very often throw the parts out of shape by overhandling.

Finishing sleeveless armholes

If sleeves are to be omitted, the armholes can be finished either with shaped facings or with bias-cut strips of the same fabric as the dress, if the material is lightweight. Usually when a pattern design is shown without sleeves as well as with, there are pattern pieces furnished for the facings. These are cut from the garment cloth and stitched into shape to form circles. The circles are then placed with their right sides against the right sides of the garment armholes. After matching the edges and pinning them together, run a seam around them ⅝ inch deep, making sure not to stretch the sensitive curved edges. Clip inward almost to the line of stitching at ⅜-inch spacings, then turn the facings to the inside of the garment. Tack the facing into position loosely enough not to cause the stitches to pull in on the outer fabric. Tacking is done about ⅜ inch apart. That's close enough.

The outer edges of the facings could be turned under once and hemmed by machine before they are attached to the armholes, but if the fabric is rather bulky, pinking would be the best kind of finish. If the heavy fabric is going to be laundered a lot, however, overcast the outer edges after running machine stitching through the single layer so that fraying is prevented. The edge could be left plain or pinked in this case.

Marking the length and turning up the hem

You are now ready to see the fruit of your work and pass judgment on the results. Should any adjustments be needed at this stage, they will be minor in nature if you have proceeded according to instructions so far. Wear the undergarments you plan to wear when the dress is finished, and also wear shoes with heels the right height, as all this has a bearing on the appearance of the finished product.

The length of the dress is usually marked from the floor up to where the garment will be most becoming on the wearer, and it is important to remember that some styles look better on the individual at one length and other styles look best at still another length, depending upon the shape of the person and the silhouette of the garment design. It is a good idea before you reach a final decision to pin up the bottom of the dress to different lengths to see which will be the most pleasing. After this important matter has been settled, the dress is marked with pins or chalk every 5 or 6 inches all around the bottom. Do your measuring with either a hem marker or a yardstick. (Fig. 19.) The

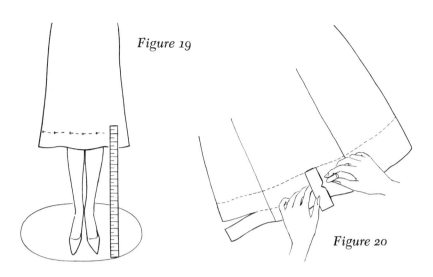

Figure 19

Figure 20

person wearing the dress should pivot on heel and toe without actually moving away from the spot; the marker or yardstick remains in one position during the marking. If you have no one to help you, you can very easily mark your own hem with one of the self-operating marking gadgets that have chalk powder in them.

Remove the garment and measure the width of the hem from the markings down. Widths of hems vary with the style of the garment and with the type of fullness featured in the skirt. The recommended width for a hem is usually specified on the pattern pieces, so cut the hem width accordingly. (Fig. 20.) Flared fullness usually is finished with a narrower hem than when the skirt is gathered, pleated, or straight.

Sew a strip of seam tape or some narrow lace to the edge of the hem, holding the strip slightly stretched during the stitching to prevent it from going on too full. Then turn up the hem and pin it into place, inserting the pins in vertical position about an inch or so apart. Sew the hem with your own favorite hemming stitch, or use mine, described below.

Don't be tempted to press the hem flat at the bottom before doing the hand sewing. Many women do this, not realizing that it is far easier to get a hem to behave well during hand stitching if you leave the bottom unpressed until your handwork is finished.

My own favorite hemming stitch is speedy, invisible on the outside of the garment and it stays in place until it is deliberately taken down; it never falls down by itself unexpectedly. You turn the garment inside out and hold the hem in an upright position. Make a knot in your thread, hide it underneath the top of the hem, and bring the thread out at the very top of the lace or tape. Now, in a direct line with the thread that is emerging from the top of the hem, take a tiny stitch into

63

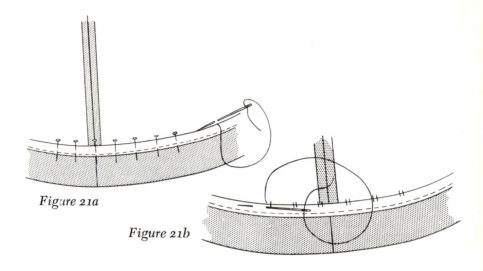

Figure 21a

Figure 21b

the garment, right above the hem; take only a yarn or two of the cloth on the needle and then pull the stitch through that tiny amount. (Fig. 21a.) Next, take a stitch into the hem, starting it directly below the thread that is coming out of the dress and making this stitch ½ inch or ⅜ inch long. (Fig. 21b.) Repeat these stitches at ½-inch or ⅜-inch spacings until the hem is finished. The stitching will resemble little "mice teeth," or ditto marks made by the typewriter. The thread should be single strand and left fairly loose in the stitching so that the stitches do not cause the outer material to dimple.

A light touch-up with the iron is all that the hem will need for pressing. Do the pressing on the lower half of the hem width to prevent the top edge from showing through on the outside. The dress is now ready to be worn!

When and how to line a dress separately

Dresses are lined for different reasons. Some are lined to prevent the outer cloth from getting out of shape. Some are lined simply to have a built-in slip inside so that they are always ready to go anywhere at a moment's notice. This is often done to a dress-up type of dress, made of good fabric—definitely not a dress that will end up in the family wash each week.

The lining that hangs separately inside of the dress is cut exactly like the outer dress, and then assembled. The neckline is cut down enough to get it to fit around the outer edge of the neck facing, and the edge is turned under and hand stitched to the dress. The seam at the center back is turned under ⅝ inch and the fold is caught by hand to the zipper tapes, the lower end of the lining seam having already been joined by machine. If the dress has sleeves, finish the armholes of the lining with just a line of machine stitching going through the single layer ½ inch in from the raw edge. Then trim away the raw edges with pinking shears close to the stitching. This is about the flattest finish you can get; it works well and doesn't fray. Some other kind of finish is apt to cause ridges to show through on the outside of the garment.

If the dress that is being lined is sleeveless, and the armholes are finished with facings cut from the dress material, the armholes of the lining should be trimmed away a bit and the raw edges then tucked under and hand-finished against the outer edges of the facings. The armholes of the lining in a dress with sleeves are left free, and not attached to the dress anywhere.

The length of the lining is measured 1 inch shorter than the dress. The hem is turned up and hand-finished. When inserting the lining into the dress, it may be put in with the raw edges facing the raw edges of the dress, so that when you look inside the dress all you see are beautifully finished lines with all the raw edges out of sight. On the other hand, the neatly finished seams, either pinked with pinking shears or zigzag stitched with your automatic sewing machine are quite acceptable if they show on the inside. In this case the only edges that would be turned toward the garment would be those around the neckline, along the zipper closing and, if the garment is sleeveless, against the facings around the armholes. This is strictly a matter of personal choice. The advantage of having a lining in the garment is there, regardless of how the lining is put in.

When the outer material is very soft or thin in texture, the seam edges and the dart folds may show through to the outside in the form of ridges. In such cases it is preferable to direct the raw edges of the lining to the inside so that the smooth finish will be against the wrong side of the garment.

3

The Glamorous Evening Dress
(with Underlining)

Every girl remembers the thrill of wearing her very first evening gown, even more vividly than she remembers the occasion for wearing *it*.

But for a teen-ager, the long-anticipated prom can turn into a disenchanted evening if she comes face to face with someone else wearing a duplicate gown. True, the clerk in the store may have said that hers was the only one like it in the store, and perhaps it was. But, don't forget, there are other stores. Manufacturers of evening gowns distribute their wares to whatever stores order them. Even though you go a great distance from your own town to purchase the gown, there is no guarantee that it will be the only one of its kind at any function.

Even expensive ready-to-wear is made in quantity, although not so much as popular-priced clothes. So the price of the dress doesn't always guarantee exclusiveness. Exclusiveness is only possible when clothes are custom-made for the individual, or made at home.

Making evening clothes is more fun than anything. The workmanship which most evening dresses entail is nowhere near as difficult as it looks. As a matter of fact, rarely is the work any more than just plain basic sewing. The fabrics are what make these gowns exciting. Most evening-dress fabrics for girls are easy to handle. For more sophisticated gowns, fabrics may be of types that require expert handling; but the taffetas, crisp organdies (both cotton and synthetics), brocades, polished cottons, and delustered satins, all create exciting silhouettes and are no trouble to work with. There are countless other fabrics to choose from in colors to make a girl as pretty as she wants to be.

Evening dress materials do not have to be expensive to be lovely. It is the effect that the cloth creates that is important. Under artificial light it will not matter whether the cloth is real silk or a good imitation.

What is "underlining"?

In the past few years it has become quite common to use an extra layer of lightweight fabric for backing the outer garment materials. This is done not only to tailored items but also to dresses and other articles of wearing apparel for adults as well as for children. This is known as "underlining," but has nothing to do with the usual conventional lining job that is done to a tailored garment before it is called complete.

The reasons for underlining garments are numerous and quite logical in most instances. One of the most popular reasons for backing the outer cloth with the extra layer is to give opaqueness enough to the garment cloth so that the seam edges and the dart folds will not show through on the outside of the finished product, which is quite apt to happen if the material used for the garment is either lightweight, light in color, or loosely woven.

Loosely woven material will especially benefit by an underlining to keep the garment in shape. Fabrics that are apt to fray readily will be helped by having an extra layer of material in the seams. Underlining provides extra body in fabrics which might otherwise be too soft and clingy to shape up into the desired silhouette. The underlining material should be about the weight of batiste or lawn.

Figure 22

A fairly basic design has been chosen for the evening dress here so that the method of underlining delicate fabrics can be fully covered. No matter what the reason is for underlining, the work entailed is the same.

When purchasing the material for the gown, match it in color with the lightweight underlining material. The underlining may be either crisp or soft, depending upon the pattern design chosen and the actual texture of outer fabric. Sales people keep up with the textures and weights of all the new fabrics as they appear on the market. Ask for their help if you do not know which type of underlining will be best for the job at hand.

Get the same amount of yardage for both dress and underlining if the fabric widths are alike, but if the outer material and the lining are of different widths the requirement for the lining will have to be figured out. Most sales people are willing to work with you on this.

We have chosen a style for our gown consisting of a bodice fitting closely to the body from the waistline up. The skirt flares out in an A-line silhouette almost to the floor, with a long zipper inserted into the center back seam. (Fig. 22.) The method of assembling the parts of such a dress, whether a formal type or one for casual wear, is exactly the same.

Take measurements each time you sew

Measurements change here and there from time to time for different reasons, and not always because the person has gained or lost weight, or has grown. The change sometimes occurs when a different type of undergarment is worn than was worn the last time the person was measured. So measure the bust, waistline, hips where largest, and the length from the collarbone to the waistline at the center back. Then hold the evening dress skirt pattern piece to the person and see whether the length is long enough. If not, add to the bottom. If it is too long, take off length at the bottom. Do all this before pinning the pattern parts to the wrong side of the cloth.

As has already been advised in the teen-ager's dress, add to the sides of the garment parts wherever the body is more generously proportioned than the pattern measurements specify. Start at the sides of the bodice and give the extra amount needed for the bust from the armholes downward, continuing in the same amount right down to the bottom of the bodice if the difference there is the same as in the bust. If, however, the waistline requires more than the bust, increase gradually as you proceed drawing the chalk line downward to make up the difference. For example, if 2 inches are needed in the bust but 3 inches are needed at the waist, you would start with the 2 inches divided into four equal parts, adding ½ inch at the top of the bodice and gradually increasing the chalk line so it is ¾ inch away from the pattern cutting line at the bottom of the bodice.

In dresses that have a joining seam running across the waistline, it is often necessary to lengthen the bodice if the girl happens to be tall, or longer-waisted than average. This addition is made at the bottom of the waistline in the same amount at back and front. Extend the darts to include them in the additions, but draw the lines with chalk straight down to the bottom of the additions instead of continuing the slant of the printed lines of the dart, to prevent getting the waistline too small.

If the person's figure is shorter than average from the shoulders to the waist, don't shorten the pattern. Cut the front and back bodice the same length as the pattern and you'll have a chance to cut off the length more accurately later on, after some of the basic sewing has been done and the bodice is ready to be fitted.

The skirt units are cut next, added to the bottom if the girl is tall, and shortened if she is short, as already stated (pp. 42–43). Add to the sides of the skirt if her waist and hips are larger, but cut like the pattern if she is smaller and the fitting will take care of this later on. Fig. 23 shows a typical layout of a style that features a waistline, showing where and how additions have to be made.

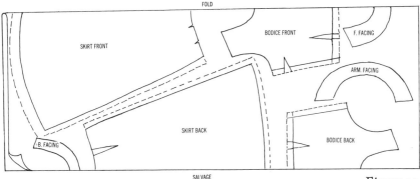

Figure 23

Now about the underlining

Cut the garment and underlining materials exactly alike, then pin the underlining material to the wrong side of the garment parts. Run a line of regular machine stitching ¼ inch in from the raw edges on each part of the garment. Next, run a line of machine stitching through the middle of all the darts, after marking them accurately from the pattern onto the underlining. The stitching goes through both layers and holds them together. Then pinch the darts together and sew them into their right shape. Without the line of stitching going through the two fabrics first, it would be impossible to sew a perfectly shaped dart through both, as the top layer would slip away from the stitching line and the outer cloth would be distorted.

Press the darts in their correct directions, the horizontal ones downward, the center ones toward the center of both front and back units. If the material is bulky, you can split the darts through their folds to within ½ inch or ⅝ inch of the points and press the seams apart, with the pointed ends flattened down so they fold in both directions.

Now insert the back zipper into the opening, but only partially. Start at the top and proceed only to within 1½ inch of the waistline, then allow it to dangle there until further progress has been made in the fitting and assembling of the different parts of the dress. Use either style of closing, the one-lap or double-fold type. You may use either machine or hand stitching, as already described. (Fig. 24.)

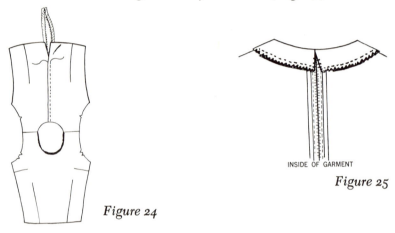

INSIDE OF GARMENT

Figure 25

Figure 24

You might also be interested in using an invisible type of zipper which now comes in synthetic as well as in metal—the synthetic ones are quite light weight and suitable for the finer fabrics. If you are already familiar with working with the regular kind of zipper, you'll have no problem following the very clear instructions for inserting this unique zipper into an opening. This zipper gets inserted completely by machine and there is no sign of either the zipper teeth or of any stitching. A special sewing-machine foot is needed to insert this type of zipper; without it the job can't be done. It is sold wherever invisible zippers are sold and it, too, comes with full instructions on how to put it on your machine after removing the regular sewing foot, and then how to proceed from there. The seam into which a zipper of this type is inserted is not stitched up first and pressed, as when working with the regular type; it is stitched up after the zipper has already been inserted. Whichever kind of zipper is to be used, however, be sure to sew it in only to within 1½ inches of the waistline and then stop.

Join the shoulder seams next and complete the neckline now. If the neck is to be finished with a facing of the garment material, underline the facing with the same material as the dress. You might even give the facing a double layer of the underlining for extra support and firmness if the outer cloth is soft and lightweight. After joining the shoulders of the facings together, sewing through the layers as if they were a single thickness, press the shoulder seams open and then run a line of machine stitching through the outer edges ½ inch in. Trim close to the line of stitching with pinking shears. (Fig. 25.)

Pin the facing to the right side of the neckline after matching it at the center front and shoulders, then stitch. The two ends of the facing should extend ⅝ inch out beyond the opening in the middle of the back. When the facing is turned to the inside of the garment, after clipping the seams inward almost to the line of stitching at ⅜-inch intervals, the two ends are turned inward and the facing is hand stitched against the zipper tapes. Note in Fig. 25 how the ends of the facings are treated; if a single lap is used over the zipper closing, the inside fold of the facing is slanted enough so it will not interfere with the workings of the zipper.

Stitch the outer edges of the facings by hand to the underlining material, making sure not to come through to the outside, or the outer material will buckle. The armhole facings can be put on after the side seams have been joined together or they can be attached right now while the sides are still open. Both ways work fine, so take your choice, and do it whatever way is easiest for you. The pressing of the armhole is somewhat easier while the sides are still open. Underline the arm-hole facings, but don't use the underlining material double here even though you did on the neck. Finish the outer edges of the armhole facings like those of the neck, and after sewing them to the armholes with right sides against the dress, and clipping almost to the line of stitching every ⅜ inch, turn the facings to the inside of the garment and press. Don't tack the facings into place as yet; you'll do that later on.

Another effective way to finish necklines and armholes is with bias-cut binding of the same material, applied to the outside of the garment as trimming, allowing ¼ inch of the bias to remain on the outside of the neckline and armholes. To keep the neck the correct size when using a binding instead of a shaped facing, it is necessary to cut away the regular ⅝-inch seam allowance with which the facing would have been sewn. Unless this seam edge is cut off before applying the bias trim, the neckline and armholes will end up being too small. How this type of finish is applied is fully covered in the chapter, "Fashion Detailing."

Locating the waistline

The more complete the bodice units are before being fitted, the better. Pin the bodice sides together with the wrong sides of front and back units facing each other, pins inserted ⅜ inch in from the raw edges and about 1½ inches apart or closer. Put on the bodice right side out and zip it closed. Move the pins here and there to get the bodice to fit smoothly; then tie a thin cord, or strong string, around the waist rather tightly so that the string will roll to the natural waistline. With your fingers, move over to the sides the wrinkles that were caused by the tightness of the string so that the "styling area" of the front and back parts of the bodice are smooth; then draw a chalk line around the waist just where the string is on the bodice material. (Fig. 26.)

Figure 26

To test whether or not the string is located correctly at the person's waist, it is a good idea, even before the chalking is done, to put a narrow belt around the waist to see whether or not the string shows either below or above the belt. If the string is peeking out from the belt, tuck it underneath the belt where it belongs. You will then be sure that the chalk line will be horizontally accurate when drawn on the front and back units of the bodice.

It is advisable to draw continuous chalk lines across the underarm sections of the bodice, from the front to the back, so that the waistline seams can be accurately matched when the garment parts are joined together permanently. Remove the bodice, chalk the inside, and withdraw the pins from the right side. Then inspect the results of the horizontal chalking.

It is very probable that the chalk line around the waist is quite wavy, especially if the upper part of the figure is shapely. The line will drop at the waistline in the area where the bust takes up extra length, and the side lines will rise slightly. The narrow belt will be of great aid in getting the waist location properly established, no matter what type the figure happens to be. Although the line undulates, an even-looking waistline will result when the bodice and skirt units are joined to each other. If the string did not show from underneath the narrow belt when you were in the process of establishing the waistline, and you were pleased with the location of the belt, you'll be just as well pleased with where the seam joins the skirt and bodice units on the finished garment.

Whatever the individual's figure problem, it will show up on the chalk line drawn around the waist of the bodice, whether the problem is in the front or back of the figure, or in the shoulders. But this method of determining the waistline successfully camouflages the figure problem. If you joined the skirt and bodice just hit-or-miss you would only call attention to the fault and make it even more obvious.

Joining skirt and bodice units to each other

Before joining the skirt units to the bodice, draw a chalk line on the right side of the skirt waist ⅜ inch down from the top. Now start at the center front, pinning the chalk line of the skirt directly on top of the chalk line on the bodice, the pieces right sides together, inserting the pins at right angles to the seam and about 1 inch apart. Work from the center toward the sides and keep the units smooth against each other. Always work with the skirt unit on top so that you can guide the pinning easily, line upon line. (Fig. 27.) Follow the same procedure for pinning the back bodice and skirt units to each other, starting at the center. The zipper will still be dangling in the middle of the back between the left and right parts, but continue to ignore it for a little while longer. You next sew the bodice and skirt parts as pinned, using large machine stitches. During the stitching keep the skirt unit on top so that you can follow and accurately judge the usual ⅜-inch seam allowance. The sides of the dress are still open.

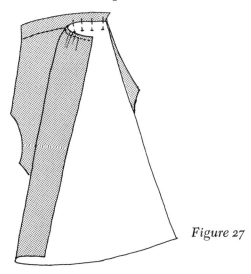

Figure 27

Fitting the sides of the gown

Pin the sides of the gown with the wrong sides together so that the raw edges project on the outside. Insert the pins vertically about 2 inches apart, starting at the waist and pinning toward the hem; then come back to the waist and pin up to the armhole. The seams should be ⅝ inch wide. If there is a slight difference in the length of the front and back bodice units at the side seams, hold the edges slightly stretched against each other and this will make them come out even. (Fig. 28.)

Figure 28

The dress is now put on and zipped up at the back, although the zipper is still free below the waistline, so pin that opening together. Move the pins here and there if you have to at the sides of the dress, but don't overfit. If the gown begins to wrinkle in the front and back, you are pulling in too much on the side seams. Seams should be even at left and right sides of the dress, unless the figure is different; in that case the seams would be different also. Inspect the fitting critically. If you are not sure the waistline is correctly located, try on the narrow belt again to see if the seam around the waist shows above or below the belt. If it does, rip the large machine stitching at the waist and change the waistline to a better location so the narrow belt will conceal the seam all around.

Before going any further be sure you are satisfied with your result so far. In the event that you have produced a crooked line in the horizontal chalking of the waist, with no justified reason for the irregularity, it perhaps is crooked because you were not quite fussy enough

74

in smoothing the bodice after tying the string, and before chalking the line at the string. All these little things are important to do along the way, and that's what brings about the eventually pleasing result.

Now remove the gown, chalk the sides on the inside, and remove the pins from the outside. Pin a piece of seam tape, or some other light-weight tape, across each seam at the waistline areas of the front and back in separate pieces, and sew these strips against the skirt waistline with regular-sized stitches this time, going through the same line twice for reinforcement. The purpose of the tape is to prevent the waist from stretching. Actually you now have three lines of stitching, because of the large-sized stitches originally made. The line of large stitches was used to make changing the waistline location easier if that was neces-sary after the fitting. To avoid bulk press the seams of the waistline in an upward direction when the top of the skirt has gathers. In styles without gathers in the skirt, the waistline seam should be pressed in a downward direction. Trim the seam down to ⅝ inch on the bottom of the bodice now that the waistline is correct, and insert the remaining length of the zipper into the rest of the back opening which continues down into the skirt section. All this is done while the sides of the garment are still open.

The side seams are pinned together next, with the material right sides together. Match the waistline seams of back and front units first, then pin down to the bottom, come back to the waist, and proceed to pin toward the armholes. Pull out the armhole facings so that their right sides are also together, and pin them as continuations of the bodice seams. Sew up side seams in a single operation from end to end, including the edges of the facings. (Fig. 29.) Press seams open.

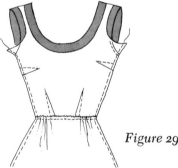

Figure 29

Now try on the gown to measure the length. When the garment is to be worn with a belt, you must put on the belt in order to measure the length accurately, as the wearing of the belt very often affects skirt length. If the belt or tie that is to be worn over the waistline is not complete, put on a belt or sash from some other garment so that it will take up the length that the actual belt will, then proceed with the hem marking.

As you can see, a hem marker is useless for arriving at the right length of a dress of this kind. You will have to experiment with the length by turning it up and viewing it first at one length and then another until it meets with your approval. If the dress is so long that it touches the floor and the fabric can be chalk-marked there, do that every 5 or 6 inches. Then use the marks as guides for turning up evenly for the actual length. Then decide on what hem width to allow and cut the excess length off below the marks. The pattern pieces usually specify what width hem is best for the particular hemlines. (Fig. 30.)

Figure 30

Use seam tape or fancy thin lace for edging the top of the hem, then turn it up and hand-finish it to the underlining only, so that no stitchings will be visible on the outside layer of the garment. If you do bring the stitches to the outside, the gown will buckle above the hem, so be sure to avoid this. A light touch-up with the iron on the lower half of the hem width finishes the gown and puts it into a wearable stage to be enjoyed.

Ribbon or velvet tied with loops and flowing streamers which reach down to the hemline may be worn around the waist to complete the dress.

Should the underlined gown be lined besides?

If the underlined gown is extra special, like a wedding dress, for example, an additional lining can be put into it to cover up all the raw edges. The lining is cut like the dress and assembled. It is then put into the dress with the raw edges facing toward the underlining fabric so that the inside of the dress is cleanly finished. The lining is then attached by hand around the outer edges of the neck facing. The armhole edges are just turned and hemmed, either by hand or by machine, but they are not attached to the outer garment at all. Hand-finish the lining against the zipper closing. Turn the hem up 1 inch shorter than the gown.

The finishing lining can be used in any type of dress, whether it is underlined or not. It can take the place of a separate slip.

Fitting Tips for Different Bodices

There are many different kinds of dress tops, or bodices. Some are meant to conform closely to the upper part of the body and others are cut fuller so they follow the body in a semi-fitted way, but do not hug it anywhere. Then there are the bodices that are cut very roomy and instead of the sides being shaped inward and closer to the body as they near the waistline, they are cut straight down from the armholes to the waistline without shaping at all. This is the type of bodice that must be gathered at the bottom and the fullness forms into blousing above the waist.

Form-fitted bodice with gathered skirt

When the dress is bouffant in the skirt and form-fitted in the bodice, it is only the bodice that requires concentration on fitting. It is then necessary to accurately locate the waistline where it will be most pleasing and correct, as already covered in the section on the formal gown. The skirt that is gathered, fully pleated, or circular is then pulled up to fit the bottom of the bodice and joined against the chalk line.

Locating waistlines on bloused bodices

Bodices that are meant to blouse above the waist are cut with more fullness and length than those meant to fit smoothly. Instead of the bodice being nipped in at the waistline with pointed darts, the fullness at the bottom of it is controlled by either gathers or folds, and the length produces the blousing. In such styles it is important that the amount of blousing be correct for the wearer's height and type, or the style will not do her justice. The horizontal fullness featured in such styles rarely needs to be altered in any way if the pattern size is right; it is only the length of the bodice that is in question.

Not all figure types wear the same amount of blousing becomingly.

Tall willowy girls and women look well in any amount of blouse, but short people, and those that are short-waisted, must limit the amount of length in the bodice of these easy-fitting garments so that the bodice draping does not overlap the normal waistline. A bloused design is becoming only when the waist of the wearer is clearly defined by a break in the silhouette between the bodice and skirt; otherwise the waistline gets lost in the fullness and the figure looks heavy in the midriff area. It is the tall, slim girl who looks best in this style.

To fix the bodice length so it will be becoming, prepare it as fully as any other bodice style, but don't put the gathering in at the bottom until after the fitting. The more complete the bodice is the better the fitting results will be. Pin the sides together, put the bodice on, and then tie a string tightly around the waist.

To make the fabric in the bodice drape properly on the body, pull the bodice down straight at the center front and in the center back. Do the same to the left and right sides, and then pull down the areas of the bodice that are in line with the bust, locating the fullness straight up and down there. Do the same in the back, in line with the shoulder blades. This draping puts the bodice in position for the next step, the one that provides you with the blousing. (Fig. 31.)

Place your hands on each side of the waist, right over the string, as if about to do a reducing exercise. Holding this position, shrug one shoulder and allow some material to pull up above the string as it wants to, but don't allow the string to shift away from the waistline— keep your hands on the string and hold it there. Shrug the other shoulder next; this pulls out more cloth on the opposite side of the bodice. Now shrug both shoulders at the same time to even up the fullness to the amount needed by the individual. The amount of extra material that gets pulled up above the string by the shrugging of the shoulders is usually the amount that will be correct for a good appearance. Now draw the chalk line where the string is, or just a bit below it. If the fullness goes right across the front and back units, run two lines of "magic stitching" about ¼ inch apart where the chalk line is,

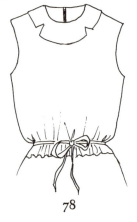

Figure 31

78

then draw the fullness up by the bobbin threads to fit the top part of the skirt that will join it.

On the other hand, if the gathers are grouped between the notches on the side front area on each side of the center, do the double row of large machine stitching between the couple of marks or notches that indicate where the fullness should be. Then trim off the excess length of the bodice to the usual ⅝-inch seam allowance. Seams around the waistline of dresses with bloused bodices are usually pressed in a downward direction for a more pleasing look. If the skirt also has a gathered top, the waistline is pressed in the direction of the part that features the least amount of gathering. Occasionally the pattern design does recommend pressing the gathered seam open at the waistline, so if you don't always know the best way, take the advice given on the pattern sheet.

The empire bodice

The style of bodice that is meant to start above the waistline is youthful and becoming if the seam is not so high on the upper part of the figure that it mounts up on part of the bust curve. The pattern should be held up to the individual and pushed close to the body to see if the curve of the bust is fully included in that part of the pattern. If the pattern part is too short, add to the bottom of the bodice pieces to make sure that they will come down a bit lower, just passing below the curves of the bust. Nothing will have to be done to the top of the skirt to compensate for this change in length, as it will not affect the skirt top in any way.

When the empire line hits the body higher than it should, it causes the figure to look heavy in the middle and the shape of the bustline is completely lost, giving the garment the look of a maternity dress.

The long bodice

Many times the bodice length is designed to come down below the waistline so that the normal location of the person's waist is not considered here, unless the long-torso bodice has seams or darts that are meant to fit and define the waistline noticeably or semi-noticeably. On the short person the long torso might be a bit too low, so she should hold it up to herself, decide just about where she would like it to come, then fold the pattern to that length at the bottom.

The tall girl would do the reverse, adding to the bottom if she feels that a longer line would be more becoming to her. In either case, it would be practical to be sure it is long enough so that the length could be experimented with after the preliminary work on the bodice has been completed and the bodice has reached the fitting stage. Once cut

79

too short, that's it! If it's too short for a long-torso look but too long for a regular waistline, you may find the skirt too short if you try fitting it at the natural waistline. So think before you cut, and you'll never be sorry.

The Flip-lined Jumper

About the easiest and quickest way to whip up a sleeveless garment, lined throughout, is to choose a flip-lined jumper. It can be worn over blouses and jerseys, or it can be made from the dressiest material and worn to the fanciest affair. The workmanship is the same in either case. Only the fabrics used make the difference.

The flip-lined garment is popular with all the female members of the family because it slips on so easily and feels so smooth and nice against the skin, especially if the skin is sensitive to different fabric fibers. The lining hangs independently inside of the garment like a slip, except that it is joined to the neckline and armholes by machine. It also takes the place of facings.

Any style that has side seams and a center front or back seam can be flip-lined. The garment fabric and the lining are cut identically. All the work is done on each of the garment parts. Sew the darts, the pockets, and if the style happens to have panels in the front and back areas, join these first. Then stitch the shoulders together. Do the same with the lining, but skip such details as pockets, of course. The side edges and the middle seams are left open on both lining and garment.

When using loosely woven or stretchy fabrics it is wise first to interface the neckline of the dress with some supporting fabric light enough in weight so it will not cause bulk. Synthetic interfacings are ideal whether the garment itself is synthetic or not, because this kind of interfacing does not wrinkle if the garment is to be washed. If the pattern envelope contains patterns for the neckline facings, use these for cutting the interfacing pieces. If there are no patterns, use the dress-pattern pieces, cut the shapes of the neckline front and back about 2 inches wide, and just pin them onto the inside of the dress parts. Then catch them into the shoulder seams when the front and back units are joined at the shoulders. It is not necessary to interface the armholes because they do not get out of shape the way the neck is apt to do if it is not interfaced.

How to attach the flip lining

Now pin the dress and the lining together with the right sides facing each other. Do this around the neckline and the armholes, with the shoulders matched correctly, and also match the center of the neckline and the ends. Sew the edges with ⅝-inch seams, being very careful not to stretch neck and armhole edges during the stitching. To retain the right shape, it is advisable, when stitching curved seams, to feed the work underneath the presser foot in a curved manner instead of holding it like a straight edge; otherwise the seams will end up stretched. Clip the curved edges inward almost to the line of stitching at ⅝-inch intervals; then reach in through the shoulders and pull each of the pieces of the back through the shoulder spaces and they will come out reversed. (Fig. 32.)

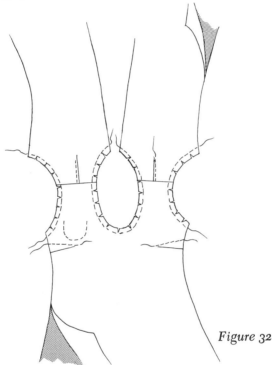

Figure 32

Baste the neck and armholes close to the edges for pressing into shape. During the basting, roll the dress edges slightly so they will overlap the edges of the lining. This will bring the seamline to the inside of the dress. The rolling prevents the lining from showing when the finished garment is worn. When pressing these curved edges, be careful not to stretch them. If a curved motion is used during the pressing, stretching will be prevented.

Sew the lower part of the center back seam of the dress and then insert the zipper. The zipper goes only into the dress fabric not into the lining, but the lining seam is stitched from where the zipper ends downward, with the top section left open. The zipper may be inserted with a one-lap finish or with the double lap, or you might like an invisible type of zipper. In the case of the invisible zipper, the seam at the lower section of the opening is not stitched up until after the zipper has been inserted. If you follow the instructions that come with the zipper, you'll have no problem.

Fitting the jumper

Pin the sides of the jumper, wrong sides together, with ⅝-inch seam allowances and about 1½ inches apart, inserting the pins up and down. Then try on the dress. Move the pins a bit if necessary to get the garment to fit as you want it. Do not pin the lining together; just let it dangle inside of the dress until further progress is made.

After removing the garment, rub chalk over the pinned seams on the inside of the dress. These will be the guides for stitching the sides together. Next, pin the dress together with the right sides of the fabric facing, inserting the pins in horizontal position and about 1½ inches apart, matching the base of the armholes and proceeding to the bottom. Come back to the armhole and start pinning the lining parts from the armhole to the hem, doing this to both sides. Stitch the sides together in one long stitching operation from the bottom of the dress to the bottom of the lining. If any alterations had been made in the dress sides, copy the widths of the seams and match them in the lining. The seams are pressed open.

Turn the raw edges of the lining under at the back opening and hand stitch them to the zipper tapes. Try on the dress once again to mark the length. Use lace or seam tape as a finish for the top of the dress hem after trimming it off to the right width. Hand stitch the hem into place loosely enough to avoid dimpling the outer material; then turn up the lining hem so it will be 1 inch shorter than the dress itself. The lining is not edged with tape or lace at the hem top, just tucked in and hand-finished.

Press the hem of the dress very lightly, placing the iron only on the lower half of the width so it will not cause the top edge of the hemline to show through on the outside of the finished dress. Give the lining hem a light touch-up and call the job finished.

4

Making Separate Skirts, Pants, and Shorts

Determine pattern size by waist measurement

Patterns for separate skirts and pants that are not parts of a two- or three-piece ensemble are sized and sold by waist measurement. If the person's waist and hip measurements compare proportionately to those of the pattern size, use the size that is comparable to the individual's waist measurement. If the hips at their largest dimension are much larger in proportion to the waist, use the pattern size that will accommodate the hips.

Cut the garment like the pattern, and the excess material will eventually be taken in during the fitting of the garment. No previous adjustments should be attempted in reducing the pattern before cutting the garment parts, except in length, as it is much easier to take care of this matter after the preliminary stitching has been done and you have the garment to the stage where it will be ready for fitting. This preserves the original styling of the garment, as only the "hidden areas" are changed.

Judging the length

Before cutting the garment parts, it is advisable to hold the pattern up to the waistline to see whether or not the length will be right. Additions are made by drawing lines with chalk on the fabric below the pattern pieces after they have been pinned into position for cutting. When the pattern pieces are too long, turn up the bottom, but be sure to allow enough for a hem. Then pin the pattern to the cloth.

When using a pattern for pants or for a skirt that is part of a two- or three-piece ensemble—a jacket, skirt, and pants set, for example—you would have purchased the pattern in the size that fits the body's upper sections. Therefore the waistline of the skirt is sized in proportion to these upper measurements. In this case additions will have to be made in the "hidden areas" of the front and back units of pants and skirt if the body measurements are larger than those specified on the pattern envelope. (See chapter 2 on how to cut dresses to the right size.) The length of the skirts and pants, however, are judged according to the instructions here.

Fitting the skirt

After you have stitched the darts into the front and back of the skirt, and joined the center back seam, pin the sides of the units together with ⅝-inch seams with the wrong sides of the material facing so that the raw edges are on the outside. Leave part of the left seam open so that the skirt can be tried on. Put the skirt on, pin the left seam closed with ⅝-inch seam allowance, then check the results so far. (Fig. 33.)

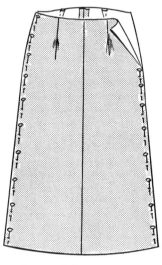

Figure 33

The skirt should require a minimum amount of fitting, if any, if the garment parts have been cut according to the personal measurements, whether the pattern size used was determined by waist measurement, hip measurement, or by the fit of the upper part of the body. When personal measurements are taken into consideration in cutting the skirt, moving the pins either a bit closer to the body or slightly farther away is about all that will be required to make the skirt fit perfectly.

The skirt that is to be finished with a waistband should be tried on with the top of it resting on the top of the hip bones, not right at the waistline. Otherwise the finished skirt will crawl up at the waistline and wrinkle below the band. The skirt should be fitted easily, just touching the body but not squeezing it.

If the skirt is to be finished with an inside facing or ribbon band, fit it right at the waistline instead of resting it on the hip bones. Look the garment over and see how the side seams fall. If they jut forward instead of falling in straight lines up and down on both sides, tie a string around the waist rather tightly with the top of the skirt under the string and pull up the skirt top at the center back until the seams straighten. Then draw a chalk line across the back where the string is, so that it will show where the extra cloth will have to be cut off, leaving only ⅜ inch there for the seam. The piece cut away will be shaped somewhat like a thin crescent. (Fig. 34.)

When the side seams of a skirt aim backward instead of straight up and down, it is the front of the skirt that must be pulled up in the center after tying the string around the waist. (Fig. 35.)

When a person's hips are not shaped alike, skirts hang to one side of the body and the hem line is farther away from the legs on one side than on the other. With the string tied around the waist, and looking at the figure full front, pull up on the side closest to the legs and continue to pull until the draping is the same on left side and right; then chalk the adjusted side. The extra material is to be cut away, leaving only ⅜ inch for the seam. (Fig. 36.)

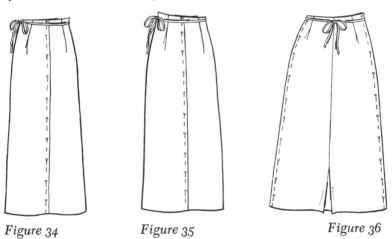

Figure 34   Figure 35   Figure 36

To remove the skirt, withdraw the pins at the left side partially so that one edge of the skirt will be released. Then reinsert the pins into the seam edge which still has the pin in it, so that it will serve as a chalking guide in the next step. Take out as many pins as necessary to remove the garment without having to struggle out of it.

Turn the skirt inside out, chalk where the pins are, and then remove the pins from the right side of the garment. In the area where there are pins only in one edge, just chalk the inside of that unit over the pins and then take those out also.

If the skirt closing is in the center back, now is the time to insert the zipper, while the back unit is separated from the front. It will be easier that way.

The side closing

When the zipper is to go into the left side of a skirt, it is a good idea to work on that seam of the garment first after the fitting has been chalked on the wrong side. Pin the left seam together with the right sides of front and back units facing each other, sew up the seam completely from end to end, and press it flat. Then open the seam from the top down to where the zipper will reach. Skirt zippers are usually 7 inches long; 9 inches for pants. Insert the zipper using your own favorite method. Then stitch together the opposite side of the skirt.

How to attach a waistband properly

You want to achieve the wonderful combination of a smoothly fitting skirt, not too snug, and a comfortable, firmly fitting waistband. You can do this by holding the work properly in your hands when you pin as well as when you stitch. Just do as the instructions say, and the results will be perfect.

Cut a waistband 3½ inches wide and 3 inches longer than the waist measurement. The band can be pieced if necessary, and the seams should be lined up with those at the sides of the skirt. Piecing should not be done hit-or-miss. When using striped material, be sure to cut the waistband with the stripes running around the waist; the effect is better.

Here's how you pin the waistband to the skirt top for best results: Place the band against the wrong side of the skirt front with the right side of the band toward the inside of skirt, allowing ⅝ inch of the band to project out beyond the skirt opening. Pin together, inserting the pins with the points in an upward direction. Hold the outside of the skirt front facing you as you start to pin. Roll the band over the fingers of the left hand with the skirt on top of it, and pin again, in an upward direction. By holding the work in this position, the skirt will be eased into the waistband evenly. Repeat, rolling over the fingers and pinning every inch around the top of the skirt. (Fig. 37.) Little ripples of skirt

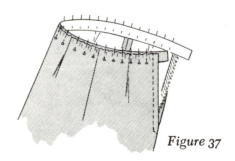

Figure 37

material will form between the pins, but they will all work in smoothly when the band and skirt are sewn together if the work is placed properly under the presser foot.

Before stitching, try on the skirt to be sure that it is the right size at the waistline. You may find that it is a little bit snug for comfort because of the easing, so just unpin the back section of the waistband and repin it without easing the skirt this time.

Now sew the skirt and band together, putting the work under the presser foot with the band side on top, the slackness of the skirt underneath, taking only ½-inch seam to make it easier to sew without puckering. Hold the skirt and band rather taut as you join them together, since this prevents puckers from forming in the seamline.

Now fold the two ends of the waistband edge to edge, wrong sides out, and sew them. Then place the skirt in an upside-down position in front of you for ease and accuracy in the final pinning before stitching. Working from front toward back, from left to right, turn the band over to the right side of the skirt and fold under ½-inch seam. Place the fold directly on top of the seam, overlapping just enough to cover the first stitching. The left hand holds the skirt and keeps it smooth while the right hand inserts the pins. (Fig. 38.) Pin 1 inch apart, stretching the work slightly as you pin, to eliminate twisting of the waistband. If the work were held in any other position, good results would be harder to achieve. If you are left-handed, follow the instructions above, but work from right to left, holding the skirt with the right hand and pinning with the left.

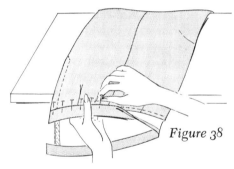

Figure 38

When you reach the little extended piece of waistband at the back part of the skirt, fold the edges generously inward so that the width is narrower at this end than on the rest of the waistband. This extended piece is a "reserve," in case the skirt needs to be altered in the future. It is also a means of achieving a neat flat closing. All well-made skirts are finished in this manner. Finishing off the waistband at the front end even with the front fold which covers the zipper is another way to keep the left side as streamlined as the right.

Stitch the waistband on the very edge of the pinned fold on the outside of the skirt, starting on the front end and continuing to the back, stretching the work as you sew. Although it is not necessary, the stitching can be carried completely around the band to include the top and ends also. This will give the band firmness and help to keep it from folding over and wrinkling, especially when the cloth is soft in texture. If additional firmness is desired, a narrow piece of grosgrain ribbon can be invisibly hand-sewn to the back of the waistband. This is easier than interfacing the band. Use small hooks and eyes for the closing, two on the front lap and one at the underlapping end.

Just in case you don't know how to sew hooks and eyes on skirt bands, here's the way you do it: Always use small hooks and the long kind of eyes that resemble little dumbbells rather than the round ones that look like tiny horseshoes. The long ones will hold the band flat against your waist. Sew the hooks ½ inch in from the front edge of the band, on the front overlap. Stitch through the holes, one at a time, and then bring the needle invisibly to the hook end and secure that with a few stitches. This will hold the band flat when closed and prevent a bulge. The little long eyes are sewn through each hole individually, with the thread transferred from one to the other. (Fig. 39.) The skirt should be turned inside out and pressed around the top of the waistband. Use a press cloth so that the easing that took place in the top of the skirt will flatten out smoothly.

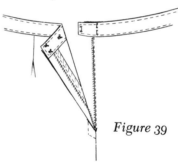

Figure 39

Another popular way of attaching a band to a skirt top is to pin it to the outside of the garment and machine stitch it into place, easing the skirt top as for the first way. Then turn in a narrow edge of the band against the inside of the skirt so that no raw edges will show, and hand-finish it by catching the stitches to those that have been done by machine. If you are using heavy fabric, finish the raw edges of the band with seam tape instead of turning it so you do not create bulk. No machine stitching will show when the band is handled in this manner, and it is a very nice way to finish silks as well as heavy materials.

When making a skirt that will not have a waistband, use 1-inch wide grosgrain ribbon to face the top edge, matching it to the color of the skirt fabric. Place the ribbon flat down against the right side of the top edge of the skirt, just as you would apply a seam tape to the top of a hem, and allow half of the ribbon to overlap the skirt and the other half to project above the raw edges of the skirt. Stitch the ribbon into place on the extreme edge that is on the skirt, and as you sew it to the skirt, hold the ribbon just a little stretched to make it go on snugly. Allow about an inch of ribbon to extend out beyond the skirt opening at both ends. Now turn the ribbon down to the inside of the skirt and tuck the ends in at the opening. Hand stitch or tack wherever there is a seam or dart in the area of the ribbon edge—this is what holds the ribbon turned after it has been pressed. The ends of the ribbon are caught by hand to the zipper tapes. If necessary, sew a hook and eye to the ribbon on the inside of the skirt. The skirt is hooked together first and the zipper pulled up afterward.

Lining the skirt

Using a lightweight but firmly woven fabric, cut the lining like the skirt and then assemble it as if making another skirt. You then insert the lining into the skirt. You can direct the raw edges outward so they will face the raw edges of the skirt, or you can wear them against yourself. Either way is correct; it is merely a matter of choice. In either case, the top of the lining is turned under so the raw edges are out of sight and the fold is pinned to the bottom of the waistband or to the bottom edge of the ribbon. At the zipper closing the edges are turned in and pinned against the zipper tapes, then the lining is hand stitched

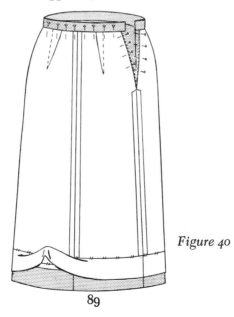

Figure 40

into the skirt, making sure the stitches do not go through to the outside. After marking the skirt length, do the same to the lining, but make it an inch shorter. Then hem them both by hand. (Fig.40.)

Fitting a wrap-around skirt

When cutting the parts of a wrap-around skirt, it is important to add to the sides if necessary, just as when making a straight skirt; otherwise the skirt will not wrap properly. After sewing the darts in all the parts, pin the left and right fronts together vertically through the centers, with the right front lapped over the left one and both fabrics facing outward. Run a line of pins across the top of the waistline also to hold the layers in place during the fitting.

Pin the skirt together at the sides, wrong sides together and with ⅝-inch seam allowance. Leave the left seam partly open to slip the skirt on for fitting; then pin it together and see how it fits. With the necessary additions made at the side edges, the skirt should look exactly like a slim skirt. If it does not look the way you want it to, the pins should be adjusted until it fits. After moving the pins, remove the skirt, chalk the side seams where the pins are, and proceed to sew the side seams. When the skirt is completed, it will wrap itself around you perfectly, with the right amount of underlay at the left side of the front, and no pulling or straining will be present. (Fig. 41.)

Figure 41

Cutting pants correctly

If your ready-made pants have been too short between the waist and the crotch, you'll find patterns will be too short also. You can correct this situation by adding extra depth to the pants at the top and getting them to fit the way they should. After pinning the pattern pieces to the cloth, draw chalk lines an inch or more above the pattern pieces at the waistline. Then extend the dart lines up into the additions, but don't change the location of the points of the darts. Checking the length of the legs is also important so you can make additions at both ends of the pants if necessary. (Fig. 42.)

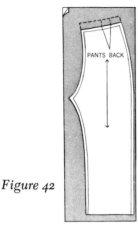

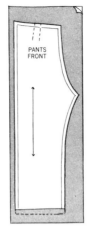

Figure 42   *Figure 43*

If the body is shorter than average between waist and crotch, and ready-made pants are too deep in the crotch, don't alter the pattern at this stage. Pin the pattern pieces to the fabric as they are. Adjustments will be made more accurately later when parts of the pants are already assembled.

Some tall people are short from waist to crotch, but their legs are long. It is very important and necessary to add generously to the bottoms of the legs of their pants; otherwise the legs may end up too short when the crotch is eventually brought up to the part of the body where it belongs. (Fig. 43.)

Another type of individual is long from the waist to the crotch, but has short legs. Only when pants are cut correctly, and then fitted as they should be, can the end result be right for each type of figure. Although many different kinds of instructions are given for cutting and fitting pants, taking measurements from one part of the body to the other, some of these instructions only tend to be confusing and make you wonder where exactly your figure differs from the average.

All this confusion is avoided when the easy method of adding and subtracting is followed at the proper stages of construction. There is no guesswork involved in this way, and you can sew with the confident feeling that the garment will fit because the right things are being done at the right time.

One of the easiest ways of preparing pants for fitting is by first sewing all the darts in all the parts and then joining the short seams in the center back and in the center front from the waistline to the crotch. Pin the front and back crotch areas of the pants right sides together, pinning from the crotch down to the bottom of one leg, and then from the crotch down to the bottom of the other leg. Stitch in one long stitching operation from end to end and then press the seam open. Now pin the pants at the side edges with the wrong sides together so that the seams are on the outside, ⅝ inch away from the raw edges. Leave the left seam partly open so the pants can be tried on.

Let it be said again, if the pants were cut according to the person's measurements, with any needed additions divided into four equal parts, and the additions made at the sides, the pants will not need any drastic fitting to make them right. The only adjustment that may be needed will be in the waistline if the person happens to be shorter or longer than average in the lower torso.

If you have made additions at the tops of the pants, or if you commonly find that your pants droop in the seat, tie a string around the waistline right over the tops of the pants and pull them up underneath the string to bring the seam up to where it belongs, to where you feel the cloth against the body. Then bend over, as if trying to pick up a dime from the floor, or as if doing reducing exercises. This movement will draw the pants down below the string to provide the amount of space the individual needs between waistline and crotch. The waistline area of the pants is then marked with chalk.

While the pants are still on, inspect the side seams to see whether they hang straight up and down. If not, an extra little tug here and there to make them hang correctly is all that is necessary, using the same technique as already covered in how to make skirts hang straight (see page 85). Remove the pants and cut away the extra cloth at the waistline so that only ⅝ inch is left above the chalk line for the seam.

If the sides of the pants have had to be refitted by moving the pins, it is best to remove the garment to make these changes and then try it on again, to be sure that the fit is pleasing before going any further. Chalk the inside of the pants after the fitting has been completed and withdraw the pins from the outside; then use the chalk marks as a sewing guide in joining the outside seams together.

Insert the zipper next, choosing either the left side or the front or back seams. You might even like to settle for an invisible zipper so that the closing gets lost in the seams.

The finish at the top of the pants can be either a waistband or an inside ribbon facing, as described for the skirt (pp. 86–89). Either way will give you a smart professional look. The pants may be lined if you wish, unless they are made of knit, which is best left unlined. The lining is cut like the pants and after the seams are joined and pressed open, the lining is inserted into the pants with the wrong sides together, pinned together around the waistline and around the zipper closing with the edges of the lining turned under so there will be no raw edges visible. The sewing is then done by hand without bringing the stitches through to the outside layer.

Try the pants on for length. Turn under the excess material and then trim it off, leaving only about 1½ inches for a hem. Make the lining 1 inch shorter than the pants legs. Do the hemming by hand and allow the lining to hang freely inside the pants legs.

The shorts with the fly-front closing

Shorts are cut exactly the same way as longer pants, with additions made at the sides and at the waistline if the individual figure demands these increases. A fly-front opening can be used on the long pants if desired, and the procedure for doing the job is no different than for shorts. The pattern featuring a fly-front closing will have all the parts needed—facings and so forth.

On the pattern piece of the shorts or pants front there is an indicator at the bottom of the crotch to show where the fly front will start. Sew from the bottom of the crotch to the indicator; then go through the same line of stitching twice to reinforce this short seam, and press the seam open. (Fig. 44.)

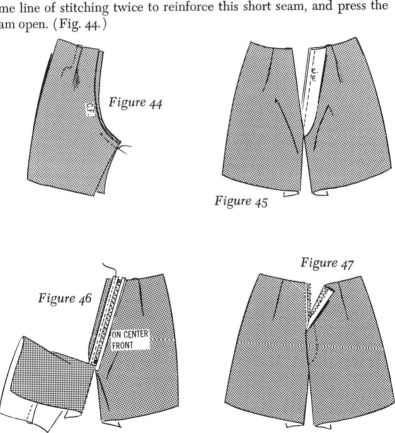

Figure 44

Figure 45

Figure 46

Figure 47

ON CENTER FRONT

Your pattern will indicate that you should cut two fly pieces, but one will be enough. Sew the fly piece to the left side of the pants, keeping the right sides of the fabric together. (Fig. 45.) Trim the seam down to ¼-inch width, turn the fly piece over to the inside of the pants, and press flat. The fly piece is frequently interfaced with a piece of old sheeting or other lightweight cotton to give it a little extra firmness when the cloth being used for the pants or shorts is soft and light-weight. This is not necessary when using firmly woven fabric.

The fly piece is pressed to the inside of the garment mainly for the purpose of establishing a trim fold line on the center of the pants front, a line which will be used as a guide for inserting the zipper easily. Now unfold the fly piece from the inside of the garment and place the right side of the zipper against the right side of the fly piece, matching the top of the tape to the top of the fly and keeping the edge of the zipper tape flush against the fold line of the flattened front seam. (Fig. 46.) Pin and sew, keeping the zipper closed during the complete operation, both for the pinning and stitching.

Now turn under ⅝ inch on the opposite side of the pants front and pin the fold to the free side of the zipper, as close as possible to the teeth. Stitch the fold next, again as close as possible to the zipper, starting from the top and working downward. Reinforce the end of the stitching by going back and forth for ½ inch through the same line of stitching a few times.

Now fold the fly piece back to the inside of the garment, just as it was pressed originally. Pin the outer edges of the fly piece into place, and do the final outside stitching through a chalk line traced from the line shown on the pattern piece. (Fig. 47.)

The construction steps for making slacks or shorts are the same for boys and girls. Inserting the front zipper is the same too, although now and then you may find girls' pants with the fly lapped over from the right to the left side of the front. With girls' things it is not serious if the closing is the opposite of what it should be, but be sure that the lapping on boys' things is always correct. All boys' things are made with the left side lapped over the right, just as shirts, sport jackets, and coats are closed.

Making pants and skirts from knits

Knits have reached great heights in popularity, especially for pants and skirts for casual wear. There are patterns for such garments marked "for knits only" and these work up very fast and require hardly any fitting. They pull over the hips without an opening, so no zipper will have to be inserted.

These special patterns marked as being exclusively designed for knits are cut somewhat differently from those meant to be made from woven cloth, or those marked "ideal for knits." There is more ease in these special patterns, and extra material has been provided at the top of the garment for the purpose of turning down and forming a casing at the waist so that elastic can be inserted.

Measure the elastic to fit comfortably around the waist but easy enough so it will slip down over the hips. Allow an inch extra for joining the ends together after the elastic has been inserted into the casing. Overlap the two ends and machine stitch them together firmly, then hand stitch the casing closed where it was left open for inserting the elastic.

Hemming the pants legs

To avoid bulk in hemming the legs of pants made of heavy cloth, including knits, use catch stitching. The top edge is left raw. With a knot tied in the thread, take a tiny stitch in the garment just above the top of the hem, then take one in the hem ½ inch to the right of the starting point, alternating from hem to garment at ½-inch intervals. If you are right-handed, proceed from left to right; but if you are left-handed, proceed from right to left. Hold the hem upright as you sew. (Fig. 48.)

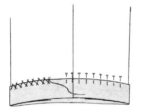

Figure 48

Skirts Made Without Patterns

The gathered skirt

A pleasing-looking gathered skirt should be no less than two yards around the bottom. The zipper closing goes into one of the seams, and the seams may be located either in the center of the front and back or at the left and right sides. They disappear into the gathers and don't show as a general rule if the design is matched carefully in printed materials or checks and plaids. If the cloth is quite lightweight and softly textured, the fullness could be even more generous and 3 yards would not be too much.

Do the gathers by machine, using two rows of "magic stitching," one row about ⅜ inch down from the top edge and the other about ¼ inch below the first line. Hold the bobbin threads firmly in one hand and with the other hand move the fullness of the gathers toward the middle of the skirt top, working from one end toward the middle and then from the other end, until the gathering has become the length of your waist measurement. Divide the fullness of the cloth from the center to the two ends so that both sides of the skirt will be alike. Secure the gathering threads by looping them into figure eights over vertically inserted pins at each end so they will not slip from their right amount of gathering as you continue to handle the cloth in making the skirt.

Because measurements elsewhere in this skirt are unimportant, the waistline is the guide for making the skirt fit. Cut the band 3½ inches wide, and 3 inches longer than the waist measures. Mark off on the band just the amount into which the skirt will have to fit, allowing ⅝ inches on the right-hand end for a seam. Then pin the gathered skirt top to the waistband, just as previously recommended for a conventional tailored skirt, finishing the opening with hooks and eyes.

The skirt with unpressed pleats

For the not-so-slim figure, a full skirt will be more flattering if it is pleated instead of gathered. The pleats may be either unpressed or pressed. Whichever style you decide to make, use at least 3 yards of material for the pleated fullness, not less.

All sorts of pleats can be used to style the skirt. All you do to make an unpressed pleated skirt is to fold the fabric either in box pleats, side pleats, or a pleat-upon-pleat arrangement for a novelty effect that is very attractive in summer cottons. Pleats can also be started from a panel of unpleated material directly in the front, with pleats folding in opposite directions on each side, to meet in an inverted pleat at the center back. Any of these styles will produce more slimming effects than a gathered skirt would. The outside pleating of the skirt should be uniform in appearance, each pleat even in width, while the underpleating should do the actual reducing of the fullness to correspond to the waist measurement. It is often necessary to do a little experimenting to determine the most becoming width for the pleats, and to find what depth to make the underpleats to fit the waistline properly. (Fig. 49.)

How to make a pressed-pleated skirt

One of the handsomest skirts that can be made without a pattern is a tailored pleated skirt, shaped to conform to the figure. The pleats are stitched down to a certain area of the figure, so that knife-sharp pleats hang gracefully and freely from there to the bottom. The pleats are

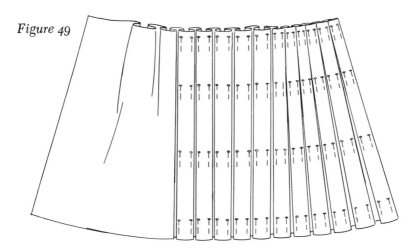

Figure 49

made differently in such skirts from the way they are made in a skirt with unpressed pleats.

To make a pressed-pleated skirt, you first measure the largest part of the hips. About three yards of fullness make a beautiful skirt for a figure with hip measurements up to about 36 or 37 inches. If the hips are larger, you can use the same amount of fullness, but make a few of the pleats skimpy on the inside to compensate for the difference. This will not show from the outside, and so don't despair if your model is heavier than you wish.

If the fullness of the skirt is less than 3 yards, the pleats will not fall gracefully in pressed folds, but will barrel out most unbecomingly at the hip area, giving the figure a most peculiar and bulky appearance. Pleats should be tailored to fit well over the heaviest part of the body. Although all pleated skirts are flattering, this particular style is exceptionally so, to everyone from the youngest to the oldest regardless of type. The narrow pleats, starting quite a bit narrower at the top and then tapering out to an inch width at the largest part of the hips flatter even the heaviest person. A slim figure is flattered by the swinging of the closely pleated fullness at the bottom. Even tiny people look well in this style. And haven't you ever admired men dressed in their kilts?

Woolen materials of medium- or lightweight texture make the most satisfactory pleated skirts because once the pleats get pressed into them they stay pleated. Dry cleaning is the best way to care for such skirts.

Two lengths of 54-inch fabric can be used, or if you are using narrower fabric, be sure to have enough fullness to make up 3 yards of width. If the wool is wider, leave the extra width there and dispose of what is not needed after the pleating has been done. It is very easy to pleat the material at home when the principles of pleating are understood.

Sew the selvage edges of the material pieces together to form a huge rectangle. Leave the fabric open and don't sew it together into a tube until the pleating is all done and the skirt is ready for the zipper. It will be easier to pleat it this way. Use a press cloth along with your steam iron to press the pleats as flat as possible and they'll stay that way, but don't bear down too heavily as you will have to do the pleating on the right side of the fabric.

How to mark the pleats

Work with the material facing right side up, because the chalk marks for the pleats will have to be seen on the right side. Fold the right-hand end of the cloth under 1½ inches from the top to the bottom for the first pleat. This fold can be merely pinned or pressed, and will be the guide for marking the rest of the pleating. The pleats will all be directed toward the left side of the skirt when worn. Mark them in the following manner:

Mark from the right toward the left, working from the first folded pleat. Place a yardstick ½ inch down from the top of the skirt, parallel with the top edge. Put a chalk mark on the top of the skirt, one inch away from the fold, and then skip 2 inches and make another mark. One inch from the last mark, make another, and then skip 2 inches again. Do this all the way across the whole skirt top. The 1-inch spaces will be the width of the pleats showing on the right side of the skirt, and the 2-inch spaces will be the under folds of the pleats. After marking the top of the skirt, do the same at the bottom, making sure that the markings are in line with one another, and that the weave of the cloth is parallel with the way the pleats will fall. (Fig. 50.)

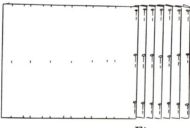

Figure 50

When the marking is done, pick up the first 2-inch space and fold it toward the one-inch space next to it, pinning the top first, and then the bottom. Then pin the center between the top and bottom. It is not necessary to mark fold lines for the pleats. The vertical lines on the diagram are only for the purpose of showing which lines should be picked up and brought over to meet the matching ones.

After the pinning is done, place the skirt with its right side up on the ironing board and press lightly with a damp cloth, pressing only a few pleats at a time. Pinning the pleats at top and bottom to the ironing board cover will help to stretch the fold of the pleats into a straight line, so try it.

The pleated fabric should measure the same as the largest part of the hips, plus one inch more. If the pleats do not work out to that measurement, it will be necessary to skimp a little on the under folds of the pleats, so that enough of them can be made on the outside to go around the hips, plus one inch more. The under folds will not show if the skimpy ones are separated and not made all in one part of the skirt.

Decrease pleat widths at waistline to fit

Pin the pleats down with another horizontal row of pins about 8 inches from the top. Then all around the top proceed to overlap the outside folds of the pleats, moving them a fraction of an inch beyond their original placement at the skirt top, gradually tapering down to the pinned area, so that the hips will not be disturbed. The amount of the overlapping of pleats depends upon the difference existing between the hip and waist measurement and how many pleats there are in the skirt. It is not necessary to be a mathematical genius to figure it out, however. Just remember, there are a great many pleats; therefore, only a tiny bit of overlapping is necessary on each pleat to reduce the top to fit the waistline. The overlapping can very easily be overdone, so be sure to try the skirt on after pinning and before stitching the folds of the pleats.

A very slimming effect is achieved when the pleats are stitched down part way. If the person is short, don't stitch too far down, for the proportions of the skirt must remain pleasing. The stitching can be eliminated for a very slim or tiny girl, to give her figure more softness. In this case you would just run a row of stitching across the top of the skirt to hold the pleats in place.

When stitching the pleats part way down the fold, do not stitch through any of the layers of pleated fabric underneath, as that would cause hardness and twisting of the cloth. Start the stitching on the extreme left pleat. The length of the stitching line can be anywhere from about 4 to 7 or 8 inches, depending upon the individual's height. Keep the line short for short girls, and longer for the taller ones. If a straight chalk line is lightly drawn horizontally across the opened skirt the right distance down from the waistline, it will help to keep the pleat stitching even. Move the folds of the under pleats away from the path of the needle as each pleat is sewn down. When all the pleats are sewed, transfer the threads at bottom of stitching to the wrong side of the skirt and tie them. The left side of the skirt has been left open to make the work easier.

How to insert a zipper into a pleated skirt

Insert the zipper into the back edge of the skirt first, about one inch away from the last fold. (Fig. 51.) Then clip and turn the fabric under at the bottom of the zipper, and stitch it into place across the bottom. Now place the front of the skirt over the back edge, with the front fold directly over the zipper. Stitch ½ inch away from the fold, boxing the zipper at the bottom. After the zipper is completely inserted, join the rest of the left-side seam, with the wide seam of the back acting as an underlay fold of a pleat.

Before attaching the waistband, press the upper section of the skirt, where the pleats were overlapped for fitting. Press on the wrong side

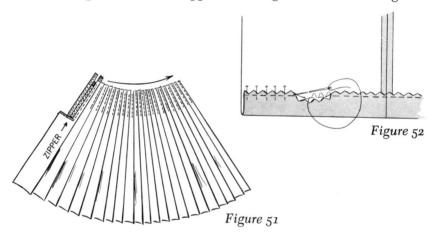

Figure 52

Figure 51

with a damp cloth so that new creases will form in place of the original ones.

Attach the waistband exactly as instructed for other skirts. Measure the hem next. Trim it to an even width, finish with seam tape, and hem by hand.

Hemming a pleated skirt

It is not practical to hem a pleated skirt first and then make it up, as some women are known to do. It is far better and easier to judge a becoming length after the skirt is finished and the waistband has been attached. Pleated skirts look best when they are not too long. Try the skirt on to mark the hem. After the length has been determined and measured in the usual way, plan to do the finishing as flatly as possible. Run a line of machine stitching through the single layer of the material at the top edge of the trimmed-off hem width, ½ inch down from the edge; then trim the raw edges off with pinking sheers. Hand stitch the hem invisibly between the layers of the skirt and the hem, catching the hand stitches to the machine ones as you proceed from one layer to the other ½ inch apart. (Fig. 52.) Another way to hem the skirt and keep it flat is catch stitching, as described for pants legs (see page 95 and Fig. 48).

Press the finished hem flat on the wrong side as if it were the hem of a plain skirt without pleats, concentrating on flattening the lower half of the hem so the top edge doesn't show on the right side in the form of a ridge. Turn the skirt right side out and slip it onto the ironing board. Rearrange the pleats at the bottom of the skirt, folding them into their right position through the original folds, which are visible enough to be used as guides. Pin the hemline down to the ironing board and press with a cloth over the pleats so they will not get iron-marked. (Fig. 53.) Press a few pleats at a time in this manner until all the pleats are flat; then turn the skirt over to the wrong side and repeat the pressing again on that side to make the underfolds of the pleats flat also. This last press job does not have to be pinned, since the outer folds will be sharp enough to keep the under ones in place.

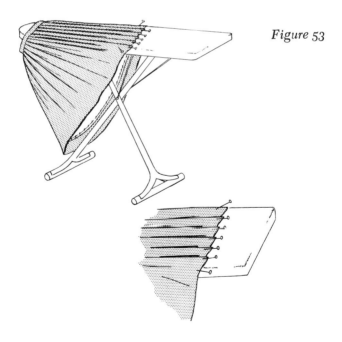

Figure 53

5

Tailoring Coats and Jackets

Except in the length of the seams, there is no difference between making a coat for your littlest child and tailoring one for yourself. The work involved in making coats, and the order of the construction steps are fundamentally basic, regardless of style changes.

Some dresses and even some blouses are much trickier to make than most coats and jackets. This is not only because the lighter fabrics are somewhat harder to handle than those used in tailored things, but also because the finer details often featured on the fussy things may entail workmanship you wouldn't be prepared to handle if your basic knowledge is at all limited.

You need a certain amount of sewing experience before you can successfully cope with binding necklines beautifully, sewing tucks evenly, applying bias-cut bands properly, and managing the countless other trimming details that are featured on so many dresses. Disappointment in sewing is usually the result of too ambitious an undertaking. Making a coat will give you sound and needed sewing experience, and it will develop your ability to make any kind of clothing without hesitation. Once the groundwork is laid, unusual sewing steps and details will not be a hardship.

Choosing the coat style

Because of its all-around usefulness and because it looks equally well on boys and on girls, I chose a classic coat with set-in sleeves and the type of collar that can be worn open or closed, making the coat suitable for fall or winter wear as well as for spring. Patch pockets are used so that they can "grow" downward on the coat after the first season's wear. This type of pocket can be moved to a better location when the hem is lowered so that the garment looks well proportioned instead of short-waisted. The pockets will be put on in a special way, so that they can be dropped easily without leaving marks in the old location. The straight lines of this style give lots of leeway for growing sideways, too. (Fig. 54.) But even if the coat you are planning to make is different in style from the one used here, the order of putting the parts together and the steps involved in completing each part will be the same.

Figure 54

About synthetic coatings and suitings

There are many synthetic coatings and suitings on the market today that look exactly like their natural cousins. They come in different weights and textures and in all types of finishes, and they can be used for garments for all seasons and purposes. They are ideal for children's wear, especially those synthetics that are machine washable and can be drip-dried or put into the automatic drier, provided that all the other materials used inside of them, such as linings and interfacings, are also made of "miracle" fibers.

These materials often come in blends with percentages of different kinds of fibers. The manufacturer's tag or label states what these fibers are, along with information on how to treat the finished garment so it will retain its new look indefinitely. The materials handle pretty much like their natural counterparts in cutting and sewing, and they will give the same amount of good service.

Underlining

It is not unusual to underline some of the loosely woven suiting or coating materials to give them support. The underlining material need not be heavy in texture, just closely woven enough to hold the outer cloth in shape. After attaching the underlining to all parts of the garment, treat the rest of the work as if you were dealing with a single layer.

About pattern guide sheets

On one side of the guide sheet that comes with your pattern, diagrams show how to arrange the pattern pieces on the fabric and how the pattern pieces are placed on fabrics of different widths. There are also larger illustrations of each pattern piece with printed information stating what part of the garment each piece is.

Look over the diagrams and then circle with pencil the one closest to your needs. If your cloth is a little different in width from any of those represented on the diagrams, settle for the one that is closest. Then separate the pattern pieces for the coat from the pieces for the lining and interfacing, and replace the latter in the pattern envelope until needed.

When the fabric has a nap or one-way direction, use a diagram that shows the pattern pieces all placed with the tops aimed in one direction. Only when a one-way direction is used in cutting such fabrics will the garment have the same color tone in all its parts, or have its plaid or printed design come out right. Look your fabric over carefully before you start, to avoid any mishaps.

It should be mentioned that the quick-and-easy tailoring methods and the order of the construction steps used in this book will be quite different from those given on the "how to do" side of the pattern guide sheet. But you should follow exactly the pattern directions for laying the pattern pieces on the fabric until you become completely familiar with doing this work on your own and know what pitfalls to avoid.

Start pinning the pattern pieces to the wrong side of the cloth following exactly the placement in the diagram. All woolen fabrics are folded wrong side out before they leave the mill. This is to keep them clean and lint-free. The fabric is ready for use, as long as it has been preshrunk.

Pinning pattern to the fabric without "nap"

In Fig. 55 a typical layout of a garment is shown. The pattern has been properly pinned to the fabric with the straight-of-the-goods symbols placed in the proper direction on each piece. The dotted lines at the bottoms of the front and back as well as at the bottom of sleeves indicate the extra material allowed so that these parts can be cut longer for future lengthening. The material in this diagram is of the type that can be used with no regard for a one-way direction, as it has

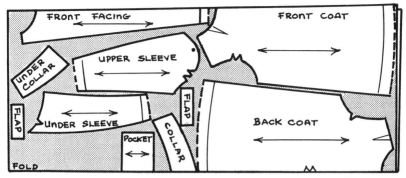

Figure 55

neither nap nor one-way pattern. The pattern pieces are placed so that the garment can be cut from the least amount of yardage without sacrificing needed length on any pattern piece.

What to do with "napped" fabric

In Fig. 56 material with a definite one-way nap is illustrated, with the pattern pinned to it so that all the nap goes in one direction. A pocket with the nap going in the opposite direction from the coat front would surely be a ludicrous sight. Note that the bottoms of the pattern pieces are all toward one end of the yardage. If you draw an arrow with chalk on the wrong side of the cloth to indicate which should be the bottom of these pieces, you will help yourself to keep from making direction errors. Extra yardage had to be used for cutting the same pattern, because the pieces couldn't be staggered without thought of direction.

When napped material is suggested for a style, the yardage requirement is specified on the pattern envelope. If, for one reason or another,

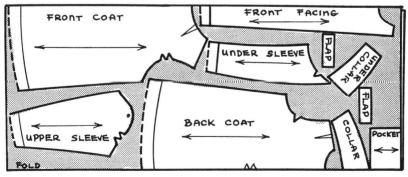

Figure 56

the style is not practical for a one-way material, you'll have to experiment with a bed sheet by pinning all the pattern pieces on to it to see how much yardage you will need if the cloth of your choice has nap. You may find that the style chosen runs into too much yardage, especially if it is styled with paneled flared fullness, like princess styles, or a fitted or semi-fitted coat for one of the girls. Never start cutting *any* material until you're sure that all the pattern parts will fit on the amount of yardage already purchased.

Cutting the coat to size

Although this important matter has already been covered elsewhere, it bears repeating again: The measurements printed on the pattern envelope are body measurements with the tape measure held firmly around the body. In creating the pattern design, allowances were made in each pattern piece to provide comfort and proper draping in the finished garment. The built-in ease must be preserved when cutting the garment, so wherever the person's measurements happen to be larger than the printed ones, make additions in the areas that do not affect the styling of the design, as indicated by the diagrams at certain points. The next larger pattern size is not the answer if the shoulders end up being too wide for the person's shoulders. A larger pattern size would also be too large in the neck. Trying to alter the upper part of a pattern, or the cut fabric, often leads to disappointing results.

Note the broken lines at the bottom and front and back units and at the sleeves. This is for reserve, so that the coat can be lengthened in these areas in the future if the cloth being used is the kind that will release old hem lines willingly. Tweeds or any of the rough textures will do this better than smooth-finished or fleecy surfaced fabrics.

Just because the side edges of the front and back have been increased where the body measurements were larger than the pattern, it is not necessary to cut the sleeves wider to compensate for the additions made. Sleeves should be increased in width only if the person's arms are larger than average. Addition is then made to the side edges of a one-piece sleeve, or a little on each of the four edges if the sleeves consist of upper and under sleeve parts. Sleeves should be about 1½ inches larger than the upper-arm measures, and even more than that if the coat will be for winter and will be interlined with warm lining throughout, including the sleeves.

Use straight scissors for cutting so that the edges are clean cut and easy to follow when joining seams together in constructing the garment. Clip ¼-inch deep in each important notch, especially the ones in the armholes and sleeves, and don't forget the one at the peak of the sleeve cap which will eventually be matched to the end of the shoulder seam. Then mark the darts on the wrong side of the fabric.

Where the pockets go

When more lasting markings are needed to show where the pockets are to be, or where whatever other detailing is to go on the outside of the garment, puncture holes through the markings on the pattern with the point of your scissors about an inch or so apart, then make chalk dots through the punctures. Upon removing the pattern, run a line of bright-colored hand stitching from dot to dot, or closer together, so the stitches will show on both the right and wrong sides of the cloth. Do this to both fronts. The proper location for the pockets will then be clearly indicated when they are ready to be attached to the garment. Just to chalk the locations would be impractical.

Mark buttonholes later

Although darts, pockets, and pleats are all marked now, it is too soon to mark the placement for buttonholes. They can be marked more accurately after the garment has been interfaced with material that gives it firmness and strength. This matter will be covered thoroughly at the proper time, along with the method of determining the most suitable type of buttonhole.

Have confidence in yourself

Now that the coat has been cut, here's a final word of advice before starting on your project. Have the utmost confidence in yourself, in your pattern, and in the infallible method you have chosen to follow. If other women have mastered the art of sewing, why shouldn't you? With this positive approach, you will surely achieve even greater re- sults than you have dreamed possible. Don't rush! You are using short- cut techniques, so work leisurely and easily. You'll finish long before you would if you were using old-fashioned methods. More speed will develop as you gain experience. Remind yourself occasionally that the ability to sew is not a gift bestowed on a chosen few. Your interest in learning is the real gift. Some women possess sewing talent without even being aware of it, and once their talent is recognized, it reaches surprising heights.

Do first things first

Progress will be rapid and the results pleasing if modern techniques are used in the preparation of each stage of the garment, doing first things first. To do this, you must have a certain amount of patience. Trying things on too soon and too often may tempt you to make adjustments that are really not necessary. The garment changes in shape and size as each stage is reached, and seeing it at too early a stage can be quite misleading. Proceed according to the steps as they are presented here and the work will be easy and the finished garment will look as if it had been made by a professional, because professional steps are being used along the way.

Pin seams together from the top toward the bottom, but you can stitch them from either end. (Fig. 57.) Each dart should be pinned from its wide end at the edge of the garment part to the point and stitched as straight as it possibly can be, with absolutely the sharpest tapered point, so that when it is pressed, the outside of the cloth is smooth without any puckers at the end. (Fig. 58.)

Seams must be a uniform ⅜ inch in width throughout the entire construction of the garment. The only place you may have a difference in seam width is at the "hidden areas" where the fitting may affect them.

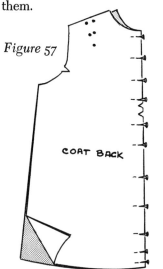

Figure 57

COAT BACK

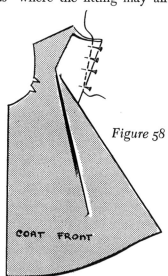

Figure 58

COAT FRONT

Steam pressing

Always press on the wrong side of the fabric when sewing, regardless of fiber content. Press seams open from bottoms up, and press darts toward the centers of the units on which they appear. In the case of the coat, the back shoulder darts are pressed toward the center seam, and the seam is separated and pressed flat. Front darts are pressed toward the center front.

When heavy fabric is used, as for winter coats, it is advisable to split the darts through their folds to within ⅜ inch of the pointed ends, pressing the dart seams open. That way bulk is avoided both in the dart and in the seams into which the darts will be stitched.

Because of their resiliency, woolens and other fabrics made from animal fibers must be pressed with a combination of heat and moisture. Use a steam iron or a regular iron with a damp press cloth. Linen dish towels make very satisfactory press cloths because they retain moisture long enough to create steam during the pressing. Too thin a cloth will dry before the garment fabric has been satisfactorily steamed flat.

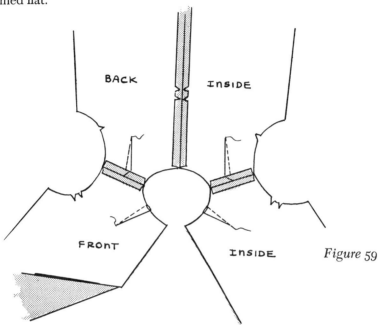

Figure 59

Pressing should be done with a light touch. Too much weight on the iron produces a shine on the outside of the material and will also flatten the surfaces of fleecy or napped materials. A steam iron is a great aid in doing the work quickly and well.

Glide the iron back and forth slowly, keeping it flat on the work without lifting it. Hopping around with the iron will only produce uneven and unsatisfactory pressing.

Although press as-you-sew is essential for satisfactory finished results, you don't have to stop and press each seam or dart as soon as it is sewn. Do as much stitching as possible on each separate unit, but be sure to press whatever has been sewn before joining one unit to another. You'll save time and effort this way, both in sewing and pressing. As shown in Fig. 59, the darts and seam in the coat back have been correctly pressed, and then joined to the coat fronts, on which the darts have also been pressed.

It should be mentioned here that if you want welt seams on the coat instead of plain ones, you should make them right from the beginning, starting with the stitching of the center back seams and the shoulders. This type of seam treatment adds extra attractiveness to a garment, especially if the fabric is heavy in texture. Full instructions for making welt seams are covered in the chapter on "fashion detailing."

Don't be surprised if you find that pressing the seams and darts in synthetics is somewhat less effective than when pressing materials made of natural yarns. Because of their stubborn nature these materials do not really crease flat even with steam pressing, but it is still very important and necessary to press as you go so that the seams and darts are caught into the next sewing step in the proper direction. This type of fabric lends itself beautifully to top-stitching details on seams as well as on the edges of collars, cuffs and garment fronts where flatness is so important to good looks.

Interfacings for different fabrics

In tailoring it is necessary and important to use a foundation fabric, or interfacing, in certain areas of the garment to give it permanent firmness and shape. Without this built-in support the parts that are meant to stay trim and tailored for the lifetime of the garment will sag and become limp and shapeless long before their time.

The best and most popular interfacing to use with wools and other fabrics made of animal fibers is medium-weight tailor's canvas, a combination weave of cotton and animal hairs. It is available in all yard-goods departments and comes in different weights and widths. The color is a natural beige. The amount required for a tailoring project is always specified on the pattern envelope.

There are also synthetic interfacing materials for garments that are made from synthetic fabrics. These usually come in colors, and in black and white.

Here's a word of caution about interfacing garments of pastel-colored coating or suiting: even though a pastel fabric may not be physically transparent, natural-colored interfacing is apt to show through as a shadow on the outside of the garment. It is much better to use white synthetic interfacing instead of the natural tailor's canvas in such garments to avoid the appearance of discoloration. Use the natural canvas with darker colors, however, because they adhere to each other better.

Aside from shaping the garment, interfacing gives it solidness in areas where one part consists of several layers of material. These layers will not separate or shift around when the garment is finished, but will act as one regardless of how many times the garment is dry-cleaned, for the right kind of interfacing gives the layers a kind of permanent cohesiveness.

Stab stitching

The layout sheet illustrates which pattern pieces to use for cutting the interfacing, and also how to lay the pattern properly on the canvas. Unless special pieces are provided for the interfacing, you may have to remove the pattern pieces from the coat facings and the undercollar, in order to use them as patterns for the interfacing too. The pocket flaps should also be interfaced to retain their shape. Cut the pocket flaps too from the canvas. By the way, canvas is already preshrunk; you needn't do anything to it.

The canvas facing pieces should be pinned accurately to the inside of the coat fronts. Work on a flat solid surface, and pick one you don't have to worry about scratching. Place one of the fronts flat on the surface with the wrong side facing upward, and pin the canvas down the front edge, making sure to pin the garment and canvas edges to one another evenly. Next, pin the neck edges together. Then lay the canvas over the pressed shoulder seam so that the canvas edge is flush with the edge of the back shoulder seam. Pin the inner edge of the canvas into place next, using the palm of your free hand to make sure that the garment material is perfectly flat under the canvas while you pin. Attach the canvas permanently with hand stitching before pinning the opposite front. The fronts and canvas will stay together more accurately when they are sewed immediately after pinning.

Here's how to attach canvas invisibly and permanently: Use a fine needle and single-strand thread in the exact color of the garment. Stitch vertically, parallel with the front edge of the garment. The first row of stitching will be done ⅝ inch away from the raw edge, and it doesn't matter whether you work from the top downward or from the bottom upward, as long as the rows go in an up-and-down direction. Only then will they remain invisible. Tie a tiny knot in the thread to secure the first stitch. Stab the needle into the canvas, penetrating through to the outside of the garment fabric; then with a quick twisting motion of the wrist, pick up a thread or two of both materials on your needle. Pull the thread through, but leave the stitch very loose. The stabbing motion is done at about 1½-inch intervals. The thread between the stitches is left so loose that a finger will fit in the loop with plenty of room left over.

Right-handed women will find it easier to do this stab stitching from right to left, while lefties will prefer working from left to right, as the garment fronts lie before them on the flat surface with the front edges closest. When the first row of stab stitching is done, cut off the thread at the end without reinforcement of any sort. Just let the thread end hang there loosely, about 2 inches long. Start a new row about 1½ inches or 1¼ inches from the first one. Repeat the rows until the complete canvas has been covered with these loose, looped, blind stab stitchings. A glance at the right side of the garment will show you how invisibly this work can be done. The stab stitching goes right through to the outside layer of material even where underlining is used as backing.

The reason that the rows of stitches must be done vertically instead of horizontally or in curves is because the vertical rows of stitches blend perfectly with the weave of the cloth, going as they do in the same direction as the cloth is woven. If the work were done horizontally, the stitches would be much more apt to show because the weight of the canvas even on loose stitches would cause dimpling on the right side of the fabric. But the combination of loose stitches and vertical rows makes them absolutely lost to view. Fig. 60 illustrates how the fronts should look after they have been interfaced.

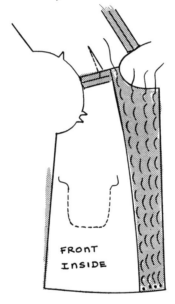

FRONT
INSIDE

Figure 60

Types of buttonholes to use on coats

With the fronts all interfaced, you are ready to consider what type of buttonholes to use on the coat. This decision depends on whether the coat is for a girl or a boy, and also whether it is for everyday wear or Sunday best. The texture of the material is also a consideration.

Girls' coats can have two kinds of buttonholes, either the bound kind or the ones that are made with a buttonhole attachment or on your automatic zigzag machine. If you do not have such equipment, the buttonholes can be made commercially after the garment is completed.

In a complete chapter, "Bound Buttonholes and All Kinds of Pockets," full step-by-step instructions are given for making bound buttonholes in the easiest possible way. If you want bound button-holes, turn to that part of the text now, follow the steps faithfully, and you'll make beautiful buttonholes immediately. It is advisable to make several samples first, however, just to become accustomed to these steps so that they can be used with complete confidence on the coat itself.

Buttonholes for boys are always made with the attachment or on the automatic zigzag machine. They are never bound. Bound buttonholes would make boys' clothes look "sissy," so don't waste your time on them. The usual type of machine-made buttonhole is known as the "keyhole" type, because the outer end is rounded and the one nearer the pocket ends abruptly.

Keyhole buttonholes are also used for girls' everyday wear, since they withstand hard use better than the dainty bound buttonholes. Bound buttonholes may not wear well on some loosely woven fabrics, and shouldn't be used with these fabrics even for Sunday clothing. That's another reason for making a few sample buttonholes first—to be able to judge whether or not the fabric can take it.

If you are going to put bound buttonholes on the coat, now is the time to make them, before the collar and facings are worked on. If you plan to use machine buttonholes, carry on with the other construction steps, and do the buttonholes at the very end.

Before you make bound or machine buttonholes in loosely woven fabrics or those that fray readily, use the press-on strips and sheets that are available at most notion counters or fabric departments. These reinforce the fabric where the buttonholes are to be made. A piece of the press-on material is attached to the inside of the garment, directly on the fabric, before underlinings or interfacings are attached, and when the buttonholes are made through the layers which include the press-on material, they will withstand wear no matter what the outer fabric happens to be.

Making the tailored collar

If you have struggled up to now with making and attaching a collar on a coat or jacket, ignore all previous instructions, no matter who or where you got them from, and you'll never struggle again, no matter what kind of a garment you'll be attaching a collar to. There just isn't any easier way of doing this job than this one. Here's the way it goes:

The collar of a tailored coat or jacket is usually cut with the upper piece on the fold and on the straight of the goods, like the rest of the garment, and the under collar is cut in two pieces on the bias grain of the cloth. The under collar is interfaced with canvas which is also cut on the bias. The bias weaves of the under collar and the canvas give the finished collar a flexible quality which makes it conform to the neckline gracefully, whether the collar is worn open or closed.

Sew the center seam of the under collar material and press the seam open. Then arrange the canvas pieces on the wrong side of the under collar with the outside edges even and the centers lapped over. Don't machine stitch the canvas at the center seam, because that would take away some of its flexibility. Just pin it into place for the time being.

Now stab stitch the canvas to the under collar, in rows closer together than those on the coat fronts, but in the same way. The center edges will be caught together with some of the stab stitching. It does not matter whether the stab stitching is started on the outer or inner edge of the collar.

Next, pin the upper- and under-collar pieces together, with the right sides of the materials facing each other. Holding the work so that the upper collar is nearest you, pin the centers first, and then the ends of the collar fronts. After the pins have been inserted into the center and ends, hold the collar pieces tense between the fingers, one hand on the center pin and the other on the pin at one collar end. This tenseness will cause the edges of the interfaced under collar and the upper collar to line up with each other evenly, even when one collar part is larger than the other. Then insert additional pins between center and ends, about 1 inch apart. Leave the neck edges open.

When sewing the collar, put the work under the presser foot of the machine with the canvas side up. This will prevent the presser foot from pushing the soft garment material out of place, the canvas being so much stiffer and firmer than the wool. This system is a "must" in stitching edges made up of garment fabric and interfacing.

The seam edge around the collar must now be trimmed off in the "customary staggered manner," as follows: Holding the canvas side of the collar nearest to you, trim away the complete canvas edge right down to the stitching. But do not cut the stitching. Don't worry if the canvas separates from the stitching here and there; the stab stitching will hold it. Cut off the edge underneath the canvas—the under collar—to ¼ inch width. Do not trim the third edge, the upper collar, at all. Leave it there to give the outside of the collar a nice appearance when it is turned over to the right side. The corners, however, are trimmed off through all the layers, as close to the stitching as possible, and at an angle so that the corner edges will not crowd inside. It is a mistake to trim the collar seam edges evenly, as so many women do. The staggering produces a nicely tapered outside edge, whereas the even edge results in a rim that gives the finished collar a very home-made appearance. Fig. 61 shows the manner of trimming the seams properly in tailored collars.

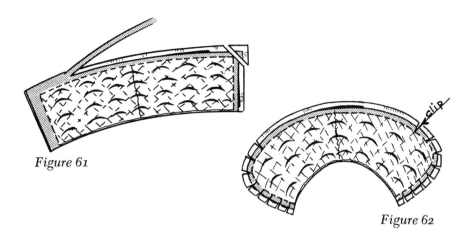

Figure 61

Figure 62

When the collar is styled with curved ends, as in the Peter Pan type, first trim the edges in the staggered manner, and then clip inward on the remaining edges, at the curves. Clip every ⅜ inch right down to the stitching. This clipping will prevent the edges from ruffling inside the collar when turned to the right side. Each little clipped section will lap slightly over the next, to give the collar a trim appearance with just the right amount of tapering. It is not necessary to remove triangular pieces from the remaining edges, as is sometimes recommended, since this is guesswork, and may cause the outer edge to be ridged (if one part is empty and another part is filled with these seam edges). Fig. 62 illustrates the correct way to treat the edges of interfaced curved collars.

Now turn the collar over to the right side. Wiggle the corners between the fingers to work out the grooves of the seam to the very edge of the collar points. It is not necessary to poke pointed objects into corners when the seams have been properly trimmed. They turn easily, and with the bit of coaxing that the wiggling gives, the corners come out trim and even.

Hold the upper collar nearest to you, and roll the seamed edge away from you so that the groove of the seam goes to the under-collar side, just enough inside of the edge of the upper collar so that the groove of the seam is not visible. If you roll the groove too far underneath the upper-collar edge, you may distort its shape. Just roll it enough to keep the seam from showing when the collar is worn. Roll and baste an inch at a time ¼ inch from the edge until you have basted all around the outer edges of the collar. Then go back and do another row of basting 1 inch in from the first one, continuing to roll the collar as you baste so that the under one will remain where it belongs. Keep on basting 1

115

inch apart until the whole collar is covered with bastings and then press the collar on the underside with a moist press cloth, but don't move the iron around or you'll push the layers of the collar out of line. Just lay the iron flat on all parts of the collar and let the steam do the press job.

If the collar, cuffs, or flaps of a garment are going to be trimmed with machine stitching, the trimming could be done now. The collar can also be done after the coat is finished, especially if the front of the coat is going to be edge stitched too. In that case, wait until the hem is turned up so that the edge stitching can be done right through the hem. If you plan to hand sew your trimming with embroidery cotton or silk twist, as is often seen on camel's-hair coats, it would be just as well to wait until the garment is completely finished, and then refer to the chapter on "Fashion Detailing" for instructions.

How to attach the collar

Often the neck edges of collars need to be trimmed, because they have become slightly uneven during the basting, rolling, and pressing. If the under collar and interfacing edges project beyond the neck edge of the upper collar, trim them off and make them all alike. But, if the upper collar is the one that projects beyond the edges of the canvas and under collar, slide the edge of the upper collar back to conform to the edges of the others, and do not trim it off. It will just give the upper collar a little more "ease."

On some collars of tailored garments, a certain amount of slackness is purposely allowed in the upper collar so that it will have a little flexibility when the collar is rolled over in wearing. This makes the collar lie flatter. Not all tailored collars have this slackness allowed in the upper collar, but when it is present, you handle it in this manner, pinning all the edges evenly together so that they will stay in place for attaching to the neck of the coat. This, of course, is done after pressing, just before attaching the collar to the garment.

There are various ways to attach collars to necklines, but none is quite so simple as the way this one will be attached. Because this method may be different from the one suggested on the guide sheet of the pattern, it is better to disregard the notches on the neck of the garment as well as those on the neck edge of the collar. Instead, mark the places on each garment front to show where the ends of the collar must be pinned. These marks are in the form of dots, triangles, or arrows at the seam line of the pattern. Place the pattern piece on the outside of the garment front, first on the right and then on the left, and mark them alike with a dot of chalk.

Next, match the center back of the collar to the center back of the neckline, pinning all the layers of the collar to the center back seam, with the outside of the collar on top and the under collar against the garment. Then, pin the ends of the finished collar to their respective coat fronts, matching the ends to the chalk dots. Hold the work so that the inside of the coat faces you during the complete pinning operation. Hold the middle and one end of the pinned work between the hands rather tightly so that the neck edges of the garment and those of the collar will conform to each other. You may find that the neck edge of the garment is slightly longer than the collar edge, or the other way around, but the stretching of the seam edges will make the two conform to each other. Pin all the layers of the collar to the neckline, starting at the middle and pinning to one end of the collar, then doing the same to the other half, until the work resembles Fig. 63. Note that the pins are inserted at right angles to the stitching line, and about an inch apart.

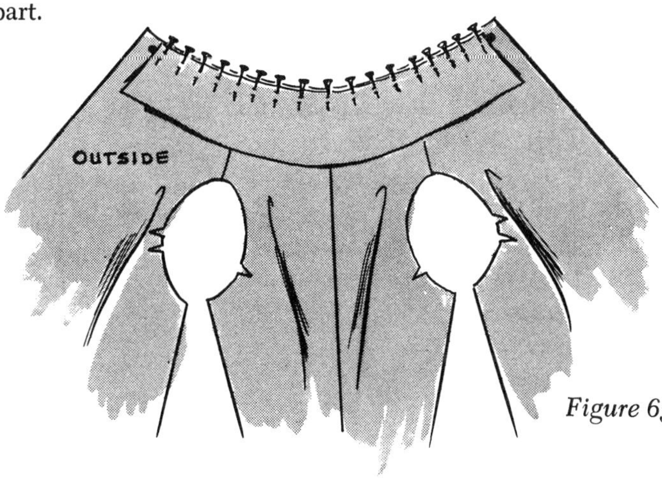

OUTSIDE

Figure 63

Before taking the next step, compare the front ends of the neckline that extend out beyond the collar to be sure that they are the same length so that the lapels will be alike when the garment is finished. Even though markings are accurately done, small differences can be magnified as the work progresses, so it is a good idea to check on yourself before you finish the stitching.

The front and back facings cut from the garment cloth are joined at the shoulders and the seams pressed flat. Pin the facing with right side against the outside of the garment, starting from the top of each front and proceeding downward with the pins inserted at right angles to the seam line; then pin around the neckline. Make sure to match the center back of the facing and the shoulders with those of the garment; otherwise the collar and lapels will not roll correctly but will twist and pull out of shape. In pinning the facing around the neckline it is advisable to partially withdraw the pins which hold the collar in place and then reinsert them to include the neck edge of the facing, but

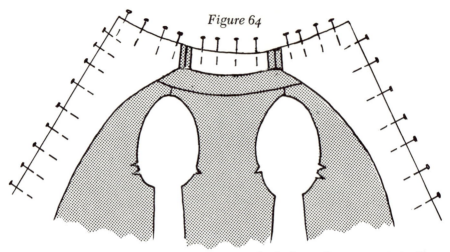

Figure 64

make sure not to disturb the way in which the collar was originally pinned to the neck of the garment. (Fig. 64.)

Start sewing the facing and garment together at the bottom of one front and proceed upward and around the neck and then downward on the opposite front. Remember to have the canvas side of the garment facing upward during the stitching to keep the coat material from getting pushed out of place by the presser foot. Only then will the edges of the three layers of fabric behave properly.

Trim away the seam edges on the two fronts in the staggered way to avoid bulk and to produce a perfectly tapered effect when finished. That is, cut off the canvas completely to the stitching line, the middle layer of fabric to ¼-inch width and let the third layer remain full seam width. Cut the corners diagonally at the top of the fronts to make them neat and flat. (Fig. 65.)

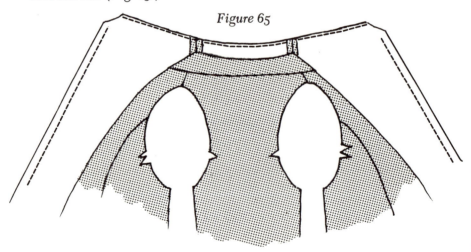

Figure 65

The neck edges are trimmed differently from the front edges. They are not staggered but cut off bluntly to a scant ¼-inch width from one end of the neckline to the other. Go back after this first trimming and cut away as much of the canvas as you can, so that there is no canvas left beyond the stitching line.

Attaching collars on winter coats of heavy fabric

There may be times when the combined layers of a finished collar plus garment and facing are too thick to get under the presser foot of your machine. In such cases sew only the collar to the neck of the coat first after pinning it into place. This will flatten the seam line area a little and make it easier to sew through when attaching the facing against the fronts and neckline after pinning them together for stitching. Just be sure to sew on the canvas side of the fronts, and then use the line of stitching that holds the collar in place as a guide when you get to the neckline.

Attaching the collar minus a back facing

For some reason or other, an occasional pattern design will not provide a pattern piece for a back facing for a coat or jacket that features a collar. In such cases the front facings are pinned into place to each front and around the neckline to the shoulders, as shown in Fig. 66. If the material being used is bulky, a line of stitching may be done through the seamline to keep the collar in place.

The facings are then stitched to the fronts and the line of stitching continued around the collar, going through the line of stitching that is

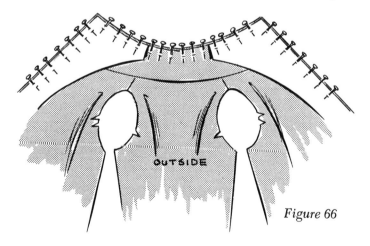

Figure 66

already there, and proceeding down to the bottom of the opposite front. The canvas side of the work is always on top when this stitching is done. The seams down each front are trimmed in the staggered way. The neck edge with the collar inserted is cut off bluntly to a scant ¼-inch width, but *only to each shoulder.* The center back of the collar and neckline are not trimmed away at all. The remaining seam provides support for the lining when it is eventually hand stitched into place. It also gives the collar neck edge the firmness it should have to make it set well when the garment is worn. (Fig. 67.)

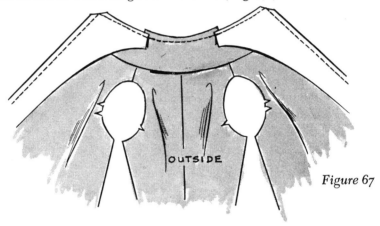

Figure 67

Turn the facings over to the inside of the garment. Wiggle and shape the corners at the tops of the fronts with the fingers so that the lapels will shape up properly, then baste them on the extreme edges for a good thorough press job. Keep the edges of the fronts and facings even from the top to the second buttonhole and baste them that way; but from there down, roll the front edge over slightly toward the inside of the coat, so that the groove of the seam does not show. Make sure to roll the edges of the fronts carefully so that the change of the groove direction is subtle below the second buttonhole where the rolling starts. The rolling should be done slightly so as not to change the grain of the cloth in an obvious way. Baste the neckline flat for pressing.

When the style of the garment features lapels and a collar which will always be worn open above the top buttonhole, since it is not meant to be worn closed, the rolling of the seam edges that join the fronts and facing together are done a little differently. This rolling is started at the top buttonhole and button, bringing the groove of the seam to the inside of the jacket or coat from there to the bottom. You then roll the edges in reverse from the top buttonhole up to the top of the lapel, which brings the seam to the underside of the lapel on each front.

Press the basted edges lightly but well, using a press cloth placed on the side of the front where the groove shows so that the side of the garment that will show when worn will not be marked with the iron. Use the small end of the ironing board for pressing the neckline seam and do the job on the under-collar side.

About Fitting the Coat

The temptation to try things on before the right stage of progress is reached in the construction of the garment has led to many needless disappointments. It takes experience and imagination to be able to visualize how the finished garment will look when there are seams still to be sewn here and there. Novices often make adjustments where none are needed because the garment has been tried on so soon that it looks "funny" to an inexperienced eye. Such a first adjustment necessitates others, and the garment soon ends up as a complete misfitting loss.

As an example, if the garment is tried on before the collar and facings are attached, the neck will definitely be too tight, because the seam allowance still surrounds the neck. When the seam is sewn and trimmed down to the usual ¼-inch width, the neck will automatically be enlarged to the right size. But if the seam is trimmed off before attaching the collar and facings, the neck will automatically be too large. This is a very common mistake.

The same thing often happens with shoulder widths. If you try on the garment too soon, the shoulder will seem to droop off your shoulders. There's a strong temptation to trim away part of the shoulder. This could be the beginning of failure. After a ⅝-inch seam is taken in the armhole seam at the shoulders when attaching the sleeves, the shoulders will be right.

Altogether, including the neckline seam and the sleeve seams, the upper part of the garment is reduced 2½ inches. These seam allowances make a tremendous difference in the fit of the garment. So beware of trying on the garment until the proper amount of work has been done. Then if you have started right, no adjustments will be necessary. On the other hand, if changes do have to be made, you can better judge the extent of the adjustment.

When you are ready for fitting, pin the sides of the coat together about 1½ inches apart, with the raw edges on the outside of the garment, and pins inserted vertically, as in Fig. 68. Try the coat on so that you can see whether or not it needs to be taken in at the side seams, or the "hidden areas." Never try garments on wrong side out. You can then see just exactly how the garment will fit, and what adjustments are needed. If there happens to be a figure irregularity,

Figure 68

proper fitting will easily camouflage it. Fitting any other way is not satisfactory, even when there is no camouflaging to do.

Pin the fronts of the coat together, just as it will be worn buttoned up, lapping right front over left if the coat is for a girl, or the opposite way if it is for a boy. Bring the collar ends right together in the middle of the neck at the front and be guided by this as to the amount of lap that the coat will have. Look over the situation, but don't be tempted to reach for the scissors if the shoulders drop off a bit. Just remember, there will be ⅝ inch taken off each side by the time the sleeves are inserted. If any further shoulder adjustments are needed, they will be done later when the sleeves are inserted. Right now, just concentrate on the sides, and take them in if and where necessary. Remember, this is a boxy coat, and should not be fitted too closely. The garment should fall freely away from the body.

If you are making a form-fitting design, like a princess style, the procedure for assembling and constructing the garment is exactly the same as for the looser type. The preparation for fitting is also the same, except that the garment will conform to the figure more closely, because of the shape of the unit parts, the upper section fitting closer to the waistline, and the lower parts falling freely. So concentrate mainly on the upper section; the lower section will take care of itself.

Changing where the pockets go

Misplaced pockets always detract from the good appearance of a garment. The patch pocket with a separate flap was chosen for our coat because it does not become outgrown nearly so quickly as another type would if the coat is for a child. The depth of the pocket keeps the coat proportioned in appearance, while another type with just a welt or flap would look too high after the hem of the coat is lengthened for growth. Another reason for choosing the patch pocket is that it will wear better than a set-in type, since it is superimposed on the outside of the garment instead of being built right into it, so there can be no weak spots to wear out. Because of the way this pocket can be attached to the garment, it can be dropped very easily if it does become too high for the wearer, and will not leave marks where it was placed before.

The placement for the pockets was marked from the pattern with brightly colored hand stitching at the time of cutting. Up to this stage of progress it was impossible to judge whether or not the indicated locations were right. Now you can see whether the pockets need to be raised or lowered. The top of a pocket should be midway between the wrist and the elbow. If the person is average in height, they'll be right as marked from the pattern, but for someone shorter or taller they may have to be moved up or down.

Make a chalk line to show where the top of the pocket should come when moved. Then mark again with the bright thread, placing the pattern back on the fronts to make sure that the shape is correct.

After the coat is fitted, turn it inside out and rub the pinned edges with chalk so that the marking will serve as a stitching guide. Hold the raw edges on the right side of the cloth with one hand and chalk on the wrong side with the other. Do this wherever there is a pin. Make the marks obvious enough so that they will be there to show you where to sew the side seams after the pockets have been finished and sewn to the coat fronts.

In the general chapter on "Pockets," you will find full directions for making patch pockets. They may be different from the instructions given in your pattern guide sheet, but you'll find them easy to do, and you'll be pleased with the results.

If you desire another type of pocket from the one suggested here, just follow instructions for the style you have chosen, using the pattern markings to guide you in the placement and size of the pocket opening. All pocket styles are covered in the chapter on "Bound Buttonholes and All Types of Pockets."

When the pockets are completed, pin the side seams together, with the right sides of the fabric together, inserting the pins horizontally, and then stitch the seams through chalk marks and press them well. You are now ready to work on the sleeves.

The two-piece sleeve

The sleeves of many tailored garments are made in two pieces, an upper and an under piece, the seams being located toward the front and back of the garment. Another type of two-piece sleeve sometimes used in tailored things has front and back sleeve pieces, an upper seam on the very top, matching the shoulder seam of the garment, and an underseam in line with the side seam of the coat. There are also sleeves that are cut in one piece, with a seam only at the underarm.

Regardless of the style, all set-in sleeves are assembled and inserted into armholes the same way, with the important notches matched to their respective ones on the armholes. First, sew the sleeve parts together and press the seams open. Use a sleeve board or a rolled-up magazine, which ever is handy. Be sure to wrap a dish towel around the magazine so that inks from the cover don't come off on your sleeves during pressing. Turn the sleeves inside out and slide them onto the board or magazine for pressing.

Usually, there is a little slackness in one of the seam edges of the sleeve, between notches in the elbow area. This slackness is to allow for freedom in bending the arm. To work the slackness in, first pin the notches together, then hold the work so that the edge with the slackness is nearest you. Drape and roll the two edges over your fingers, with the slack piece on top. The draping and rolling will even up the slackness and make it fit the shorter seam edge. Pin the edges together 1 inch apart. Sew with the full part underneath the shorter edge, holding the edges slightly stretched as you sew, to prevent puckers from forming. If the fuller edge were on top, the presser foot would push the slackness into tiny pleats between the pins during stitching.

Inserting set-in sleeves should cause you no hardship. (Women have been known to shun patterns with set-in sleeves even though they consider themselves capable of doing good work with other styles.) The experienced sewer who has had unsatisfactory results with set-in sleeves can now gain added faith in her ability by following the instructions for inserting sleeves into a dress given in full in Chapter 2 (see page 59).

The "magic stitch" simplifies the operation of inserting sleeves into armholes on every type of garment in which a set-in sleeve is featured, whether it is a dress or the most tailored type of apparel. (Fig. 69.) The principle of how the work is held in the hands and how it is placed underneath the presser foot does not change; it is always the same. In suits and coats the fullness in the cap of the sleeves between

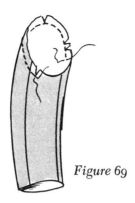

Figure 69

the shoulder notch and those at front and back is greater than it is in most dress styles. Therefore, it is even more important that you hold the job in the "steering wheel" position to be sure that the trimness that a tailored garment must have is achieved with ease.

You may find at times that there is more fullness on one side of the sleeve top than on the other, but if your notches are matched at the left and right as well as at the top of the sleeve, don't worry. The fullness was meant to be there for one reason or another, so trust your pattern.

Even such a small matter as knowing which side of the work should face upward when sewn can make the difference between an easy job and a hard one, between pleasing or shoddy results. It is as simple as that. Always start to sew sleeves at the underarms, and always inside of the tunnel, and be sure to take an exact ⅝-inch seam allowance and not less.

In case the shoulders are too wide

As was mentioned previously, the shoulders can be narrowed more satisfactorily now than at any earlier stage in the construction of the coat. If found to be a little bit too wide, simply rip the sleeve out of the armhole across the upper section, from the notched area in the front to the notched area in the back, directly alongside the "magic stitch" but not disturbing it. (Fig. 70.) Don't disturb the underarm seam either.

Now, try on the coat and pin the sleeve top to the shoulder seam in a more becoming location; then remove the coat. Place a pin where you intend to restitch the sleeve on the outside of the garment, and then, working inside the garment as before, and looking inside the tunnel, start repinning the sleeves into the armholes. Place the top of the sleeve at the mark on the shoulder line, and pin at right angles to the seam line. Keep the original ⅝-inch seam allowance on the sleeve itself, since this alteration is only being made in the armhole, and not

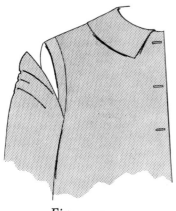

Figure 70

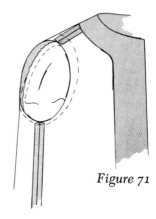

Figure 71

in the sleeve. Continue pinning toward the notched areas, allowing the sleeves to taper back gradually to the original seam line of armhole as the notched areas are reached. Do not trim away the extra width of armhole seam at the top of the shoulders, because it acts as a support to the rest of the garment and is not noticed from the outside. (Fig. 71.)

With the shoulder fitting well, the sleeves sewn without a pucker, the notches matched and each sleeve in its armhole, you will now perform a little trick that will make the tops of the sleeves forever smooth and that will prevent later rippling. To do it, trim away the seam edge of the *sleeves only* next to the magic stitch, from the notches in front to the notches in back across the tops only. Leave the underarms as they are. The firmness of the complete seam width is needed there to support the shape of the armhole. See Fig. 18, which shows just how this trimming of fullness is done.

Here's a bit of very pleasing advice for a change. This advice is what *not* to do, and it is stressed with the same emphasis as for any "must." This is it: never press the seam around an armhole after the sleeves have been inserted. Many, many sewing instructions stress the importance of pressing, shrinking, steaming, and otherwise torturing seams here, of all places. Yet such pressing has often been the only reason for disappointment in the finished garment.

Shoulder shapers for set-in sleeves

In the past large shoulder pads were used inside of garments to give an exaggerated appearance to the shoulders. As time went on the pad became smaller and smaller so that today pads are just a firm flat imitation of what they once were. Although the trend is for natural-looking shoulders in most clothes, it is sometimes a good idea to build a little extra firmness into tailored garments at the armhole and sleeve areas of the shoulders to support the joining seam which might otherwise collapse and lose its shape, especially if the material is soft and loosely woven. Even garments made of firm-textured cloth benefit from some built-in shaping if they are in tailored styles.

These shaping devices have a rise of about ¼ inch or less at the edge that fits into the armhole in the area where the end of the shoulder and the top of the sleeve cap meet. They usually come covered with tailor's canvas and are available at most notion counters. (Fig. 72.) They make the person's shoulders look alike whether they are or not and they also camouflage faults very successfully. If after the shapers have been inserted into the garment, the shoulders still look uneven, make a small roll of some scrap material in the shape of a small hot dog and hand stitch this to the underside of the shaper on the lower shoulder, and *voilà!* The shoulders will now look exactly alike without any alterations whatsoever on the garment itself.

The shapers are inserted into the armholes by sliding them in so they project into the tunnel of the sleeves about ½ inch. Pin them in place from the outside of the garment. (Fig. 73.) The armhole edges are directed into the inside of the sleeves as the pinning is done. Pin from the shoulder downward on each side of the armhole, smoothing the garment cloth over the shaper as you pin. If you notice wrinkles forming in the armhole and sleeve seams during the pinning, it is because the seam edge of the armhole has been allowed to slip in the wrong direction, so *direct it into the sleeve.*

Shapers are always sewn permanently by hand, from the outside of

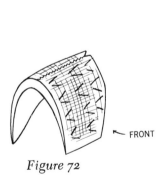

← FRONT

Figure 72

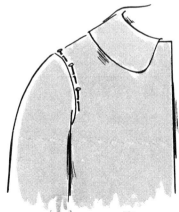

Figure 73

the garment, to be sure that smoothness is retained. A tiny backstitch is used, made directly through the groove of the armhole seam. The stitches are 1 inch apart, starting at one end of the pad and ending at the other. The tiny stitch remains on the outside of the garment directly in the groove of the seam, and if it is not drawn too tight, it will blend right in with the weave of the fabric. Just be sure not to pull it so as to cause a dimple on the outside of the garment. Pick up just a thin layer of padding when doing this tacking, so that the stitching doesn't make a dent in the coat. (Fig. 74.)

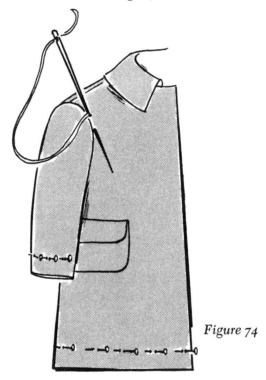

Figure 74

Shapers for kimono and raglan sleeves

Shoulder shapers for kimono and raglan sleeves are designed somewhat differently from the set-in type. The outside ends are rounded and made to cup over the shoulder, producing the soft natural lines that kimono sleeves require. When buying these pads, refer to them as "cup-shaped" pads. (Fig. 75.)

Pin the shaper and garment together through the long seam that extends from the neckline down to the bottom of the sleeve, stopping just before the edge of the pad is reached. A seam line usually runs horizontally across the thick section of this kind of pad, and if the

128

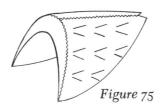

Figure 75

pinning is done only to that seam, the shape of the upper area of the garment will be smoother. Tack into the garment just as for the first padding, starting at the neckline area and stitching by hand through the long seam. The parts of the pad that hang down each side of the shoulder inside the garment will be held in place eventually by the lining.

Marking the length of the coat and sleeves

The coat is now ready to be tried on to determine the finished length. Girls' and women's coats should always be 1 inch longer than anything that will be worn underneath them, so that nothing shows below the hemline. With boys, the coat is usually measured just about to the knees if they are little fellows, or a bit longer if they are school age.

Put the coat on and pin the front together as if buttoned. Mark every 5 or 6 inches all around the bottom, using a hem marker or a yardstick and chalk or pins. Have your model stand naturally, and not in any exaggerated pose that might affect the hang of the coat.

The sleeves can also be marked for correct length at this time; and then you won't have to try on the coat again.

The finished length of the coat sleeves should come right to the wrist, neither longer nor shorter. The garment will look oversized if they're too long, and outgrown if they're too short, even if the rest of the coat fits perfectly.

Turn up the bottom of the coat to judge what length will be most becoming and then proceed to mark. Judge sleeves the same way, first turning them up to see how they look and then doing a more complete marking. Fig. 74 serves a dual purpose. It illustrates how you back-stitch the shapers through the groove of the armhole seam and shows how the hem and sleeves are marked for turning up.

Reserve extra material for letting down when making coats for growing children. Four or 5 inches turned up for the hem is not unusual. Four or 5 inches should be turned up for sleeve reserve also, as arms and legs grow rapidly.

When making fitted coats, however, there is a limit to the amount that can be successfully left in the hem for letting-down purposes. The hem gets too full at the top edge if too much is left to turn up, so in such styles it is wise to turn up just the amount recommended, plus an inch or so, to avoid making the hem look bulky and nonprofessional.

Because of the way sleeves taper inward at the bottom, it is sometimes necessary to rip part of the seam that will eventually be covered by lining, so that when the bottom of the sleeve is turned up, it will fit the larger section of the sleeve above the wrist. The opened seam will separate to allow for this. So, pin the sleeves with as much extra left inside as you want, and pin into position with pins inserted up and down an inch apart. (Figs. 76a and 76b.)

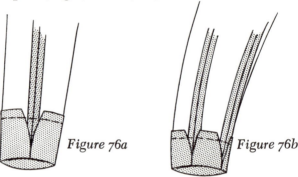

Figure 76a   Figure 76b

Many coat hems are finished with the lining left free at the bottom, so attach a seam tape by machine to the top edge after cutting the coat hem evenly all around the bottom. Place the tape on the right side of the hem top and hold the tape slightly stretched as you sew it into position to prevent it from ruffling and becoming too full. Arrange 3 or 4 inches of the tape on the hem edge and stitch that much, then stop with the machine needle inside of the stitching job, and arrange another 4 or 5 inches and sew that, keeping up this stop-and-go procedure until you have gotten completely around the coat hem. This work is usually easier if you don't pin the tape to the hem first and then stitch, but arrange as you go along.

Only the coat needs seam tape. The lining is hemmed later without tape, with just the top edge tucked under so raw edges will be out of the way, and then hand finished. Turn up the hem of the coat to the right length, and match the seam lines, placing the seams of the hem against the coat seams, and pinning these areas first. Insert the pins vertically. Next, pin the hem between the seams. Spread the fingers of both hands as if you were going to place them on a typewriter keyboard, on top of the hem between two pinned seams to break up the slackness. Remove one of the hands and use it to insert additional pins into the hem an inch apart, while the other hand holds the hem in its arranged position, the pins going in vertically. When hems are handled

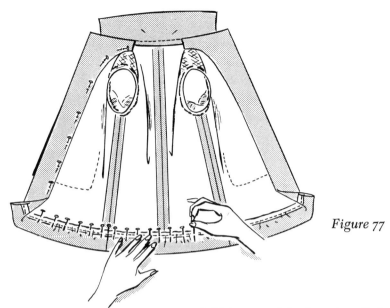

Figure 77

in this manner, you avoid the need to fold the top of the hem into little pleats to get rid of top slackness in the hem, which would give the hem a homemade look. (Fig. 77.)

Next, pin the facing into position. Place the garment on a flat surface and work on the inside, arranging the facing over the shapers in the shoulder area, and then continue pinning downward, using the palms of your hands to keep the garment and facing smooth against each other as you pin. Insert the pins parallel with the facing edges about 2 inches apart. Lap the bottoms of the facing over the turned-up hem. Unless the material is extremely bulky, it is better to leave all the hem there, both on the garment and the facing, although the interfacing should be trimmed away at the turn of the hem to get rid of the bulk. If the edge of the coat front, the part where the garment is joined to the facing, is directed away from the interfacing and aimed toward the facing at the time the hem line is being turned up, some of the bulk will be reduced. But if you allow this seam edge to rest on the canvas, or separate it by pressing the seam open, you will make the bottom of the garment bulkier. All this is not as complicated as it seems, as you will discover when you try it.

How to sew a hem

Now that everything is pinned into place, sew the hem by hand, invisibly, using the stitch described on page 63. It is a very speedy stitch that stays up until you voluntarily take it down, and it never needs reinforcing. You may have to work along with the text for 3 or 4 stitches, but you'll soon get the swing of it. Before starting it, you should know that a hem should never be pressed around the bottom until the top has been sewed into position. Some women do this, thinking that they are making their work easier. The opposite is true, for premature pressing makes the top edge of the hem hard to handle. Leave the pressing of all hems until the very last.

Hand sew the loose facing edges to the garment fronts, starting at the top of the shoulders and attaching them to the pads at the shoulder area, using an in-and-out method of stitching, similar to basting. This is done ¼ inch away from the facing edge, with stitches about 1 inch long. Below the pads, sew the facings to the canvas edges, making sure not to come through to the right side of the coat. Stab stitch back facing to garment loosely.

Now turn up, pin, and hand sew the bottoms of the sleeves. Use stab stitching to secure the hem of the sleeves, working very loosely so that stitches will not show on the outside of the coat. These stitches should be about 1 inch apart and ¼ inch from top edge.

Give the coat a final touch-up with the iron wherever it needs it so it will be ready for the lining. Press the hem carefully and lightly and concentrate mostly on the lower half of the width. Placing the iron on the whole hem width will make a ridge on the outside of the garment, so don't, especially when the cloth is heavy. A light pressing on only the lower part of the hem is enough so that a soft fold results instead of a sharp crease. This makes the job of lengthening the coat later on much simpler because there is no sharp crease to try to press out.

Use a moist press cloth and let the steam do the job instead of your weight on the iron. When the press job is finished, the hem should not be visible on the outside of the garment. If it shows in any way, it could be because your hemming stitches are too tight or too close together, or you might have pressed more heavily than you realized.

About coats with flared fullness

Some coats for growing girls and misses are designed with flared fullness, like princess styles, for example. The parts of these garments are cut into shaped panels and when they are joined together, they produce a smooth fit from the shoulders to the waist and then flare out gradually. The fullness forms into ripples at the hem.

This type of garment does not have quite the wearable lifespan of styles that hang freely from the shoulders to the hem line without defining the waist location. When a girl grows, three locations are affected: the bottom of the garment, the sleeves, and the waist, and although some letting down can be provided for, not much can be done about a lengthening waistline. In a flared coat, also, the amount that can be added to the bottom of the garment for letting-down purposes is limited because of the shape and fullness of the hem.

The normal hem width allowed on pattern pieces for flared styles is usually less than for garments cut along straighter lines, but you can successfully add an extra inch to the original hem width if you wish the garment to give extra service. The top edge of the hem is quite full when turned up, but if a line of large machine stitching is done ¼ inch below the raw edge, you can draw up the fullness so that the hem will fit more flatly against the part of the garment where the stitching is to be done.

It is easier to get such a hem neat if seam tape is omitted at the top edge, so that the fullness can be more easily shifted with the fingers as the hand stitching is done. In that way the fullness will work in evenly all around the hem. In turning up the hem, match seams of the hem to those in the garment and pin these parts first, inserting the pins parallel with the vertical seams. Next pin between the seams, drawing up on the large machine stitching to gather the top of the hem a little so it will lay flat on the inside of the garment, inserting the pins about an inch or so apart, and proceeding in this way until the whole hem has been pinned up. Then stitch the hem by hand as invisibly as possible with the stitches left loose enough so they do not dimple the fabric on the outside of the garment. Press the lower half of the hem lightly.

You are now ready to make the lining in the same way whether it is to hang independently from the coat at the bottom or to be hand stitched to the coat hem. All this will be explained in full detail when the lining is ready to be inserted into the coat.

Interfaced hems on coats and jackets

To produce a permanent smooth shape at the bottoms of coats and jackets for girls and misses, insert between the hem and the outer layer of the garment a strip of interfacing material cut on either the straight or cross-weave of the grain. The interfacing should be about

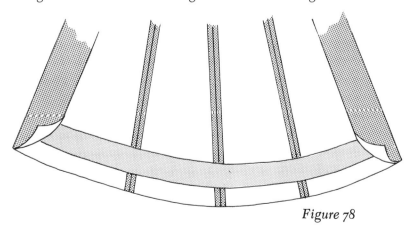

Figure 78

133

the width of the hem itself, or just a bit wider. Attach the canvas with rows of stab stitching about an inch or so apart, very loose, and when you turn up the hem, hand stitch the top edge of the garment hem to the top of the interfacing. (Fig. 78.)

The canvas adds to the shaping of the silhouette, especially if the material used for the garment is soft and loosely woven. It also prevents the hem width from showing through when the garment is finished, so that a professional appearance is achieved. The canvas can be used whether the hem is to be finished with seam tape at the top edge, or the lining will lap over the top of the hem.

Quite frequently the pattern instructions show a strip of canvas placed at the bottoms of the sleeves also to hold them in shape. This is a good idea when the bottoms of the sleeves are not too narrow and the cloth is lightweight and stretchy. Otherwise the bottoms become quite bulky. Try the canvas, but don't use it if the end result is too thick and chunky. If you wish to keep these sleeve ends in shape, use some lightweight cotton instead of the interfacing material and this will do the supporting without bulk. Interfacing the bottoms of sleeves is beneficial if the sleeves are cut all in one piece, as in kimono styles. Such sleeves are not on the "straight grain" of the cloth, but usually quite bias. The interfaced bottoms will stabilize the weave of the material and keep the hems of the sleeves in shape. Such sleeves are rarely cut along slender lines. They are usually flared at the bottom with plenty of room to accommodate the extra supporting layer of interfacing.

About Linings, Interlinings and the Zipped-in Types

The lining for coats and jackets should be of good sturdy material that will last as long as the outer fabric. There are many different kinds of linings to choose from, but the most popular ones are the good quality rayons which come in a large variety of weaves, from the fanciest satins to the most casual twills. They wear very well, and are equally suitable for boys or girls. They come in all the usual colors and weights. These materials outwear most silks.

Rayon linings make the garment easy to slip on and off, an important consideration if it will be worn over wool or other fabrics with a certain amount of adhering quality. Struggling in and out of clothing is hard on both the seams and on the cloth, not to mention how hard it is for the youngsters to dress themselves.

The yardage requirements for the lining are specified on the pattern envelope. Most of the time the same pattern pieces are used for cutting the lining as were used for the coat or jacket. The pattern pieces are

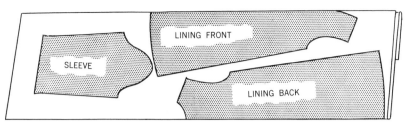

Figure 79

clearly marked, showing which parts to use for the lining and which must be folded out of the way. The layout chart shows how to place the pattern on the wrong side of the lining fabric. If additions were made in the "hidden areas" of the garment, do the same to the lining and add to the bottom of the hem and sleeves if necessary.

Cut the lining with the same precision as the coat, clipping in for the notches wherever they are needed. The lining layout diagram will show allowances for a pleat in the center back. Once the lining has been cut with the pleat included, forget that it's there. It will take care of itself naturally when the lining is inserted into the garment. The allowance for the pleat gives more ease and freedom, and if the lining should shrink at the cleaner's, the fit would not be affected seriously. (Fig. 79.)

Assemble the parts just as if you were making another coat. Insert the sleeves into the armholes even though the pattern instructions tell you otherwise. Just remember, you are doing it the easy way. Press the lining seams open, as it is being put together.

About interlining winter coats

You can choose from many interlinings to make clothes cozy and warm for winter wear. Interlinings do not have to be bulky and thick to be warm. As a matter of fact, the best interlinings are very thin with loose, open weaves, making the garment lightweight but warm. Woolen interlinings are most popular, with synthetics a close second. Cotton flannels are also used for this purpose. Some of the cotton interlinings are made with one side fleecy and the other tightly woven to act as a windbreaker.

Interlinings are cut exactly the same as linings. They are then incorporated with the lining pieces and sewed as one item. First, the outer lining material is placed on the interlining and pinned on all edges. The parts are then joined and treated as one. When the interlining is a bit heavy, some of the seam edge can be cut away after stitching, but this is not always necessary. Do it only when you need to reduce bulk.

135

Because interlining never shows, here is an opportunity to put to use some old lightweight woolen clothes that are taking up space in your closet. One or two straight skirts would serve this purpose nicely. Take them apart and see how easily they can be utilized. The fabric would surely equal the quality of the higher-priced interlinings. Do you have a lightweight blanket that has seen better days? This too would cut up into a wonderful interlining. Just be sure that the colors of these things are not so dark that they show through lighter-colored garments. Save the dark things for heavy or opaque fabrics. If you must piece to make a part large enough to fit the pattern piece, overlap the raw edges and sew through without making a regular seam; then treat the pieced sections as one. The interlining will never be seen, and the joinings will be flatter this way.

Pile and fur linings

Fake furs or any other fuzzy materials make handsome linings inside of winter coats, and are as warm as can be. They sew right up on the sewing machine without any difficulty and when completed you insert them into the coat the same way you do linings and interlinings made of other fabrics.

When using the fluffy type of lining, it is necessary to choose a coat that is designed with deep armholes and plenty of room in its styling so that there will be enough living space in the garment to accommodate the lining material. Even a semi-fitted design with a pile lining looks lumpy and gives the person a heavy appearance. The loosely designed garment is best.

The sleeves of furry linings are always of another kind of material. A good quality rayon twill with a lightweight interlining makes ideal sleeves to insert into the armholes of a furry lining. This makes the coat more comfortable to wear.

There are also on the market linings that are woven with one side of good quality rayon satin and the other side fleecy for warmth. The satin side is worn as the finished side of the lining. Such a fabric would be a good choice for the sleeves in the "fur lining."

The furry lining does not have to be interlined with another fabric, as the "fur" itself will provide enough warmth in a winter coat. The same is true of the double-faced material mentioned, with satin on one side and fleece on the other. This type of material also takes the place of the separate lining and interlining layers.

Many people have used a millium lining and found it to be not quite warm enough for a winter coat, unless it is used along with an interlining, and that is exactly how this specially treated material should be used when putting it into winterwear. The single layer of millium will act only as a windbreaker; it will not generate heat, so if your blood circulation requires boosting, do include interlining along with the millium and it will then provide warmth enough for the winter coat.

How to insert lining into coat

Whether the coat is lined with a single layer of lining fabric or interlined, the procedure for inserting the lining is the same. To keep the interlining from separating from the lining, hand sew the outer edges of fronts and neckline ¼ inch in from the raw edges, using a long basting stitch. If this little precaution is not taken, the interlining will slip away from the lining cloth after the two have been inserted into the coat and cause lumping. So do anchor them together before going any further after assembling the parts.

Now slip the sleeves of the lining into those of the coat, matching tops, and pin the tops of the lining to the shoulders of the coat, or to the shapers, if they are being used, inserting the pins on the right side of the lining. Then reach underneath the lining and hand sew the armhole edge to the shaper at the shoulder end, or to the shoulder seam of the coat, right where they are held together with pins. Use a double thread and go back and forth from one layer to the other several times to form a durable thread "shank" about ¾ inch long between the garment and the lining. The "shank" will hold the two layers together, but will allow for enough independent action between them to prevent strain on either.

Use the shank stitching again at the top of the side seams where they meet the bottom of the armhole and after pinning the lining and garment together there, go inside of the lining and repeat the shank stitching operation. Make sure that the seams of the armholes are in their natural upright positions or else the garment will wrinkle underneath the arms.

Pin the side seams of the lining and coat together temporarily, to make the rest of the pinning job easy. Starting at the base of the armhole, match the side seams of the lining to those of the coat, looking underneath the lining each time to see that the seams are exactly aligned against each other as you pin. Insert the pins about 2 or 3 inches apart on the outside of the lining and in horizontal position so that they will hold better.

Pin the fronts of the lining into place next, starting at the top of one front, turning under ⅝ inch of the lining, and placing the fold onto the coat facing ⅝ inch in from the raw edge. Pin vertically this time, about 2 inches apart on each front. Continue the pinning at the shoulders, placing the lining against the facing and proceeding toward the center back. In the center back make a one-fold pleat of the material that will be left over.

Quite frequently it is necessary to clip the edges of the lining along the back neckline to make it fold back willingly, especially if the material used for the lining is somewhat stiff or heavy. The clipping is done about ¼ inch deep about ⅝ inch apart and this makes the edges turn under without puckering the outside of the lining. The pleat gets pinned into place about two inches down from the neck and it is eventually stitched through by hand with cross-stitching. (Fig. 80.)

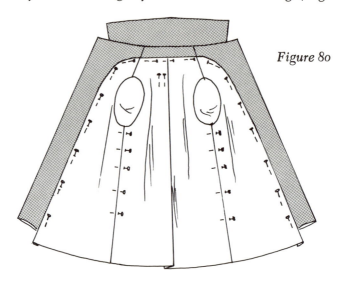

Figure 80

Measure the bottom of the lining 1 inch shorter than the coat, and if the coat is for a growing youngster, turn the whole hem so that it can be let down later, but limit the width of the lining hem if the coat is for an adult. Some of the interlining material can be cut away at the hem line to reduce bulk if you wish; but if it is not too heavy, it can stay.

Sew lining into place with the bridge stitch

Hold the lining side of the garment toward you and start stitching at the bottom of the left front if you sew right-handed, or at the bottom of the right front if your left hand does the sewing. Follow instructions for this most invisible and most versatile stitching, even though you may have to sew "one word at a time" until you become familiar with the simple steps. Tie a knot in the end of your thread, which should be double strand for double strength. Take a stitch into the fold of the lining, hiding the knot inside the garment. Now take a stitch ¼ inch long into the coat facing, starting the stitch directly alongside the thread coming out of the lining fold. Then take a ¼-inch stitch through the fold of the lining, starting that stitch exactly alongside the thread that is coming out of the facing. You will be working from right to left, from the bottom of the left front toward the top. Continue to work around the neckline and then proceed in the same manner downward on the opposite front to the bottom of the lining. If you are left-handed, of course, you'll work in the opposite direction. In the alternating process of this stitch, working from the lining to the facing and then back again, the threads holding the two together form into horizontal "bridges." If the stitches are not made directly alongside each other, the threads will show. When the stitches are properly pulled up to the right tension, after first taking four or five loose stitches, the bridges disappear completely. The lining will appear as if it had been machine sewn together to the inside of the garment. As you progress with bridge stitching, you will realize how closely related the motions of this type of stitch are to those of the "mice-teeth" type of stitching. The only difference between the two is that in this case the stitches are even lengths in the alternating process, while on the hem the stitches were short on the dress and long on the seam tape. (Fig. 81.)

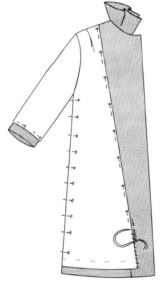

Figure 81

The pleat at the center back is caught into position about 2 inches below the neck with cross-stitching which should be copied from some ready-made garment in your closet. Study it a little and try to imitate the stitches as closely as you can, being sure not to stitch through to the outside of the coat. It's always a good idea to check with a ready-made article when confronted with sewing problems. They are a great help in showing how certain details should look, so imitate if you can't be original.

Do the hem of the lining next. If the lining is made of a single fabric, and not interlined, use the same "mice-teeth" stitching as on the hem of the coat. If the coat is interlined, use the bridge stitch, catching the stitches to the interlining. At the bottom of the facing, below the fold of the lining hem, there are some raw edges showing. These should now be tucked in with the tip of the needle and hand-finished neatly. The hem between the coat and facing is an open tube, and this should also be stitched together by hand with loose bridge stitching. If the stitches aren't loose enough, they will cause the fronts of the garment to pull up and buckle.

The lining — when there is no back facing

When the coat or jacket is minus a back facing of the garment fabric, the lining cloth is cut to reach right up to the seam line at the back of the neck so that it covers the raw edges of the collar. With the lining fronts pinned into place, bring the back of the lining over the shoulders and up to the neckline seam where the edge is folded under. Continue pinning around to the center back. Work first from one shoulder toward the middle and then from the other, meeting in the center back where the extra material is folded over into a pleat. (Fig. 82.)

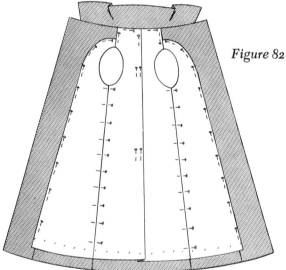

Figure 82

Sleeve linings

Next turn the sleeves inside out and arrange them so that the seams of the garment and those of the lining are matched perfectly against each other; otherwise the finished sleeves will twist into diagonal wrinkles. Measure the lining sleeves so that there is a little "play" in the length. This will prevent the lining from pulling up on the outer

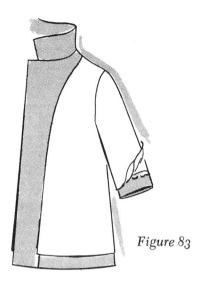

Figure 83

sleeve and causing distortion. If the lining is first measured to the full length of the sleeves and then the fold of the lining pinned against the top edge of the sleeve hem, there will be just the right amount of slackness in the lining to prevent any kind of problem. (Fig. 83.)

The attached lining — how to handle it

When the bottom of a lining is to be attached to the hem of the coat instead of being left to hang free, the general pinning of the lining is done in the same way as has already been covered, but the bottom is treated differently. Extra lining length must be allowed for ease so that the finished garment doesn't buckle, but not so much that it sags below the hem. There is a foolproof way of arriving at just the right amount of extra lining to have at the bottom to keep the garment smooth so that sagging and buckling problems are avoided.

With the lining already pinned in everywhere, measure the lining at the direct side seams, which are still pinned together to the coat seams, and see that it is turned under at the same length as the coat and pinned through the fold, but free of the coat hem as yet. Do the same thing to the center back, holding the lining taut and in a straight line from the middle of the back neckline to the bottom, then turn the lining under and pin it through the fold. The two fronts of the lining are now measured to be ¾ inch shorter than the length of the coat, and that part of the hem is turned under and pinned. The five pins that are now holding the lining hem turned under will be the means by which the right amount of slackness will eventually result.

Stretch the folded lining hem by holding a pinned area in each hand so that a continuous fold results from the stretching, and pin hori-

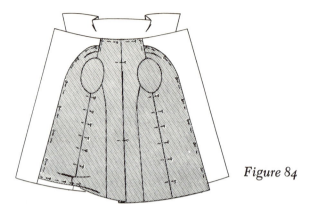

Figure 84

zontally between the pins so that a more solid fold is formed. Do this from the fronts to each side, and then do the same thing from the sides to the center. When the whole hem has been turned under in this manner, you are ready to pin the resulting hem of the lining to the hem of the garment.

Now pin the lining to the bottom of the coat, starting at the side seams and working toward the fronts, sliding the fold of the lining up to 1 inch above the bottom of the coat. Insert the pins parallel with the fold of the lining hem and quite close together. Do the two fronts first, then slip the lining up, working now from the sides to the center back. Make a pleat of the extra fullness of the lining there, folding it in the same direction as at the top. Note Fig. 84, which shows how the lining has been handled at the hem line as well as how it has been treated at the shoulders when a back facing is omitted.

Now you are ready to stitch the lining completely into the coat by hand. A light touch-up with the iron, and the garment will be almost ready to wear, except for making the buttonholes. If you have made bound buttonholes, the facing will have to be cut through where the buttonholes are located on the garment front and finished according to instructions given in the chapter on "Bound Buttonholes and All Types of Pockets."

Coats and jackets with zipped-in linings

Tailoring coats and jackets into which cozy and warm linings can be zipped at a moment's notice is not too different from making coats that are lined or interlined in the usual way. If you have already had the experience of making a lined coat, the deviations from the regular steps taken in putting parts together will present no problem.

The construction steps in tailoring the garment are applied in the order presented earlier, but they do change after a certain point has been reached. This point occurs when the canvas is already in place on each front, bound buttonholes have been made into the right-hand front through the outer material and the canvas (if there are to be machine-made buttonholes, these come after the garment is completed, so they are not considered at this time), and the pockets have been taken care of, and the collar has been finished and pinned to the neckline of the garment.

Stitch together the front and back facings at the shoulders and after pressing the seams flat, turn the inner edge of the facing under ⅝ inch and press carefully to form into a fold, being careful not to stretch the edge in handling. Purchase a separating-type of zipper in the color closest to the garment fabric and in a length that will go from about 6 inches above the hem at one front of the garment, up and around the neckline, then down the other front to about 6 inches above the hem. These zippers come in different weights, but you will not need the heavy type here. The zipper may have to be specially ordered from the fabric shop or department store in the length required, since they are not always stocked in all sizes.

Before attaching the facing to the garment, attach one part of the separating zipper to the inner edge of the facing by laying the folded edge wrong side down against the right side of the zipper, overlapping the zipper teeth so they do not show, and leaving the zipper closed while you are applying the fold over it. It's easier that way. In pinning the zipper and facing edge together, start at the middle of the back of the neckline and in the middle of the zipper, and pin in opposite directions to the zipper ends. Then sew the fold over the zipper teeth about ½ inch in from the folded edge. If you think you will find it easier to sew on the wrong side of the work with your zipper foot, do so, as long as the fold looks even when the job is finished. (Fig. 85.)

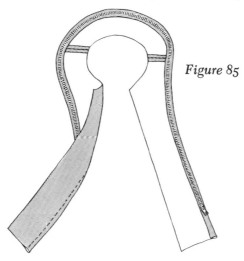

Figure 85

143

Now separate the zipper parts and put the free one to one side until later. Proceed to pin the facing to the fronts and neckline edge of the garment and sew it in the usual way. Trim the seams correctly, turn the facing to the inside of the garment, and press flat. Leave the facing edges free without pinning them down to the garment.

Continue constructing the garment by sewing the two sides together and then insert the sleeves. Also complete the regular lining and have it ready to be inserted.

Slip the lining sleeves into the garment sleeves and attach the shoulder areas together with shank stitching. Do the same thing to the tops of the side seams, making sure that the armhole seams are kept in their natural position all around. Pin the side seams of the lining to those of the garment so that they are in line with each other to make the handling of the lining easy. Start the pinning at the top of the side seams and proceed to the bottom.

Smooth the fronts of the lining toward the canvas interfacings, lifting the regular facing up and out of the way, then pin the extreme front edges of the lining against the canvas interfacings from the top down, first on one front and then on the other. Pin around the neckline at the back last. Use ½-inch running stitches to hand sew the lining to the canvas with double thread, but be sure not to go through to the outside of the garment.

The garment facing is now brought over to cover the raw edges of the lining and pinned into position flatly all around, first working on the two fronts, then on the back of the neck. Hand stitch the facing permanently to the fronts and back neckline edges, using double strands of thread and stitching through the machine stitching that holds the zipper in place, but do it as inconspicuously as possible. Use backstitches for more security. Go through the lining and canvas carefully so you do not go through to the outside layer of the garment material. The inner edge of the facing will look loose when the hand stitching has been done where the zipper is, but the zipper teeth will not show. The backstitches should be about ¼ inch apart.

Preparing the zipped-in lining

The material used for this special lining is cut like the regular lining, except that the center back pleat is omitted to prevent bulk. It is also cut somewhat shorter than the garment and no hem is allowed. Use a fabric of lighter weight for the sleeves if fake fur is being used, but use a lightweight interlining fabric for warmth. Then sew all the parts together, including insertion of the sleeves.

Bind the outer edges of the zip-in lining all around for less bulk, using a commercial bias tape in a color matching the lining, or cut your own bias from a lightweight lining fabric. Many times the zip-in lining

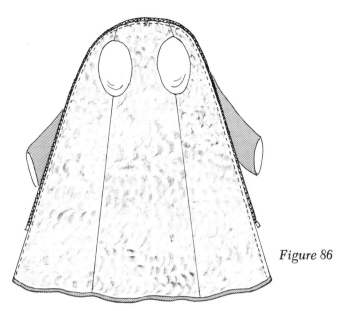

Figure 86

is sleeveless, and in that case the armholes are also finished with the bias tape.

The part of the zipper which has been laid aside is now pinned with its right side up against the wrong side of the lining. Start the pinning at the center back of the lining neckline and work toward the two ends alternately. Attach the bound edge of the lining right up close against the zipper teeth so that the teeth project out beyond the edge of the lining. Machine stitch in one continuous operation from one end of the zipper to the other to complete the lining. (Fig. 86.)

The sleeves of this lining are directed into those of the garment and regular lining and allowed to stay free without any tacking anywhere. They are hemmed either by hand or by machine and should be an inch shorter than the garment sleeves. To insert the zip-in lining match the zipper ends at the starting point, and pull the lever up and around the neckline and down on the opposite front.

Making Sport Jackets and Blazers

The workmanship on sport jackets and blazers is the same as on coats, whether for the smallest male member of the family or the largest, and here's where the real savings come in. Sport jackets are expensive to buy ready-made no matter what size they are, but making them at home entails exactly the same type of workmanship as making a coat, with the exception of the length of the seams. Picture your pleasure in seeing two fellows wearing matching sport jackets, one tiny and the other huge! This fun is possible only if the lady of the house makes the jackets herself. Otherwise such duplicates are out of the question.

If the jacket is for outdoors, not a suit jacket style, you can make a zip-in lining to go into it on really cold days, when it would be worn for ice skating or skiing.

If the jacket is a suit type, the construction as well as the lining is a little different. In this style, everything is done like the coat up to the stage of attaching the facing to the jacket fronts. The facing and lining fronts are joined together by machine and a bound pocket is then inserted into the assembled right-hand front of the lining. Follow the instructions given in the chapter on pockets. Then pin the facing to the fronts and collar, right sides together, and sew upward from the bottom on one side, going around the neckline and down on the opposite front to the bottom. If there are curves at the two fronts at the bottom, start the stitching at the beginning of the curve on one front and end beyond the curve on the opposite front. These curves usually start where the inner edge of the front facing and interfacing ends.

After trimming the neck and front seams correctly, fit the jacket and insert the sleeves. When the shoulders have been padded—and most sport jackets do have shoulder shapers—pin the front lining into place and baste it firmly around the armhole edges of the jacket. The underarm seams of the lining fronts are then turned under ⅝ inch and the fold is pinned down against the groove of the jacket side seam, covering only the edge of the front unit, while the seam edge of the back unit remains exposed. If you happen to be somewhat confused, this is a good time to inspect the inside of a purchased suit jacket belonging to one of the males of the house for a better understanding of these instructions, and do remember that you are not the only one to feel this way when working on a brand-new project. Hand stitch the folded edge as pinned down to within 5 or 6 inches from the bottom and then stop so that the next step can be done easily. You'll eventually come back and finish the hand stitching here. Bridge stitching is the best for attaching the lining to the side seam.

Before continuing with the rest of the lining, finish the seam edges of the jacket, since the back lining covers only the upper part of the inside of the jacket, and some of the seams will show. The seams that will be visible should be bound with bias-cut strips of the lining material. Do not be tempted to use commercial seam tape for this job, as it would cause bulk and might also make the seams pucker. Cut the bias strip 1 inch wide and sew several strips together for this purpose, using some of the scraps from the lining. Press the seams flat before you apply them to the jacket edges.

Sew the binding to the right side of the seam edge with ¼-inch seam, and stretch the bias strip slightly while stitching it. Next, wrap the binding around the garment seam edge and bring it to the underside. Then sew it from the right side of the seam, directly through the groove of the seam that holds the binding in place, and right alongside the binding. Finish all the exposed seam edges of the garment in the same manner.

The flat center back seam is also bound with bias strip. Finish the back or side vents, whichever style the pattern happens to feature, according to pattern instructions. Bind the bottom of the jacket with a bias-cut strip before the hem is turned up. Use "mice-teeth" stitching for the hem, as on the coat hem.

Assemble and construct the back lining according to the pattern. There are several types of linings, some full length and some not, each a little different from the other. It is advisable to use the type suggested by the pattern. The lining is hand sewed with the bridge stitch to the groove of the side seams. Most frequently, the linings of jacket sleeves are inserted by hand, so put the "magic stitch" on the sleeve lining first to make it easier to work in the fullness between the notches. Fig. 87 shows the inside of the jacket, and how the bound pocket is inserted through the lining and facing, using the lining material for bindings, and pocket lining too, to avoid bulk.

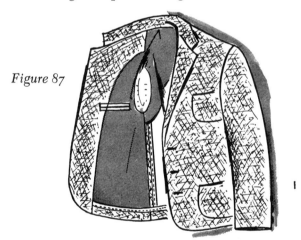

Figure 87

How to mark the garment for machine buttonholes

The placement of the buttonholes is the last consideration before the garment is finished. The size and location of the buttonholes rarely need to be changed from the position given on the printed pattern piece. First you must fold away the seam allowance on the pattern edge to be sure that the buttonholes will be the right distance away from the front edge of the jacket, then pin the pattern to the left side of the jacket front, matching the edges correctly and insert the point of the scissors into each end of the buttonhole marks as indicated on the printed pattern piece. Mark the holes with chalk which has been sharpened to a pencil-point sharpness. When you remove the pattern run a line of bright-colored hand basting between each set of dots. This is where the machine buttonholes will be made.

Beware of making the buttonholes on the wrong front of the garment. Girls' garments have the buttonholes on the right-hand side, while boys' are on the left. A very young and unobservant individual may not notice if the buttonholes were put on the wrong side, but once this fact becomes known, even the very young will refuse to wear something that is not traditionally correct, especially if this youngster happens to be a male.

In some ready-made coats that are made of materials suitable for girls as well as boys, in styles that can be worn by either, there are buttonholes on both front edges so that the coats can be worn lapped from left to right or the other way around. So if you ever get the buttonholes on the wrong edge, just make another set on the opposite side and tell everybody you are copying ready-mades. In this way even the kids may be convinced that you did it intentionally. While they are young, you'll get away with more little errors than later on. Charge these mistakes to experience and they will surely pay off in the future.

Changing the location of buttonholes

If an individual is taller than average and wishes to add an extra buttonhole on a coat, measure the distance between the buttonholes printed on the pattern and just add another one to the bottom, spacing it like the others and making sure that it is located the same distance from the front edge. On a short jacket, however, it is usually a better idea to increase the space between the buttonholes so that the lowest one comes down a bit lower than originally marked on the pattern, rather than adding another. There isn't always enough extra space on jackets to accommodate an extra buttonhole and button, and yet make the closing look balanced.

If the garment is for an individual shorter than average, it is better to space the buttonholes closer together if a change is desired, rather than eliminating the lower buttonhole. Try raising the buttonholes a bit first; if this doesn't solve the problem, the closer spacing of them will.

When machine-made buttonholes are to be made in jackets and coats, they should be the keyhole type, just as they are in ready-made apparel of this type. If you have your own automatic sewing machine which makes buttonholes, or an attachment that does them, follow the markings you have already made. The same markings will do if you have the buttonholes made by a commercial establishment that provides such services.

How to sew on buttons

Use fairly strong thread to sew on buttons, or use buttonhole twist, which is available in most colors and at most notion counters. It comes in ten-yard lengths on tiny spools. This is the type of twist that is usually used for hand picking or saddle stitching on the edges of collars and fronts of camel's-hair, cashmere, and other plain-colored coats, so if you wish to do this kind of trimming on your project, the thread would be suitable for both purposes. This trimming is discussed in chapter 11.

Whether the buttons have holes or metal loops or shanks, they must be sewed on to the garment with sufficient extension of thread to allow freedom between the button and the garment fabric when the coat is buttoned, so that it won't appear to be thumbtacked on. Button placement is marked on the pattern, although it is easy enough to find the places by trying the coat on your model. On single-breasted coats, the buttons usually run in a straight line from the end of the collar down the middle of the front, so that the collar ends come right together when buttoned up. On double-breasted styles, it is advisable to use the pattern markings for button location, for both the functional row and the ornamental row.

Here's how to sew on buttons: Place two paper matches on the spot where the button is to be sewed, and then place the button on top of the matches. Sew the button on, inserting the needle next to the matches as you sew through the holes or shank of the button, going right through to the facing of the coat every few stitches to give the button a firm foundation. Sew with double thread. At the beginning of the stitching, the knot of the thread should be worked underneath the outer fabric by jabbing it between the cloth yarns if possible. Take about 6 or 7 stitches, then withdraw the matches after the thread has come through from the button part of the work. Wrap the thread around the thread shank formed by withdrawing the matches, and keep wrapping until you get down to the garment. Here you tie a knot in the thread and insert the point of the needle into the upper layer of the garment fabric, then bring it through about an inch or so away from where the knot is. Cut the thread off right to the garment fabric, and the end will disappear inside the garment.

Tiny flat buttons are often sewed on the inside of the garment directly underneath the outer buttons, to cover up the stitching on the facing side and also to give a firmer foundation to the top buttons.

A light touch-up with the iron on the outer edges of the lining and over the buttonholes completes the tailoring job. When pressing has been properly done during the construction of the garment, the light pressing is sufficient to put it into a wearable condition. However, if the material pressed poorly while being worked on, no matter how much effort you put into it, a pressing job done by your good neighborhood tailor will help to make the garment professional-looking in every respect.

6

Little Girls' Dresses for All Occasions

The girl wearing a pretty dress her mother made is proud and happy, and her mother is equally pleased. Because of the endless variety of fabrics that are easy to work with and care for, no mother needs to hesitate to make the kind of dress that once took hours of time and effort to wash and iron. Such a garment can now be freshened up and made to look like new with just a swish or two in mild sudsy water. Allowed to dry on a hanger, it will be ready with no ironing, or just a touch-up.

Synthetic materials, which are such naturals for garments for growing youngsters, can also be washed in the automatic washer, using a "synthetic" setting, then put into the drier for a short time. If the garment is immediately when the drier stops, it can usually be worn without any further attention. These materials retain their new appearance for their lifetime. But remember, when you buy the trimmings for dresses made of these miracle fabrics, be sure they are also made of synthetic fibers so that they do not cause laundering problems.

A complete dress wardrobe can be made from these great fabrics, which are available in many weights and finishes. There are crisp textures and soft, sheers and opaques, prints and solids, florals, checks and polka dots, plaids and embroidered surfaces. They make excellent school wear as well as clothes for Sunday best and parties, and are suitable for wear in all seasons.

Fashions for little girls

Styles for little girls' clothing do not change as rapidly or as drastically as do those worn by her mother or her older sisters. Some styles just live on and on. Patterns are readily found in the catalogues for whatever kind of dress is desired. A very good way to decide which style will be best suited to the material you have in mind is to study the designs in the catalogues and try to find one illustrated in a fabric closely resembling yours. This will give you a pretty good idea of how the finished product will look, and will help simplify your choice.

It is a very good idea when sewing for girls, and even for boys, to let them help you in this choice. They'll be much more pleased with the finished product. Some subtle compromise will have to be made from time to time, but you might be surprised at some of the young ones' good suggestions, so let them in on the fun.

Clothes should fit when new

Some mothers make the mistake of buying or making for their children clothes that they must "grow into." This is false economy. It is while the garment is brand-new that it is most attractive and most enjoyed, not when the best part of its life has been worn away. When the finished product is a misfit, there are two very disappointed people—the person the garment belongs to and yourself. The misfitting garment is also an eyesore to the observer who had nothing to do with it.

The fit of the garment is very important. If the fabric chosen is the kind that can be let down in the future, all the better, especially if hems are treated with respect in pressing during construction of the garment and later on. Today's hems are not meant to be knife-edge sharp at their bottoms. In the first place, some of the synthetics do not press sharply anyway, and on many even a light press job will hold, so extra special care should be taken when pressing this part of the garment. This matter is important not only at the hem of the garment but at the bottom of long sleeves, wherever they appear.

Children's clothing need not have a complicated design to be attractive and becoming. Styles may be quite simple, requiring only basic sewing knowledge to make them. When they are made from materials that behave the way you want them to, in colors that do full justice to their wearers, they just can't miss being masterpieces. With an occasional change in the style or shape of a neckline, or the style of the sleeves, even the simplest design can be used over and over again, and each dress will look quite different because of the effect created by different fabrics. A design made up in gingham with a plain belt around the waist looks entirely different when made of crisp pastel-colored nylon or cotton organdy with a wide ribbon or bias-cut sash tied in a butterfly bow in the back. The fabric plays a very important part in the attractiveness of a child's dress, much more than the actual cut of the design. If the dress fits well, and is cut from the correct pattern size, the color, the kind of fabric, and the silhouette of the design will do the rest.

As an example, the fitted bodice with a full gathered skirt will never go out of style. It is just about the easiest kind of dress to make, so the beginner is sure of results that will make her happy. In this dress only the bodice requires fitting. The fullness in the skirt hangs gracefully from the bottom of the bodice and needs no fitting. Only the hem will be measured later on.

Styles and fabrics for the average-sized girl

If a girl is considered fairly average in height and size for her age, she can wear any style, made from all kinds of materials, as long as the pattern and the cloth suit each other, and the fabrics listed as suitable on the pattern envelope take care of that. The color should be flattering to her face. Hold the cloth up to the face, covering whatever is being worn, and look to see what the color of the cloth does. One tone of color will be more becoming than another, and only by trying them against the face can you really see which is the best choice. Some girls can wear any tone of any color; others, who may be pale, need to look more glowing. The right color and tone will do this.

Light colors around the face are sure to enhance the girl as well as the dress, so see that the collar and cuffs, or the yoke of a dark dress are of a light flattering color. Some of the dark materials in prints, checks, and plaids make terrific school things, and a touch of lightness at the face will flatter. Untrimmed, dark wearing apparel makes some young girls look pallid when they really aren't.

Fashions for the very thin girl

Thinness is easy to camouflage. An appearance of dainty slimness is produced by dresses that are not skimpy in design. Dresses with gathered skirts, or unpressed pleated ones, puff sleeves, yokes from which fullness drapes over the body, and which can be worn with or without a belt, are all good choices. Rounded collars instead of pointed ones flatter the face, and double-breasted coats and jackets are sure to make a thin girl look pleasingly average.

If the girl is tall, she will look less thin and somewhat shorter if her garments of striped material are cut with the stripes running crosswise, instead of up and down. This will add to her width and so camouflage her thinness very successfully. Fabrics should have enough body so the garment does not cling. It is very important when cutting styles that feature a seam joining bodice and skirt to each other that you hold the pattern of the bodice up to the girl's shoulders to see how much extra will have to be added to the bottom of the bodice so that the finished garment doesn't end up short-waisted. Once this has been determined, check the skirt also. If you have to lengthen it, do so at the bottom after pinning the pattern to the cloth.

Short thin girls should wear stripes running up and down so they will look taller, but the styles should be cut with fullness to produce a lovely bouffant silhouette which gives the girl a pleasingly petite appearance.

Styles for the chubby girl

To make the chubby girl look slimmer her clothing should never be fitted too snugly anywhere, nor should she have too much fullness in her skirts or sleeves. Modified fullness in each of these parts will give the ease a garment needs and the limited amount of fullness will make her look more average. Instead of gathered skirts, hers should be folded over in unpressed pleating. In this way the fullness will be there, but the bulk will be missing. Streamlined fashions, like easy-fitting shifts, A-line designs, and princess styles are all great choices.

Belts are becoming if they are not too wide. Plaids and prints, as well as checks should be small in size. Up-and-down stripes will create the slim look she wants. Solid colors may be as bold or loud as desired. Jackets and coats that are single-breasted are best as there will be fewer layers of cloth over her midriff. No girl has to look exactly as she is if she doesn't want to! She will look more pleasing in clothes that are chosen with an eye for dramatizing her good parts, and minimizing those that are out of proportion with the rest. This is true not only where it concerns little girls' clothes, but with mothers and older sisters also.

The fitted bodice and full-skirt design

When the style of a dress consists of a bodice and skirt and the figure is long-waisted, additions are made to the bottom of the bodice to locate the seam at the person's natural waistline. Extend the darts down in a straight line, not tapered, so that the waist does not become

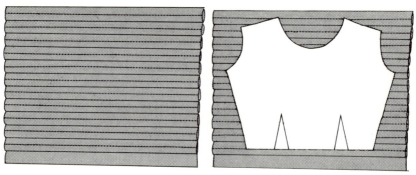

Figure 88a   *Figure 88b*

too snug. In this style only the bodice needs to be fitted after the preliminary sewing has been done to bring the front and back units to the stage for fitting. Leave the side seams open.

If the girl is shorter-waisted than average and needs the bodice shorter than the pattern, cut the bodice according to the pattern and then shorten it later, before the skirt is joined to it. It is easier to judge just where the shirt will look best if you can hold it up to her while she is wearing the bodice for a fitting. The location of the waist can then be moved up or down to please the eye, and the extra length from the bottom of the bodice can be cut off.

Creating different effects on the bodice

Women with creative talent and imagination can do a lot to make their daughters' clothes more interesting. A simple pattern will make it possible to do this. For example, a plain bodice pattern used for the cutting of material that you have decided to tuck horizontally, just to see what would happen, turns out to be a very interesting and expensive-looking creation. After tucking the material in the size of tucks you have decided to make, all you do is lay the basic bodice pattern on to the tucked cloth and cut it into shape. The back of the bodice can be left plain, or you can tuck that also if you wish. (Fig. 88.)

About fake smocking

Smocking on children's wear has always been a favorite with mothers. It is not necessary to give smocking instructions here, because there are excellent instructions right in the dress patterns that use it. The transfer pattern for stamping the smocking design on the right side of the fabric is included in these patterns, and the actual how-to-do-it smocking instructions are on the pattern guide. Smocking is so easy that even a beginner will smock beautifully right from the start.

If you do not have time to hand smock, you can still make attractive smocked things on the machine. They will be smart and effective in appearance, whether you use self-colored thread or a contrasting or harmonizing color. Most dress fabrics are suitable, but the sheer cottons, nylons, and any of the lightweight synthetics work up especially well.

A very good way to make all-over shirring for a bodice front is to cut a piece of cloth just about the length of the bodice, measuring from the shoulders to a little below the waistline, and about twice the width of the front. Make horizontal chalk lines with a ruler or yardstick, spacing them according to how close you would like the shirring or fake smocking to be. About 2 inches apart is a good distance for these chalk lines.

155

Next, run machine stitching through the lines, using a slightly larger stitch than is used for ordinary sewing. When all the lines have been sewed through, do additional rows of stitching below the first ones, about ¼ inch apart. Two or more rows can be done at each marking, with the remaining space left unsewed. Four closely stitched rows make a rich-looking bodice.

When all the rows are stitched, hold the bobbin threads in one hand at one side of the material, and with the other hand shirr the cloth toward the middle. Do half the width from the left side of the fabric, and the other half from the right-hand side, pulling all the bobbin threads at once in each group of stitching lines. The cloth is shirred up to the widest part of the bodice, the bottom of the armhole area. To produce a nice evenly shirred appearance, steam the shirring. First, tip the iron so that the bottom is up and cover the bottom with a damp cloth. Then, hold the top and bottom of the shirred material rather taut and run it over the iron. This steaming is done only once, so that the gathers can be blocked into a straight up-and-down direction. They will remain that way for the life of the garment. (Fig. 89.)

A strip of seam tape can then be hand sewed to the wrong side of the shirring, the hand stitching caught to the machine shirring. Or it can be attached by another row of machine stitching, done through

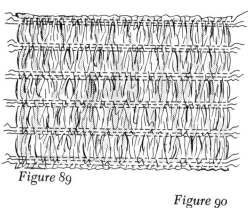

Figure 89

Figure 90

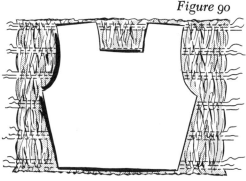

156

one of the rows already there. The tape is for reinforcement; it keeps the shirring from pulling out duiing handling, both while making the bodice and while wearing it. Now place the pattern over the shirring and cut to size from the shirred material. If you want the back shirred, do it in the same way as you did the front. It is not necessary to shirr the back, though, especially if a wide crushed sash is worn with the dress and tied in a large butterfly bow in the back. This will be decoration in itself. (Fig. 90.) From here on, treat the bodice like any other. Stitch around the neckline to hold it to its original size.

If you have an automatic zigzag machine that does fancy stitching, here's your chance to use it to good advantage. When the shirring has been pulled up to the right size, run some of the fancy stitches over the regular ones, either in the same color or in a contrasting color for an added attraction.

You can even imitate hand smocking once you have pulled up on the gathering stitches. Embroidery stitches, such as you often use in doing needlepoint or crewel, when used over these machine stitches give the job a thoroughly hand-done look.

Smocking fullness in a dress designed with a yoke and letting the fullness fall straight, or caught in at the waist with a sash, is another way of getting your automatic sewing machine to give you a hand in decorating your daughters' or granddaughters' or nieces' dresses. (Fig. 91.)

Figure 91

Adding pockets of different types, doing a bit of embroidery on the ends of collars, running rows of lace horizontally on bodice and skirt, add artistic touches to a simple pattern design. A great number of changes can be made without involving too much extra time and

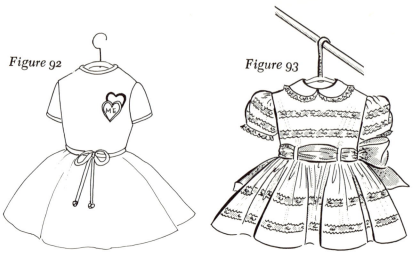

Figure 92

Figure 93

effort, or sewing knowledge either. Such additions make the job fun to do! (Figs. 92 and 93.)

For elegance, triple the hems of sheer dresses

When using sheer materials, allow extra fabric at the bottom of the skirts on girls' dresses so that the hem can be turned over twice instead of only once. The finished hem will then consist of three layers instead of the usual two. This can only be done to hems when the garment is cut with straight fullness around the bottom, not flared in any way. This kind of hem is equally effective on adult dresses when the style is right.

The width recommended for an attractive-looking hem is specified on the pattern pieces, and all you do is double that amount, or a little bit more, and you'll have enough to produce a triple-layered hem. The raw edges of the hem will now be down at the bottom fold instead of at the top and there will be no straggly raw edges showing through to spoil the appearance of the hemline. The extra layer of sheer will provide interesting contrast by giving the rest of the garment a look of even greater sheerness.

Collars and cuffs of sheers

Triple layers of sheer enhance the appearance of collars and cuffs also, because the raw edges around the stitched side do not show quite as much through the sheerness and yet an airy appearance is retained. One side of the triple collars and cuffs will look better than the other, so after trimming the seams to a scant ¼-inch width and turning the collar and cuffs to the right side, look over both sides. Use the better-looking side on the outside.

Attaching collars and other finishes to the neck

Collars are attached to dress necks with either a shaped facing cut from a pattern piece provided for this purpose, or the neck edge is finished with a narrow bias strip of cloth. It is often necessary to use your own judgment as to which will be the best way to finish the neckline on which a collar is featured. The most practical and attractive way depends upon the kind of material used for the garment. If the fabric is opaque and a shaped facing will not show through, use the shaped facing and follow the pattern instructions for doing the job. If the material is transparent, however, skip the facing and use a bias-cut strip of either the dress cloth or the collar material, if the collar is of a different fabric than the dress, so that nothing will show through on the outside to spoil the appearance of the finished garment.

Cut the bias strip about 2 inches wide and fold it right side out lengthwise. After pinning the collar to the neck of the garment with the right side of the collar up in its wearing position, pin the raw edges of the folded bias to the edge of the collar, holding the strip slightly taut as you pin it into place. Sew through all the layers around the neckline, then trim away the raw edges bluntly to a scant ¼-inch width. Direct the fold of the bias downward and hand finish it neatly to the outer layer of the garment as invisibly as possible.

A collarless design looks fine when finished with a bias-cut strip sewn to the outside of the garment neckline, stretching the bias a little as you sew it into place with ⅝-inch seam allowance. Trim the seam down to a scant ¼-inch width, then turn the folded edge over to the inside of the garment, leaving ¼ inch of the bias strip showing on the outside for a trimming detail. Catch the folded edge by hand to the machine stitching on the inside of the garment. The sleeveless armholes of a garment are also effective when finished this way. The bias strip for this purpose is cut about 2½ inches wide and then folded over.

Assembling dresses the easy way

If the step-by-step procedure for putting garments together according to pattern instructions puzzles you, follow the instructions here instead and you'll find it easy. For example, do everything possible on the front and back bodice while the side seams are still open. Attach the collar, the pockets, or whatever other detailing appears on the upper part of this type of dress. The sleeves in young folks' dresses may be inserted while the sides are still open. (Fig. 94.) Use the "magic stitching" in the way already described (on page 59) and when nothing else needs to be done on these units, pin the sides of the bodice together and try it on. Take in on the side seams, or let them

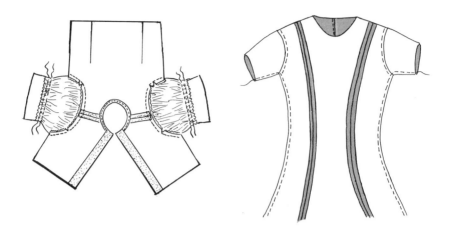

Figure 94

Figure 95

out; then chalk the sides of the garment after removing it. You then sew the sides of the bodice together permanently, running the seams through the sleeves also. While the bodice is being fitted, the gathered or pleated skirt should be held up to it to see where it will look best. Then attach the skirt to the bodice at the most becoming location.

In assembling other styles, like princess designs or A-line shifts, for example, you also do all that is possible to do while the side seams are still open, inserting the long zipper down the back, and so forth. You then pin the dress together with the right sides facing each other, matching the armpit first and continuing the pinning to the bottom of the sleeves. Come back to the armpit again and pin from there to the bottom of the garment, inserting the pins crosswise so that they can hold the layers firmly during the stitching, although you can pull the pins out when you come to them if you wish. Insert the pins about 2 or 3 inches apart for this job. Each of the side seams are then done in one long stitching operation, either from the bottom of the dress up to and including the bottom of the sleeves, or from the bottom of the sleeves downward to the bottom of the dress—it doesn't matter, as long as the pinning was correctly done. (Fig. 95.)

The final fitting of the dress

The dress should be completed before it is tried on to mark the length. Belts should be tied, zippers closed, buttons buttoned, shoes on, and the girl should stand naturally, not as if posing for a picture. Only in this way can the marking of the hem be done accurately.

Lengths are measured from the floor up to where the garment will be worn, and a chalk mark or a pin every 5 or 6 inches should indicate where the skirt will be turned up.

When the garment is removed, the hem width is trimmed to a uniform amount and the top finished in the way that is best for the kind of a dress it is. There are different hem finishes for different types of materials and for different skirt styles. The various ways of finishing hems are covered on pages 174–176.

Combining leftover fabrics creatively

Most women who sew have a natural love for fabrics and want to put every leftover piece to use if at all possible. They collect these pieces, just waiting for the right inspiration to come along.

When there are small girls around the house the inspirations come along faster. Often you can combine one material with another to complete a dress, so before setting out to shop for fabrics, see what you have on hand that can be used in some attractive fashion. Many a dollar is saved this way, but even more pleasing than the financial saving will be the feeling of satisfaction gained, and the fun of working out your own ideas. Collars, cuffs, yokes, and even a pair of sleeves can be made from left over fabrics. You might convert a jumper pattern into a dress, a collarless design into one with a pretty collar, and you have a wealth of possibilities for bandings, belts, and other details. The ideas are endless.

Of course, it is important to analyze the materials you plan to combine to see that they are of the same washable quality and fast color; otherwise they will present problems in this respect. If one fabric is drip-dry but the other is not, you will, when the garment is laundered, have to iron the part that is not made of the drip-dry material. Fig. 96 gives some ideas on how pieces of your collection can be used in interesting ways. They will surely help you to create a "specialty shop" appearance in your finished garment.

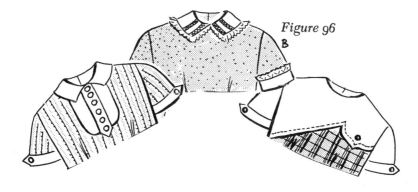

Figure 96

7
All About Shirts

Not every garment is worth making at home. Some items of wearing apparel, sport shirts among them, should be purchased ready-made when the fabric and workmanship are of good quality, the right size is easy to obtain, and the price is reasonable.

So you should have a good reason for making sport shirts at home. Is it because you can save about two thirds the store price and still make a sport shirt to compare well with the expensive ready-made kind? Are you duplicating an expensive corduroy or flannel shirt? Do you want a really well-made plaid sport shirt? Plaids are not always carefully matched at every seam in ready-made shirts unless the price is high. Do you have in mind a certain color that can't be obtained in a ready-made shirt? Does the shirt have to match or harmonize with a special skirt or pants? Is the person hard to fit in ready-to-wear? Do you have an unusual and interesting fabric that would look superb in a sport shirt? Do you have a special style in mind that you can't find in the store, for which you can either make your own pattern or adapt one of the commercial patterns?

These are all good-enough reasons to warrant your putting in valuable time making sport shirts. But you should think hard before deciding to make one. The workmanship on sport shirts is different from that on other types of garments. The inside of the shirts must be finished so that there are no raw edges showing.

Patterns for men's and boys' shirts

Shirt patterns for men and boys come by neck measurements and the patterns should be purchased in the same size as their ready-made shirts. If the arms are shorter or longer than is considered average for the size of the pattern, the adjustments are made at the bottom of the sleeves just above where the cuffs will be attached on full-length sleeves.

Pattern sizes for girls' and women's shirts and blouses

Patterns for women's and girls' blouses and shirts are sized according to the chest or bust measurement. Pick the size that fits in a ready-made garment. If the body measurements are more generous than the standard measurements specified on the pattern envelope, add to the shirt at the sides of the front and back units, just as you do when cutting other garments.

Although girls' and women's shirts can be finished with regular seams, they will look more tailored and professional if they are treated in the same manner as the male shirt, so that the inside of the garment has no raw seams.

How to make flat-felled seams

The shoulders of the front and back of the shirt should be sewn first. To make flat-felled seams, you first sew the ⅝-inch edge, with the raw edges on the outside of the garment and the wrong sides of the fabric together. One edge of the seam is then trimmed down to ¼-inch width, and the remainder is folded down over it and top stitched. The easiest way to do this last row of stitching is to tuck in a ¼-inch edge of the wide seam with the tip of your scissors, instead of basting or pinning, and then sew an inch or two before arranging another length. (Fig. 97.) Inspect a ready-made shirt to determine which seam edge to trim off and which to lap over, depending on the part of shirt being sewed, and then imitate. Ready-mades are always good guides when you are in doubt.

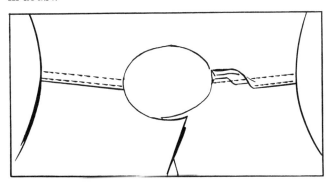

Figure 97

The collar on a shirt is usually interfaced to keep it permanently trim in shape and to give added body. Permanently finished lightweight cotton or synthetic interfacing for this purpose is readily available in fabric departments. Even when the shirt fronts are not interfaced, as is sometimes the case when using firm-textured cloth, the collar always

163

is. Construct the collar in the same way as you did the coat collar (see p. 113), but do not stab stitch the interfacing to the under collar. Instead, place the interfacing against the under collar and catch it into the stitching when the upper and under pieces are sewn together around the outer edges. Then trim the seams in the staggered way and cut off the points diagonally for smooth finishing. If the outer edges of the collar are to be trim stitched, now is the time to do it.

How to attach a sport collar on a shirt

Pin the collar to the neck edge of the shirt, starting at the center back and working toward the fronts, matching the ends of the collar to the marks indicating the spot they must match on each front. Continue to pin 1 inch apart through all the thicknesses from the shoulders to each front, leaving the back unpinned as yet with just the center pin holding things together. Next, pin the facings to each front, but the inner edges should first be finished with a ½-inch edge turned over to the wrong side and machine hemmed close to the fold. Do not finish this edge with a double fold; once is enough. If interfacing is used, place it against the facing and treat it as one layer of cloth here, incorporating it into all seams and hems.

Now place the facings on each front, right sides together. At the shoulders, the facing edge which will eventually fit across the shoulder seam should be turned ⅝ inch to the wrong side of the cloth and pinned into place in that position, to be eventually caught into the neckline seam.

Before stitching, clip through all the layers of the seam edges the depth of a seam width at the shoulder area where the facing edges were turned over. Now sew in the following manner: From one front end to the shoulder seam, sew through all the layers of the combined edges; stop with the needle inserted in the work; lift the presser foot and lift up the upper layer of the collar at the clipping; continue

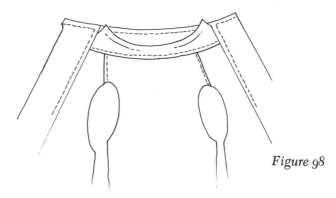

Figure 98

sewing through the layers of the seams underneath it. When the opposite side of the shoulder area is reached, again raise the presser foot, leaving the needle in the work, and again arrange the upper collar edge to be included in the remaining part of the neckline seam. Only the top layer of the collar will be free at center back. Trim the seam edges down to ¼-inch width, but leave the free edge of the collar full width. (Fig. 98.) This edge is then tucked neatly under and the complete center back seam is directed upward and into the collar, while the two front seams will automatically go into a downward position. Then sew the collar edge at center back by machine, as close to the fold as possible. Once in a while this seam is hand sewn invisibly. Either way is correct.

Making and attaching the collar with a neckband

Collars on some shirts and blouses have fitted stand-up neckbands into which the actual collar is placed. The collar folds over the band when the garment is worn. This is the type of collar that is usually used on men's and boys' dress-up shirts, although it is sometimes found on sport shirts also. If the shirt you are making has one of these collars, here's what you do:

Make this collar the same way you make any other type, and interface it with preshrunk cotton or permanent press interfacing to give it the necessary firmness. Place the interfacing against the under-collar section when putting the three pieces together. When the collar has been completed and pressed, trim stitch it around the outer edges if

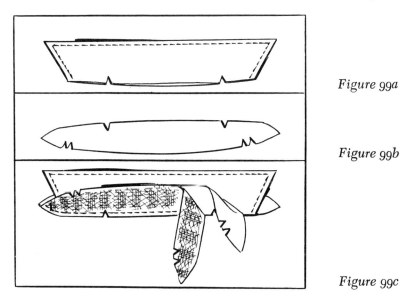

Figure 99a

Figure 99b

Figure 99c

you wish. Most collars of this type are edge stitched, either ⅛ inch or ¼ inch away from the edge. (Fig. 99a.)

Next, the collar band, Fig. 99b, is attached to the collar. The band is also interfaced. The neckband edges are so similar in shape to each other that the notches must be carefully matched to shirt neck or you may end up by putting the band on upside down—and the collar won't fit.

Place one neckband on the outside of the collar and the other on the underside of it, matching the center backs and notches, and pin at these places through all thicknesses. Now place the interfacing against the wrong side of the inner neckband, the one that will be worn closest to the neck. (Fig. 99c.) Withdraw the pins and reinsert them to include the interfacing. Then sew through all the thicknesses, from one end of the band to the other. Trim all the seams off to ¼ inch and press well in a downward position.

Now pin the inner neckband, the one with the interfacing against it, to the inside of the shirt neckline. This position will direct the raw edges of the seams to the outside of the garment. Then turn the outer band under ¼ inch, place it over the raw edges, and sew it down as close as possible to the edge of the fold (Fig. 100) making sure to conceal the row of stitching that was made on the inside of the garment.

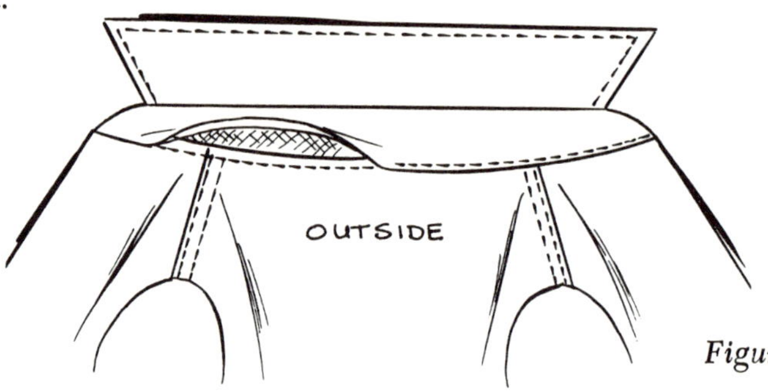

OUTSIDE

Figure 100

Inserting sleeves into sport shirts

Insert the sleeves into the armholes before the side seams are sewed, just as for small children's dresses (see p. 159). It is easier to make the flat-felled seam around the armhole if the garment is flat during the sewing. First, run a row of "magic stitching" around the top of the sleeves from the front notches to those in back, making sure to have this stitching exactly ⅝ inch away from the edge. Pin the tops of the sleeves to the shoulder seams with the wrong sides of the fabrics together, and the raw edges on the outside of the garment. After matching the notches, pin the sleeves 1 inch apart, then sew with the sleeves held on top during the stitching so that the fullness can be properly manipulated and worked in with the tips of the fingers.

166

Trim away the sleeve edge to ¼-inch width, and then turn under the armhole edge ¼ inch and place it down flat against the sleeve. Sew close to the fold, using the tip of your scissors to tuck in the seam edges as you proceed. Some women press this seam edge before sewing, but this is not a good idea because of the tendency of fabrics to stretch, especially on curves. Just allow the edges of the armhole to do what is natural for them and you'll encounter no difficulty in making flat-felled seams. (Fig. 101.)

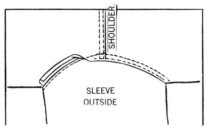

SHOULDER

SLEEVE
OUTSIDE

Figure 101

Pin the sides of the shirt together, and if the sleeves are a bit too long, shorten them if the shirt is for an adult, but if it is for a growing youngster, leave it a little long because the arms grow quite rapidly and before long the extra length will be used up.

The continuous-lap sleeve opening

A very popular finish for boys' and girls' sleeve openings just above the cuffs of their long-sleeved shirts is a continuous lap. Cut a strip of fabric 1¼ inches wide on either the straight or cross-weave of the material. Place it against the wrong side of the slashed opening—the pattern indicates where this slash is to be made—and machine stitch with ¼-inch seam, no wider. (Fig. 102.) If the slash is pulled apart and flattened down as much as possible, so it looks as if it is doing the "split," there will be no problem in stitching the end of the slash without getting a pucker there. After stitching the strip from end to end, bring it over to the right side of the sleeve and fold under a tiny edge of it, about ¼ inch. Place this fold over the line of stitching, covering it. Sew down on the extreme edge of the fold, making the opening do the "split" again for neater and easier sewing. (Fig. 103.)

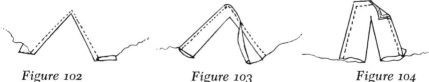

Figure 102   *Figure 103*   *Figure 104*

The continuous lap is actually an extended placket that keeps the opening of the shirt sleeve together. When the placket is directed to the inside of the sleeve it folds over with one lap forming the top of the opening, the other the bottom. No tacking is necessary to keep them in their proper position; the cuff will hold them when it is attached.

The faced opening

Another good way of finishing the bottoms of sleeves before cuffs are attached is to slash up the bottom of a sleeve where indicated by the pattern and then apply a slashed facing. This is a flat finish, suitable for use on blouse sleeves as well as on shirts. Cut the material that will be used for a facing about 3 inches wide and an inch or so longer than the slash in the sleeve. Turn the three edges of the facing over to the wrong side about ¼ inch and machine stitch a hem, leaving the bottom edge of the facing raw. Slash the middle of the facing to the same depth as the slash in the sleeves. Place the right side of the facing against the right side of the sleeve and sew the two together from end to end with ¼-inch seam, or a little narrower. Hold the slash as if it were doing the "split," so only the tiniest amount of seam is taken at the slashed point to prevent puckers. After turning the facing to the inside of the sleeve to press it flat, you might have to do a bit more clipping if puckers spoil the top of the slash. If so, reverse the facing and clip until the opening presses smooth and flat. (Fig. 104.) The cuffs go on next and the corners of the facings are caught into permanent position by hand.

The tailored shirt-sleeve opening

The truly elegant sleeve finish is the tailored placket; the most expensive shirts are finished this way.

When the slash for the opening has been made at the bottom of the sleeve, clip ¼ inch at an upward angle on each side of the end of the slash. Now attach a strip of fabric about 1¼ inches wide to the wrong side of the opening, on the edge that will be toward the back of the sleeve. The strip should be about 1 inch longer than the slashed opening. Sew the strip with a ¼-inch seam, the raw edges visible on the outside of the sleeve. Then bring the strip over to the outside of the sleeve, and turn under ¼ inch. The folded edge of the strip, called an underlap, is then placed over the raw edges on the right side and sewed down close to the folded edge. (Fig. 105.)

The tailored overlap is cut next. It should be 3 inches wide and about 2 inches longer than the sleeve opening. Sew the right side of the tailored lap to the wrong side of the front edge of the slash with ¼-inch seam, starting evenly at the bottom. Then bring the overlap to the

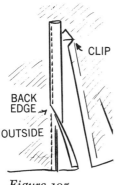

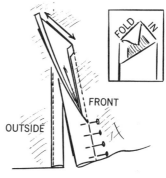

Figure 105 Figure 106

outside of the sleeve. Trim off the top edge of the overlap at an upward angle, starting at the seamed edge and aiming toward the opposite edge. It is much easier to make a nice even triangular trim at the top of the overlap in this manner than it would be if you tried just cutting a triangle. When a pattern is provided for this piece of overlap, use it, but if you are improvising your own placket piece, follow these instructions and you'll have no problems.

Pin the loose edge of the overlap over the raw edges and arrange neatly over the underlap. (Fig. 106.) Fold the fabric into a triangle at the top of the opening. Trim off the excess fabric on the underside of this trim, after the shaping has been done and before it is sewed, to avoid bulk. Stitch on the edge of the pinned fold, carrying over on the opposite side of the placket to the level of the ending of the slash. (Fig. 107.) The little triangle that was cut at the beginning is now tucked under and caught into place with the stitching that is continued across the top of the opening for extra reinforcement.

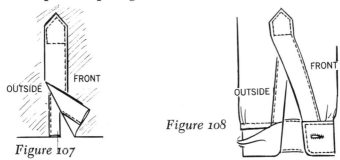

Figure 107 Figure 108

The long, continuous side seam

The flat-felled side seams are sewed next, starting at the bottom of the sleeves and continuing to the bottom of the shirt, if the shirt is straight across the bottom, or to the area of the side seams where the

169

shirttails start to curve away from the side seams. Trim off the back edges of the seams to ¼-inch width and lap the front edges over. Turn then under ¼ inch, lay them flat on the back sections, and sew the folds as close to the folded edge as possible.

It is sometimes a problem to sew flat-felled seams inside a sleeve because of the confined space. This is particularly true when making small garments. You can make this work easier if you sew the folded edge part way up from the bottom of the sleeve, and part way down, your stitches meeting halfway inside of the sleeve. In this way you will be working toward the hard section from both ends.

Finish the bottom of the shirt with a narrow rolled hem done by machine. Draw up the bottoms of the sleeves to fit the cuffs, either by gathering them or by laying the fullness into pleats.

Construct the cuffs the same way as a collar, interfacing if the fabric needs extra body. If French cuffs are to be used, cut the cuffs twice the width of ordinary cuffs so that they can be doubled over and worn with cuff links. But whether they are French cuffs or the ordinary kind, the work in attaching them to the bottom of the sleeves is the same.

The under part of the cuff with the interfacing against it is placed against the wrong side of the sleeve and sewed from end to end. Turn under a seam allowance on the outside layer of the cuff material and place the fold over the raw edges. Pin the fold into place and top stitch on the edge of fold. (Fig. 108.) The stitching can be continued all around the cuff edges if you wish.

Mark the buttonholes on the shirt front and the cuffs last. Those made at home, using the attachment, are suitable. For boys the buttonholes go on the left side, and for girls on the right side of the shirt.

8
Putting New Life into Outgrown Clothes

The length is usually outgrown first in children's clothing. When this happens to her favorite dress, it is a matter not very lightly taken by most girls, large or small. The seriousness of this mini-tragedy is quite apt to overshadow the thrill of having attained the extra height, unless Mother's ingenuity and imagination, and her desire to stretch a dollar here and there, come forth with some artistic way to make the garment wearable again.

A leisurely session or two with her growing youngster, trying on the clothing that has become outgrown, will help to reveal what procedures will be best to follow. Not all clothes left from a previous season warrant the time and effort necessary to make them wearable again. Unless the material is still in good condition and attractive, it is a waste of time. If there are many items to judge, divide the sessions into a few short ones instead of trying the clothes on all at one time. Most children get bored to tears when they have to stand on ceremony too long, even when this concerns their own clothes.

Treating these trying-on sessions like "fashion shows" might make them a little more interesting to the "model," especially if you discuss your plans for doing the job and ask her to make some suggestions too. Taking part in these decisions will make her appreciate the finished product that much more.

The clothes that are worth salvaging often turn out to be as attractive-looking and as pleasing to their wearers as they were when new. Some of them, after a few neat and simple tricks, can be changed so entirely in appearance that they are hardly recognizable as garments from a past season.

Letting down the hem

The first thing that comes to mind when the length of a dress has been outgrown is to drop the hem and face it with a strip of matching material, but this does not always work out satisfactorily, especially if the hem has been pressed over and over again during dry cleaning or laundering. Most creases left by old hems are impossible to press out, and to add to this grief, a line of discoloration also remains, left there by the soil that has become ground into the bottom of the garment as it was being worn. This just adds to the eyesore.

Unfortunately, no matter how faint the old markings are, they still detract from the appearance of the garment, but there are various ways of camouflaging these old hem marks. Most of them can be achieved quite simply and quickly without a lot of work or expense. One way to lengthen a dress is to let down the present hem and press it flat, then make a narrow tuck or two on the outside where the old hem was, bringing the old hem crease to the underside of the tuck so it is out of sight and pressing the tuck down over it. Then face the bottom of the dress with a strip of lightweight material in the color of the garment and hand finish it on the inside. The width of the facing should be about the same width as the original hem.

When the full width of the hem is needed to lengthen the garment, a decorative braid or banding of some kind may be used to hide the crease and to make the dress look pretty at the same time, especially if such trimming is carried to other parts of the dress—the neckline and the sleeves or on the pockets. There is a world of attractive trimmings available for such purposes. They come in different widths, made from natural fibers as well as from synthetics, and include bandings, laces, rickracks, fringes, braids, and side-by-side floral appliqués. There are decorations for use on the daintiest sheer party dresses as well as for casual denims and corduroys.

The trimmings are sold by the yard and also come packaged in practical amounts to complete most jobs. It is wise to take the garment that is to be lengthened with you when shopping so that the most suitable and effective trimming may be chosen. The decorative findings come in quite a range of prices. They do not have to be expensive to be effective, but it is important that they be suitable for the garment on which they will be used. If they are to go on a washable dress, they must be fast color and washable. This information is usually printed on the package or on a tag or label. If it isn't, ask the sales clerk about it. Otherwise you may run into washing problems later.

Some very interesting and attractive effects can be produced by combining a couple of trimmings on one article, as we did on Fig. 109a. We used a giant-sized rickrack on the hem crease and the mini-type rickrack above and below it. The three rows of trimming may be all the same color, or each in a different one, whichever is most appealing to the individual. Some of the braid was then introduced around the collar and cuffs, although this last is optional.

On the outgrown A-line shift, another combination of trimmings

were used. A cotton braid covers the line of the old hem, and then some fringe has been added below the braid just for fun and to give the dress a mod look which most kids love. The same trimmings were used around the neckline and the bottom of the sleeves. (Fig. 109b.)

A dress that is styled with a fitted bodice and a fully gathered or pleated skirt usually gets outgrown in two places at once, at the bottom and at the waistline. Such styles can be lengthened very attractively by adding a border of a complementary fabric to the lower part of the skirt to give the extra length needed there, and then inserting a strip of the same material as a set-in band after the skirt and bodice have been separated. This brings the waistline of the dress to a better location and changes the entire character of the dress in a very pleasing way. To carry the decoration even further, some of the border fabric may be used for a touch at the neck and sleeves if you wish.

Some delightful combinations can be used to put such dresses back into use. For example, add a printed border to the bottom of a dress made of solid-colored material, or a plain border to the printed dress, choosing a color from the print. Another idea is to add a sheer border to the bottom of a dress made of opaque material or vice versa. Combining two such different textures is very effective whether they are in the same color or in harmonizing ones. Picture a pink sheer dress bordered and belted with the same tone of color in polished cotton! Two different tones of one color also make an attractive combination. Such ideas are endless and can also be used for original styling when making new things. (Fig. 109c.)

The turned-over hem on dresses

Hems should be invisibly finished so that the stitches do not show through on the outer layer of the garment. They should also be loose enough to prevent the thread from puckering the fabric. If the stitches are spaced about ½ inch apart, the hem will have a professional look. Taking stitches closer together might not produce this appearance.

One of the most popular and practical ways of finishing the hem edge of a dress that will be constantly washed is to allow ½ inch extra cloth to the width of the hem so that the edge can be turned under and a line of machine stitching made through the fold before the hem is turned up to the inside of the dress for finishing. There will be nothing to get worn out from the frequent launderings of such a dress. This type of finish may be used on medium- or lightweight fabrics.

The hem is turned up into place with pins inserted vertically about an inch apart, and the garment is turned inside out for hemming. The hem is held with its top in an upright position, the needle in the right hand, if you are a right-handed sewer, and you proceed with the work from the right toward the left. Use a fine needle and a single strand of matching thread for the sewing job. If you do most things best with your left hand, these procedures are reversed, holding the needle with the left hand and sewing toward the right.

Tie a knot in the thread and hide it underneath the hem top, taking the first stitch in the fold at the top. Then take a tiny stitch in the garment directly above the top of the hem, in a straight line with the thread emerging from the hem. Next take a ½-inch stitch through the single layer of the folded top, starting by inserting the needle into the single fold of the hem edge, in line with the thread emerging from the garment and coming out ½ inch away from the starting point, either to the right or left, depending upon whether you are right- or left-handed. (Fig. 110.)

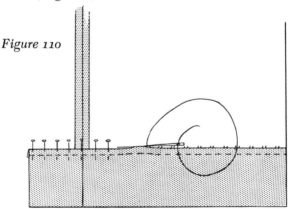

Figure 110

You may have another way of hemming that works just fine for you. Use it, of course. Just don't let the stitches show, and leave them loose so they don't cause puckering and dimples. That's what is most important.

The machine-stitched top finish is of advantage when the dress is styled with flared fullness in which the top of the hem is always fuller than the part of the garment to which the hem will be stitched. On such hems the machine stitching can be easily pulled up some to reduce the fullness at the top so that the hem will lay in a flatter position on the inside of the dress for the final finishing. Use a fairly large machine stitching for this purpose so that it can be pulled up easily. (Fig. 111.)

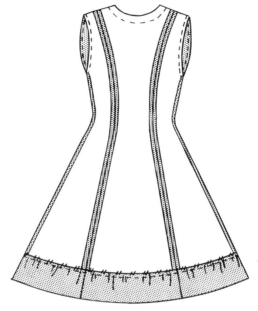

Figure 111

The taped hem

The hems of dresses made of heavy fabrics like corduroy, denim, knits, linen, woolens, or any other fabric that is bulky, should not have a turned-down finish at the top of the hem. Seam tape should be used as a finish instead to avoid bulk. When stitching the tape to the top edge of the hem, it is advisable to hold the tape slightly stretched so that it does not go on too full and ripply, which it is very apt to do unless the tape is held taut. Sew the tape close to the edge that is lying on the top of the hem; the other half is off the hem. The method of stitching on hems that are finished with tape is covered in detail in chapter 2 (see page 63).

Another satisfactory way of finishing the top of a hem when the material is too heavy to be turned under is with your automatic sewing machine. Put a zigzag finish on the top of the hem and then catch the hand stitching to the threads of the zigzag stitch. This is an ideal finish for corduroys and knits.

The blind-stitched machine hem

Your automatic zigzag machine will do blind hemming, but you must learn how this is done. If the instructions are given in your machine manual, follow them carefully. Otherwise have the sales-people who sold you the machine demonstrate how the blind hemming is done. Then go home and try it on your own machine. It requires patience and practice to become an expert, but it will save a great deal of time when altering the hems of clothes for the family.

What? Hems without stitching?

Sewing departments everywhere are constantly coming up with surprises to make your work easier, faster, and more interesting. Get yourself aquainted from time to time with the new things that are featured there, and try them out—perhaps on the old clothes that you are going to put back into use again! This will give you the experience you need and allow you to judge whether these items are practical for you.

There is available a bonding net that holds two layers of fabrics together firmly when pressed with a warm iron. The net comes in different sized "sheets" as well as in strips. The narrower widths come in strips of 3-yard lengths and are used for putting up hems on both indoor and outdoor wearing apparel; the garments will go through laundering and dry cleaning without the net losing its grip. To take down the hem that has been fused into place with this stripping all you do is press it again with a warm iron; the layers will separate easily if pulled apart while the fabrics are still warm, so changing hems is no problem.

The bonding strip is placed between the outer layer of the garment and the turned-up material, just below the already finished top edge. Whether the hem has been taped, turned down, or zigzag finished, the bonding net will hold it in place once it has been pressed.

Converting Original Garments into Accessories

There are very few articles of wearing apparel that cannot be turned into something useful and attractive, even when they have been out-grown and have reached their limit in lengthening. If the fabrics are still worth putting to use, study them a little and you'll be surprised at the number of ideas you will come up with, especially after browsing through the accessory department of a department store, or looking through the pattern catalogues for ideas.

For example, once the princess-styled dress has been outgrown in length, cut it off even shorter, hem it, and let it be worn as a tunic over pants. The same can be done with any shift-styled dress, which can get real wear as an overblouse with skirts or worn underneath jumpers, or both.

If some of these items are a bit snug around the chest area, remove the sleeves and finish the armholes with a facing or with binding. You'll have plenty of material from the sleeves to do this with, and the sleeveless style will be more comfortable. If the lower part of a dress is too snug, open the side seams after cutting the dress to the blouse or tunic length, finish the raw edges with some of the cut-off material and you will have a Chinese type of overblouse with slits.

A very attractive and useful two-piece outfit can be made from the outgrown dress that was originally designed with a fitted bodice and a full skirt. Just rip the top and skirt apart at the waist and separate them. The top of the dress can be converted into a midriff type of blouse. Finish the hem by turning up even more material and hemming it into place by hand, or with a double row of machine stitching. Or decorate the bottom of the midriff with ball fringe or the regular kind. It can be made with or without the original sleeves.

The fully gathered skirt can be finished with a machine-stitched hem at the top an inch or so wide, which becomes a casing through which elastic can be drawn to make the skirt fit around the waist. No opening is necessary; the skirt will slip on and off through the elastic top. The skirt may be trimmed with some of the fringe used on the top, or left plain. With bare skin showing between the bottom of the midriff and the top of the skirt, you have an outfit that would be great to wear to the beach or to picnics. (Fig. 112.)

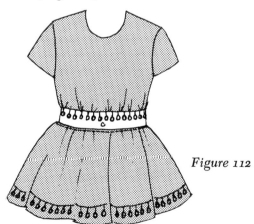

Figure 112

The dress that is styled with a gathered or pleated skirt usually has enough width in the skirt section to allow you to cut the material into a pair of shorts which can be worn with the midriff top. The top of the pants can be finished with a casing for elastic or with a zipper opening and a waistband. (Fig. 113.)

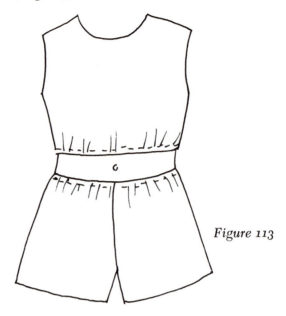

Figure 113

Last year's coat is this year's topper

Coats also become outgrown and eventually cannot be worn as full-length garments. When this happens, cut them off even shorter and convert them into very useful toppers or jackets. Worn over skirts and pants, they will provide service for another season or more. Try the coat on its owner and experiment by turning up different amounts to see which length will be best. Once the matter has been settled, cut off the extra cloth, but leave enough for a 2-inch hem. Study the way the old hem was handled and copy the workmanship as nearly as you know how.

If the lining and the coat were joined together at the bottom originally, treat the hem that way now. Or use bonding net between the hem and the outer garment and you won't have to do any stitching. If the hem of the lining is to be left loose without joining it to the hem of the coat, use the bonding net on the lining's hem also.

Directions for attaching the lining hem to the coat hem are given in chapter 5, "Tailoring Coats and Jackets," so refer to those instructions if this is the finish you intend to use.

No doubt the sleeves will also require lengthening if the garment belongs to a growing youngster, so let down and press the hem creases in both sleeves and the sleeve linings as flat as possible. The bottoms of the sleeves may be faced with some of the material cut off from the coat bottom. You make a pair of tubes to fit the bottoms of the sleeves and attach them to the bottoms of the sleeves with a narrow seam. Then turn the added material to the inside of the sleeves and hand stitch it into place after deciding the new length of the sleeves. If the sleeve facings are cut deep enough, it may not be necessary to lengthen the sleeve linings; they can simply be attached to the top edges of the applied facings.

When there isn't enough old hem to let down to make the sleeves long enough, a cuff can be made from the material that was cut off. Start this kind of a lengthening job by cutting a pair of tubes 6 inches deep. Sew one edge of the tube to the bottom of the sleeve with right sides together. Then try on the garment and adjust the tubes to form cuffs at the bottom. Turn the rest of the width inside the sleeve to form the hem. Unfortunately this kind of lengthening does not suit boys, but on girls the cuffs look well. To press the bottoms of sleeves nice and flat, whether they are plain or with cuffs, roll up a magazine, wrap it in a dish towel, slip it through the sleeves, and press carefully, using a moistened press cloth. Plain sleeves can be pressed on the wrong side, but those with cuffs are pressed with the magazine inserted inside of the sleeves so the cuffs can be pressed in their natural positions. If you have a sleeve board, use it instead of the magazine.

Just as it is possible to turn dresses into accessory items when they have outlived their original use, so it is with coats and jackets. If the fabrics are still good, make jackets into weskits or sleeveless vests. Turn them into short boleros or cardigans. All you have to do is study them for a little while and you'll see many possibilities. Look through catalogues, pattern books, and newspaper advertisements from your local department stores. You'll get lots and lots of ideas.

Skirts, skirts and more skirts

Skirts can be made from more things than you can imagine. By cutting off the top of a dress, jumper, or coat, you can make a skirt without even using a pattern. All you have to do is sew in a few darts into the front and back, fit the sides a little, and you've got yourself an extra skirt. A short zipper in the side or back does the rest. If there isn't enough material for a waistband, face the top with a strip of dime-store ribbon in the color of the cloth, measure the length, and that's it. Coat materials make dandy skirts for school. Usually coats are made from fairly firm-textured fabrics and in weights that hold pressing and shaping. Put your old coats to good use by converting them into great-looking skirts for your teen-aged daughters or yourself.

9
How to Handle Various Fabrics

Laces

Underline laces in the areas of the garment that require extra support, such as the bodice, using sheer material in the color of the lace so that its airiness is not lost. The lace and the underlining material are cut alike and then the lace is mounted on to the underlining. A line of stitching is done through the two layers ¼ inch in from the raw edges on each part of the garment before the parts are joined together. In joining the double layers, treat them as a single layer. Underlining gives just the right amount of opaqueness to prevent seam edges and dart folds from showing through on the outside of the finished garment.

Delicate silks

Besides giving the delicate silks a rich appearance, underlining helps to prevent seams and darts from pulling away from the stitching—a very common problem with many delicate silks. The supporting cloth is cut like the silk and the edges are included in the seams and darts.

Chiffon

Chiffon garments look exceptionally rich and luxurious when this material is used double instead of in single layers. Seams and darts do not show through the doubled chiffon. Long sleeves should be made single, so that the contrast between the garment and the sleeve produces added interest and attractiveness, whether the sleeves are styled with fullness caught into cuffs, or are fitted closely to the arms. Cuffs are underlined, or the chiffon used in double or triple layers, to make them opaque enough not to show the seams where they join the bottom of the sleeves.

In making short sleeves of any plain-colored sheer material try cutting them double so there is no finishing required at the bottoms. This is done by folding the material crosswise, placing the pattern with the line which indicates the finished length on the fold, and then cutting the sleeves that way. Each sleeve is now a double piece of fabric, as shown in Fig. 114. Pull the layers apart, sew the length of the underarm seam, and press it open. (Fig. 115.) Put the caps of the sleeve together with the raw edges of the seams against each other. Be sure to have the notches of each layer together also, and don't forget the ones at the top of the cap. Run the "magic stitching" through the two layers, then insert the sleeves as if they were a single thickness.

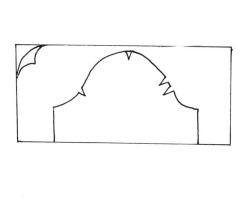
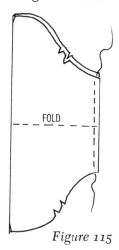

Figure 115

Lamés and other glamour fabrics

Most metallic materials are underlined not only to prevent them from fraying but also to make them more comfortable to wear. Besides the underlining, they are often lined with another fabric so that all raw edges are covered. Metallic-looking yarns are rough against the skin and the extra lining takes away the roughness. It is often necessary to face necklines and sleeveless armholes with another material instead of the lamé for comfort. To look as it should, the material used for such facings should be matched very closely in color and weight to the outer material.

Some of the materials with blistered or quilted-looking surfaces are best faced with smoother fabrics in the necklines and armholes of dresses so that a flatter finish can be achieved. They should be underlined if they stretch, unless the designs into which they are cut are easy-fitting ones; in that case only the necklines need to be interfaced or underlined, but the smooth-finished fabric should still be used for the finishing wherever the cloth must be double.

Working with some prints

It is always a good idea to study the pattern design for which you expect to use a printed material, especially if the print is large and splashy. Do not cut up the fabric into any more seams than are necessary for the shaping of the silhouette. Too many seams tend to detract from the good looks of the finished garment. Let the print speak for itself by leaving the design as whole as possible. Simplicity in pattern design will do this.

When the background of a print is light and the printed colors are dark, they will show through wherever the cloth must be used double, as in collars, cuffs, facing for collarless necklines, front facings, and hems. In these parts underlining or interfacing will provide the right amount of opaqueness to prevent the printed design from showing through and will also give the special support the fabric needs.

Working with velvets, velveteens, and corduroys

As a general rule when using these pile-surfaced materials, the smoothness of the nap is directed upward so that the rich jewel tones of the dark colors show up clearly. When the smoothness of the nap runs downward, the colors show up several shades lighter and they take on a rather attractive frosty appearance, especially in the lighter colors, the pastels. The nap may be run in either direction, whichever tone you prefer. Just be sure that all the garment parts are cut with the nap direction alike.

Panne velvet has been processed so that the nap lies perfectly flat against the base fabric and the surface looks almost like satin, it is so sparklingly lustrous. This material is always used with the smoothness going downward.

In some of these materials the pile on the surface is so erect that the nap direction is hardly noticeable either in looks or by touch. It is, nevertheless, advisable to use this cloth the same as the ones with an obvious nap direction, maintaining one end of the yardage for the bottoms of the garment parts and the other one for the tops, so that the color of the finished product will be the same tone throughout. In cleaning or in the wearing of the garment, a nap direction may develop unexpectedly, so play safe.

Collarless necklines and sleeveless armholes are best faced with another firmly woven fabric as the self material for these parts would cause too much bulk. It would be impossible to press the edges flat enough without marring the outer cloth. Taffeta has always been a good material to use for such facings because it gives support and finish at the same time. Velvets, as a rule, are not underlined with a supporting material throughout, but in some parts they may need underlining for special effects that the pattern features. The pattern will specify this when necessary.

Matching Plaids and Large Checks

Simplicity of design is the keynote when choosing patterns for plaids and fabrics with large checks, as too many seams detract from the design of the material. Conflicting lines, such as curved seams, not only make it more difficult to keep the horizontal lines of the plaid matched, but the vertical direction of the plaid is apt to become distorted at the same time. Then neither the material nor the pattern design is shown off to good advantage.

To do a good matching job of plaids, it is necessary to first cut the ends of the yardage straight along a horizontal line of the plaid design from one selvage edge to the other. The selvage edges are then pinned together so that the designs match. Continue the pinning about 2 inches or so apart for the whole length of the yardage.

If matching the ends and selvage edges causes the middle fold to twist or buckle, meaning that the fabric is off-grain, the cloth will have to be reblocked so that the folded fabric lies perfectly flat on the cutting table when it is prepared and matched for cutting. Otherwise the garment parts cannot be matched at the seams.

Cotton plaids are simply dipped into lukewarm water and when partially dry the cloth is folded so the selvage edges are evenly matched. The same thing is done with the ends. Press the material and the job is done.

If the material is a drip-dry type, regardless of what the fiber content is, you are not likely to reblock it successfully if the fabric was purchased off-grain, as the condition has been permanently set into the cloth in the processing that gives it the drip-dry quality. Some of these off-grain fabrics can be used for certain articles if they happen to be in solid colors, but a plaid or a print is another story. Avoid buying such fabrics.

The even plaids

There are some plaids on which the pattern design can be pinned with tops and bottoms going in either direction, and as long as the notches are placed on matching lines of the plaid, the seams can be made to come out perfectly matched.

The uneven plaids

One-directional plaids cannot be reversed. They must be used just like materials with napped surfaces. Otherwise it is impossible to match the plaid designs at the seams. Look the plaid material over at the time of purchase and get enough yardage to allow for matching as well as for cutting the garment parts with all bottoms going toward one end of the yardage and the tops in the opposite direction.

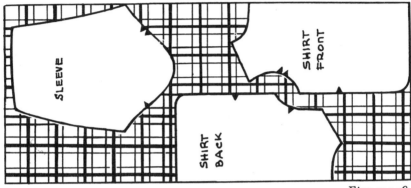

Figure 116

An evenly designed plaid is shown in Fig. 116 with a shirt pattern pinned to it. Note how the notches on the edges of the pattern pieces are matched to similar lines of the plaid to make it possible to bring these designs together properly when stitching the seams. Also note that the notches on the sleeve edges are on the same kind of line of the plaid design as the notches on the armholes. This will produce exact left and right fronts and sleeves with seams all matched.

The same pattern is shown pinned to an unevenly designed plaid. All the bottoms are directed to one end of the material only. The notches have to be matched as in the first plaid so that the seams can be joined together properly. (Fig. 117.)

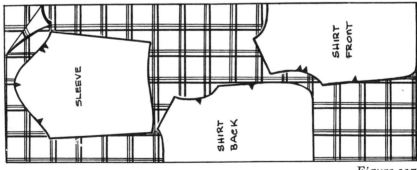

Figure 117

184

A Word about Stretch Fabrics

Stretch materials come in a variety of weaves and knits, and in different weights as well. These materials are ideal for garments that will be worn for certain purposes, like sports, for example. Although woven they will "give" like knits. They look well, whether the individual is in action or not.

Some stretch materials expand only up and down; others stretch only sideways. Still others have expandability in both directions. If you're planning to make a ski outfit, test the cloth you have in mind to buy to see which way it stretches. Then plan to use it to best advantage. In the pants part of the outfit, use the stretch up and down; in the jacket part it will be best to have the stretchability of the cloth expand sideways. Many of such materials look alike in both directions of the weave, so the top and bottom of the outfit will be alike even though the stretch has been used in different directions.

Synthetic threads and ball-point machine needles should be used for stitching these garments so that the seams will "give" as the fabric does.

The Fabulous Knits

Knit materials are irresistible. They are handsome to look at, comfortable to wear, and they come in all colors—solids, prints, plaids, and checks. They have very attractice surfaces that closely resemble different types of weaves—waffles, jacquards, crepes, satins, bouclés and many others—and some even look like what they really are, *knits*.

Most of the knits made from synthetic fibers are machine washable and dryable and do not require ironing. They don't wrinkle in wearing either. They also come in natural fibers and in blends, and these also have some fine qualities. These modern knits snap back to their original flatness when the strain put upon them is released, so they do not require lining to give them shape or to keep them that way. When the garments are lined, it is only to make them look pretty on the inside, as in jackets and coats.

If knitted material is listed on the back of the pattern envelope under the heading of "suggested fabric types," simply handle this fabric exactly as you would a cloth that has been woven.

Although knits do have a lot of "give" compared to woven fabrics, it is still necessary to make the required additions to the side edges of the garment units if the body measurements are greater than those printed on the pattern envelope. Otherwise the garment may end up smaller than expected.

As has already been mentioned, when using these expandable materials, greater liberties may be taken in the fitting than when working with woven materials. Knits can be made to fit closer to the body without too much regard for the amount of ease needed for freedom of movement, as the stretchability of the cloth will prevent constriction. However, let the choice of the amount of ease your garment should have be your own, and not just an accident, or a gamble, because you didn't add on at the time of cutting. Even if the amount needed for the addition is small, it is well to have it there. If you feel that you would like the garment to fit closer to the body than it does at the first fitting, you can always remove the excess.

When the allowances that are needed are not made, the garment is apt to look strained across those parts of the body that are larger than the pattern measurements. This calls unwanted attention to those parts of the body.

To stitch knits, hold the seams slightly stretched, with one hand ahead of the needle and the other behind it. This will provide ease in the line of stitching so the thread will be loose enough in the stitches not to break when the garment is strained in the process of wearing.

Using a ball-point machine needle prevents weakening the fibers of the knit, whatever they happen to be, as the needle goes through the fabric between the yarns instead of piercing them. Polyester thread, or any thread made of synthetic fibers, is best because it stretches.

Dresses made of knit fabrics will drape more softly and look better if left unlined. Only in the parts of the garment where interfacing is usually used when making garments of regular woven materials is it necessary to use an interfacing fabric. Interfacing is used inside of collars, under the facings of collarless garments, and inside of fronts featuring lapels and button-down closings. Without interfacing of the right texture and of the right fiber these parts would neither take shape nor stay in shape, whether the material was a natural or synthetic knit.

Occasionally a lining is used inside a knit dress, because the material is white or a pale pastel, and the seams and darts would otherwise show through on the outside of the finished garment. The lining is a lightweight woven lining material, of a fiber to match that of the outside knit. It is attached by hand around the outer edge of the facing at the neckline and along the zipper closing. If the dress is sleeveless, the lining is hand stitched around the armholes, catching the stitches to the outer edges of the facings without going through to the outside. The lining is hemmed 1 inch shorter than the garment.

If your sewing machine is the modern automatic type with a setting for knits, you should use that setting not only for the seams but also for finishing other parts of the garment that require special handling.

Hems of knits

If your machine is not an automatic zigzag type, run a line of machine stitching at the top edge of your hem about ½ inch down from the raw edge and either leave the edge that way or pink it with your pinking shears close to the machine stitching. When sewing the hem by hand after pinning it up into position, catch your hand stitches to the machine ones on the hem, then take a tiny stitch into the garment, doing the stitches in between the two layers ½ inch apart, alternating from the hem to the skirt (see Fig. 52). Using seam tape on knit hems makes the top of the hem show through, but when tape is omitted the hem is hardly visible.

The lacy knits

Some very loose knits are designed like lace, with large open spaces as part of the designs. Such materials must be underlined with a lightweight material so that they do not sag out of shape either during the time they are being worked on or when being worn. Handle lacy knits in the same way as other lightweight fabrics. Mount each piece of the knit on a piece of underlining material cut in the same shape, and use a line of stitching on the outer edges to hold them together. The underlining should be placed on top of the knit during stitching so that the knit lace does not get stretched. Stitch ¼ inch in from the raw edges. Usually the sleeves are not underlined. Bare skin showing through the mesh of the lace makes for added interest, as well as contrast.

The underlining material does not have to be the same color as the lacy knit. Some attractive results can be produced by using another color. Picture white lace over black or black over white or ice blue!

In hemming an underlined knit, be sure not to bring the hand stitching through to the outside layer of the lace. The top edge of the underlined knit hem can be neatly finished with a strip of seam tape or a fancy lace edging.

Special patterns that are marked "designed for knits only"

The pattern companies have put out special patterns which they have labeled in their catalogues as "designed for knits only." These designs are cut along rather plain lines with very little shaping and with a limited number of darts. Many have no darts at all. These fashions are mostly for casual wear and are meant to drape easily on the body with hardly any fitting at all. Shaping is done by running elastic through casings around the waistline of skirts or pants; dresses are pulled in at the waist with belts or sashes, or worn loose, the material draping itself naturally on the body contours. It is the fabrics used for these specially designed patterns that make the garments interesting and eye-catching.

These patterns come in different sizes, just as other patterns do. They should not be used for woven fabrics or for knits that are bonded. Such materials would not drape properly when cut from the special patterns and the results would be disappointing, both in fit and in appearance.

Bonded fabrics

When purchasing bonded materials, knits or weaves, it is necessary to inspect the right side carefully to see if the grain of the weave or knit has been properly aligned to the under fabric. Some of these materials come through the bonding process quite off-grain and nothing can be done about straightening the weave or knit direction, making it impossible to match plaids, stripes, checks or any other prints for that matter.

It is often necessary to place the pattern pieces on the right side of bonded material to cut garment parts so that lines that need to be matched can be seen well enough to do the job correctly, as the under material and the bonding agent cover up the lines of the outer design of the material. The best way to cut parts of garments that must be matched is to cut them one piece at a time instead of through the double layers.

If the weave of the fabric has been badly bonded to the under cloth, don't invest either your time or money in making something from it, as the garment is very apt to end up as an eyesore. Do inspect bonded fabrics carefully before you buy them. Some are very well bonded together, but not all, so watch out!

When a part of a garment must be cut on a fold of the cloth, it is a good idea to cut that piece of pattern from folded tissue paper so you have a complete pattern piece instead of a half pattern. Then lay this onto the right side of the bonded plaid or check fabric. In this way it will be easy enough to shift the pattern piece a bit to make the notches come on similar plaid or check locations on the left and right sides so they can be eventually matched to their joining parts.

Most slim skirts made of bonded fabrics have to be lined to keep them in shape, as they do stretch. This is true of not only separate skirts but the skirts of dresses also.

Sewing Leather Garments

Leather garments can be made at home on your regular sewing machine if you are an experienced sewer. Sewing-machine needles, made specially for working on leather, have either a flat point or one with three sides, instead of the usual round kind, and these penetrate through the leather seams without any problem.

It is a very good idea to make up the pattern you intend using for the leather garment from some muslin first so that you can make whatever adjustments the garment requires on the muslin test pattern and no such adjustments will have to be made on the leather itself. Needle marks stay in the leather once they are in it, so ripping is not possible without spoiling the looks and weakening the seams.

Skins come in different sizes and in different finishes—suede, smooth leather (calf, kid and so on), and reptile skins. The suedes have a "nap" surface, so it is advisable to use them with the nap going in a downward direction, just as the skin grows on the animal. You can readily distinguish by the shape of the skin purchased, which end is the neck and which is the tail end. Mark the wrong side with spearhead chalk marks pointing to the tail end to remind you that all the bottoms of the garment parts go one way, and all the tops go in the opposite direction. Pin the pattern within the seam allowance, not where the pin holes might show when the parts are joined. Cut one piece of the garment at a time for a cleaner cutting job, and use straight scissors.

Smooth leathers and the reptiles do not usually have a one-way direction, so they can be used one way or the other. Many leather garments are joined with welt seams, because they do not press flat. When plain seams are desired, glue the edges down after they have been stitched, using a fabric glue.

Use mercerized thread and about 8 to 10 stitches to the inch. To get the corners to lay flat, it may be necessary to pound the layers of leather with a flat piece of wood about the size of a brick, covered with some cloth. Hems are also glued down as a rule; so are front facings.

Zippers are usually inserted into openings with a double fold which meets in the middle right over the zipper teeth rather than by the one-lap method. If the side edges of the seam are glued down first it makes the zipper job easier.

Leather dealers have a very clever way of converting the yardage requirement in a pattern to the amount of leather that will be needed for your particular project. Before buying the leather pieces be sure you have enough for the whole garment you wish to make. You should buy all the leather pieces at one time so they can be matched in tone of color and also in thickness. Dealers advise that pattern pieces should not be placed on the off-grain of the skins. The garment will stay in shape better if the up-and-down grain is observed in all parts of the garment.

Here is a trick that will make sewing smooth leathers easier on your sewing machine: Skins such as kid or patent leather, as well as imitations of such leathers, tend to stick to the metal parts of the machine during the stitching, causing the stitches to be uneven and twisting between edges and top stitching. To overcome this problem rub a little machine oil on both top and bottom layers of the leather where the stitching will be done. The stitching will then go through without a hitch, and the oil will rub right off without leaving spots. This treatment is not recommended for suedes or other leathers that are porous, as these will absorb the oil and change the color of the skins. This warning applies to imitation leathers also. Use oil only on shiny and nonporous finishes.

Those Honest-Looking Fakes

The "leathers"

The leather imitations are so great you actually have to touch them to know whether they are real or not. They are made to resemble all kinds of animal and reptile skins and come in finishes that look like suede, kid, patent, tooled leather, and many others. These materials handle more easily than real leather because their bonded backing allows them to go through the stitching process without the seams balking, as they often do when stitching real leather.

The imitations are suitable for many different kinds of wearing apparel, and the choice of pattern design depends upon their suppleness or lack of it. The suedes are quite soft, so they will fall into soft lines when cut into princess styles, as well as into straighter lines. Since the stiffer leather fabrics do not ease, they make up best in styles that do not have parts that require much "easing." For example, when the "leathers" have firmness they make up more satisfactorily in a pattern with the raglan sleeves rather than the set-in type.

Use mercerized thread for stitching the seams and be sure that stitches are 8 to 10 to the inch. The needle holes do not disappear, so the work has to be done right the first time. Just as it was advisable to make a test garment from some muslin, or some other throw-away material, before cutting into real leather, so it is with making apparel from these good-looking imitations, because redoing things is not practical. All the necessary alterations should be made on the cloth garment, and then the pattern used in conjunction with the corrected test pieces for cutting the synthetic leather.

The "suedes"

The suede materials should be used with their "nap" going in one direction only, or the color tones will not be alike throughout the complete garment. Usually the nap is brushed downward in the real leather, and this should be done with the imitation, unless the color of the cloth is more pleasing when the nap runs the other way. In either case the bottoms should all be directed toward one end of the yardage when placing the pattern on the cloth, and the tops toward the other end. Nap directed downward will make the suede lighter in color tone and upward will make it darker.

The "furs"

There are all kinds of "furs" from which to make your own coats. They imitate spotted cats and baby seals, minks and broadtails. Others have such densely covered surfaces that you could easily mistake the fabric for real lambskins of all types. Some fur materials are shaggy and long-haired; others are curly and flat, some looking like expensive Persian lamb.

The flat-type "furs" are used with their nap going in a downward direction like the coat of a real animal. When the materials are not too bulky they can be stitched by machine in the usual way with the ⅝-inch seam allowance. The seam edges are then pressed apart with a light touch. But some of the heavy "furs" must be cut like real fur pelts. This is done by removing the seam allowance and then joining the pieces together by hand, using a dense overhand stitch. This type of stitching is done very close to the raw edges with the furry sides of the work together. When the joining is finished, the seam is flattened out with the fingernail of your right or left thumb, depending upon whether you do things with your right hand or the left.

All these materials are best to cut singly, even the ones that are cut with a fold through the middle. A full-sized pattern should be made from tissue to cut such pieces. Place the pattern on the wrong side of the fur fabric for cutting. Where darts are shown on the pattern, cut away the fabric on the chalk line you've traced from the pattern and catch the dart together as you would a seam with overhand stitches. No seams show on the outside of such materials.

When you've finished the seams, go around to the right side of the seam and pull out any of the long hairs that come out willingly when you use a large needle to slide underneath the stitched-in fur pile. The seams will look better as a result and will also be less bulky on the inside.

Coats made from fur fabrics are treated pretty much like those that are made from regular coating materials. Interfacings are used down the fronts and inside of collars for shaping and support. Instead of buttonholes, however, frogs or covered hooks and eyes, like those on real fur coats, are used to keep the coats closed. Braid or cloth loops are also used, inserted into the front edge of the garment and caught securely by hand to the canvas inside of the front and facing layers. Choose a style with the least number of seams, as seams produce bulk; the fewer there are in the style of the coat the better. The "fur" itself creates the attractiveness of the garment and does not require any detailing. The materials dry-clean, unless the manufacturer has specified on the hang tag or on the bolt that they are washable, and many of them are. Be sure that everything you put into the making of a washable "fur" garment has the same washable qualities so you won't have a washing problem.

10
Bound Buttonholes and All Types of Pockets

How to make bound buttonholes

There are several ways of making bound buttonholes, but none compares in simplicity and ease with the way recommended here. The method is foolproof. Try it and see!

As I mentioned earlier, bound buttonholes are used on girls' and women's clothing, but rarely if ever on any masculine garments. If they appear on a man's very fancy silk vest, for example, it is an exception and not the general thing. For men and boys, machine-stitched buttonholes are the rule, or the kind that are hand embroidered. It is not unusual to make machine buttonholes, and then go over them with hand stitching, if you want the handmade look. Machine-made and hand-embroidered buttonholes are suitable on wearing apparel for both male and female.

Bound buttonholes should be made only on garments that will be dry-cleaned, not on casual wear that will go into the washing machine and drier. They would fray and fall apart in no time from such treatment. If a garment that you plan on laundering at home does have bound buttonholes, wash it separately in a wash basin, swishing it around in warm sudsy water and squeezing it gently. It should not be wrung; just press out the excess water by hand. Either roll it up into a fluffy bath towel to dry to the stage where it can be ironed while still moist, if it is the kind of fabric that requires ironing, or just hang it and let it drip-dry if it is made of no-iron material. Bound buttonholes treated in this way will last as long as the garment will.

Before attempting to make bound buttonholes on any garment, you should first make a few samples using the garment material. With each buttonhole made you will discover how much fun it is to make them this special way and how easy it is to get each one perfectly aligned with another, so they all end up the same length and the same distance away from the garment edge. Make your mistakes in the samples and you'll know how to avoid them in the actual garment. If you make your first samples from wool, this being the easiest material with which to work, you can later make bound buttonholes on more difficult-to-handle fabrics.

To make the work really easy, put a brightly-colored thread in the bobbin, but use the garment-colored thread on the spool. Do this also when actually making the buttonholes. It will give visual aid, and make it easy to achieve precision workmanship, both in sewing and cutting the buttonholes. This thread guidance is especially important when you are making buttonholes on fabrics that have a busy texture, like some tweeds, or loosely woven fleecy things. The bright thread will be concealed completely on the final step; it will not show anywhere.

You are safe in trusting the size of the buttonhole featured on the pattern pieces of your project. The sizes and the spacings between each one, as well as the distance from the outer edge of the garment fronts, have been carefully planned in the manufacture of the pattern design.

Before you start, prepare the strip which will eventually be the finish on the buttonhole edges. Cut this strip 1 inch wide, from the crosswise or lengthwise weave of the cloth, whichever way will fray the least. The bindings can also be made from small scraps of garment fabric, since they will be cut into small lengths anyway. Just be sure that they all run in the same direction of the cloth weave.

Fold the strip through the center lengthwise, with the right side out. Then sew through the strip exactly ⅛ inch away from the fold and trim away the raw edges along the stitching line, leaving only ⅛ inch there. The machine stitching is now in the direct center of the strip. The width of the fold and that of the raw edge must be identical, because the raw edge acts as a spacing device for the folded half when the buttonhole is finished. If these widths of fold and raw edge are not alike, the buttonhole will not be perfect. So check to see that you are starting right. (Fig. 118.)

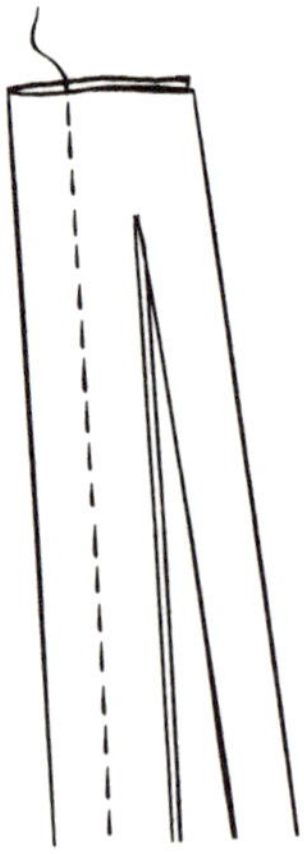

Figure 118

Follow the instructions for each step as set forth here, reading one sentence at a time, just as if you were making a cake from the recipe in a cookbook. This, too, is a reference book and should be used as one. It is not necessary to remember each and every step from one sewing venture to another. Refer to the book each time, and the more you repeat a performance, the more versed you will become in the whole procedure. That is how confidence and efficiency are achieved. As these will only be sample buttonholes, make them any size you wish. Make them in different sizes for really good experience.

Step one

With chalk sharpened to a pencil point, mark the length of the buttonholes on the right side of the fabric in the form of a miniature "goalpost," such as seen on football fields, or like a giant letter H. (Fig. 119a.) The horizontal line of the symbol represents the length of the buttonholes, and should be drawn directly parallel to the cross-weave of the fabric. The guideposts at the ends of the line should be parallel to the up-and-down weave of the fabric. The first step, the marking, is finished.

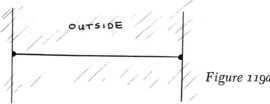

Figure 119a

Step two

From the binding prepared before starting, cut two strips, each an inch longer than the horizontal line of the symbol. Place one of the strips above the horizontal line, with the ends projecting evenly beyond the sides of the goalpost and the raw edge of the strip resting on the horizontal line. Stitch through the strip from post to post, making sure that the stitching is done directly through the contrastingly colored preliminary sewing. (Fig. 119b.) Cut the thread ends at the start and end of this stitching to 1-inch lengths, but no shorter, for reinforcement. Now place the second binding below the cross line of the goal post, with the raw edges butted right up against the ones on the first strip, and sewed the same way.

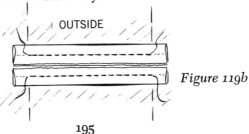

Figure 119b

Step three

This step will be done on the wrong side of the cloth. Mark the center area of the buttonhole between the two rows of stitching with a "bull's-eye," a dot, with the chalk. (Fig. 120a.) Pierce the dot with the point of the scissors. Insert the point of the scissors into the hole at an angle and cut directly to the end of one row of stitching, cutting only the uppermost fabric to which the bindings were sewed, not the bindings on the other side of the cloth. Reinsert the point of the scissors in the same manner to cut all four ends of the stitchings, starting from the "bull's-eye" each time and not cutting any farther than the ends. The cuts will resemble an "X." (Fig. 120b.)

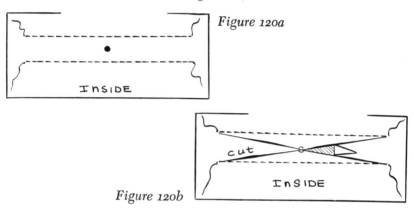

Figure 120a

Figure 120b

Step four

Before starting this step, get the sewing machine in position for stitching by turning the wheel by hand so that the needle is inserted into the needle hole in the plate, and bring the threads toward the back of the machine to keep them from snarling when the stitching is begun. Now, pull the bindings through the cut buttonhole, from the right side of the cloth to the wrong side and finish the ends in the following manner: The garment is placed to the left of the machine needle with the right side of the buttonhole facing upward. Fold back the cloth at the end of the buttonhole nearest to the needle, so that the triangle and the bindings underneath it are visible on the wrong side of the garment. Slide the work, holding it in that very same position, directly against the needle until you can't slide it any closer. Lower the presser foot, and stitch downward on the projecting buttonhole parts, keeping just as close as possible to the fold without catching any of it into the stitching. (Fig. 121.)

When a single buttonhole is featured, as at a coat neckline, for example, or at the waistline of some jackets, the goalpost symbol is used. However, when a group of buttonholes are to be made on the

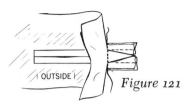

Figure 121

front of a garment, they are marked with a symbol that resembles a ladder with rungs. Then all the buttonholes can be made exactly the same length and spaced alike from the outer edge of the garment front.

Here's how to make the ladder: First, pin the pattern to the interfacing side of the right-hand front, matching the edges of the pattern to those of the interfacing and the garment fabric accurately, and pinning through the seam allowance to hold the pattern in place. It should be mentioned here that the buttonholes should be marked only after the canvas foundation has been accurately stab stitched to each of the fronts. Rarely are buttonholes made without some kind of foundation to give them strength. Even when buttonholes are used strictly for decorative purposes, they are interfaced to make them look neater. To mark buttonholes, puncture a hole in the pattern at each end of the buttonhole marking and then put a pencil dot at these ends. When each one has been marked, remove the pattern from the garment and draw two parallel lines directly through the dots from the top to the bottom, using a ruler for accuracy. Now draw in the "rungs" of the ladder, where the dots are, then run a large machine stitching in an obvious color directly through the long parallel pencil lines, working on the interfacing side of the garment so that the ladder symbol is produced on both sides of the front. (Fig. 122.) This will make it easy to make all the buttonholes the same size and to place them in a straight row. You can easily check their accuracy by the marking on the canvas side. When the buttonholes have been checked, remove the machine stitches. They will leave no marks.

When several buttonholes are featured on a garment front, all the bindings are stitched to the horizontal lines on the right side first. (Fig. 123.) This gives you an opportunity to inspect the stitching on each of the bindings by looking on the canvas side to see that they are correctly lined up. If they need to be corrected for one reason or another, now is the time to do it. Each pair of stitching lines that hold the bindings in place must be exactly even at both ends, otherwise the finished buttonhole will have slanted ends instead of straight ones. After correcting the faulty lines of stitching, rip out the large "ladder" stitches carefully. They have served their purpose.

Mark a "bull's-eye" in the center of each buttonhole on the inter-

197

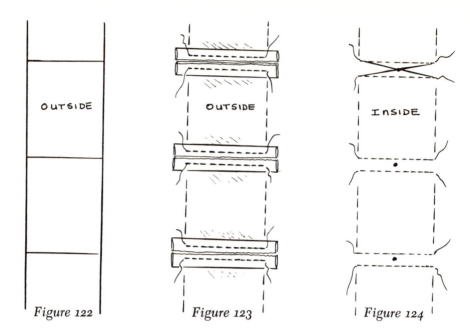

Figure 122   Figure 123   Figure 124

facing side of the garment, then cut the buttonholes through, finishing each one completely before cutting the next one, to prevent the canvas and the outer cloth from fraying. (Fig. 124.) Trim off the ends of the bindings to ¼ inch when finished so that they will lie flat inside of the garment. If they are left too long, they cause bulk.

Baste the bindings together on the right side of the garment, then press the buttonholes on the wrong side, after they have all been cut and basted. This will block them closed and keep them in shape. (Leave the basting in the buttonhole bindings until the garment is finished and ready to be worn.) The facing material is cut through next. Insert pins at each end of a buttonhole to penetrate through to the inside of the garment; then cut the facing from one pin to the next in a straight line. Finish the raw edges by tucking under a tiny bit of facing with the tip of the needle; then hand sew the fold to the buttonhole bindings, making sure that the stitching doesn't go through to the outside. Take two extra stitches at the ends of the cut facing, where there will be no fold to tuck under, since this is a straight cut. The extra stitches will reinforce the raw edges and prevent them from fraying. Check the bound buttonholes on a ready-made garment and see if yours look as well. Finish one buttonhole at a time on the facing side, to prevent fraying and to keep the facing flat. When all buttonholes have been finished, give them a light touch-up with a damp cloth and a warm iron.

All about pockets

When the bound buttonhole steps are understood, set-in pockets will be no problem to make, since they are constructed using the same basic steps and precision workmanship. Different pocket styles are produced by varying the steps slightly.

Because fabric textures play an important part in the way the finished pocket will look, it is smart to make a sample pocket first, using the garment fabric. You can then judge how suitable the material is for the style of the pocket chosen, and can analyze how it will look in the finished garment.

The bound or buttonhole pocket

This pocket is made just like a giant-sized buttonhole, with a pocket attached behind it. It is a very popular pocket for all types of coats and jackets, and is often seen on the back of shorts and trousers.

Mark the placement of the pocket on the garment, and interface the material in that area if the garment fabric is loosely woven or soft. This will make the pocket stronger and also keep the garment in shape. A piece of lightweight cotton such as sheeting is good for this purpose. Pin the interfacing into place, or baste around it with large hand stitches, just to keep it in place while making a pocket through it. A goalpost should be drawn with chalk on the right side of the cloth, and bright stitching run through the chalk lines in case the chalk rubs off.

Make the bindings for the pocket any width you like. We shall now refer to these bindings as "welts," the right title when they pertain to pockets. Welts can vary in width from ⅛ inch to a full inch. The weight of the cloth used is often the deciding factor in choosing the width. Making a sample first will help decide the matter for you. The welt can be made on the straight or cross-weave of the fabric, as well as on the true bias.

Fold the welt right side out and stitch it ¼ inch away from the fold. The raw edges are then trimmed off to the exact width of the folded edge, ¼ inch. Cut the two welts generously long, about one or 1½ inches longer than the horizontal line of the goalpost. Sew one welt above the goalpost with the raw edges resting on the horizontal line and the ends projecting equally beyond the goalpost on each side. Sew through the original stitching, just as you did for buttonholes. The end threads should be left fairly long, about 1 inch at least, to be caught into the following steps. Sew the second strip of welting below the goalpost, with the raw edges of both touching each other, and stitch through the first row of stitching that was made on the welt. (Fig. 125a.)

199

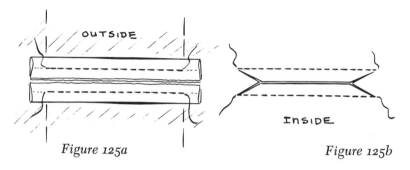

Figure 125a

Figure 125b

After inspecting the stitching on the wrong side of the garment to see that the stitching lines are equal in length, cut the pocket through from the wrong side of the garment. Slash horizontally through the center of the space between the two rows of stitching, but stop 1 inch away from each end. Here, continue the cutting at angles, coming as close as possible to the end of each stitching line, without cutting the stitches. (Fig. 125b.) The welts are pushed through the slash from the right side of the garment to the wrong side, and left that way until the lining pieces have been prepared. The welts may be hand basted together at this point to make the work easier.

Cut two pieces of pocket lining from some sturdy fabric. Use the material from which the garment will be lined, if it is sturdy enough. Each piece should be cut generously wider than the horizontal line of the goalpost, or as long as the welts, and about 3 or 4 inches deep. Coat pockets can be deeper than those used on other clothing, so the above depth is approximate. It is easier to make pockets when the lining materials are left fairly generous in size; they can be trimmed off later when the pocket is finished. To the top of one of these pocket linings, attach a strip of garment fabric about 1½ inches wide, joining the two with a ¼-inch seam. This is called a pocket facing. Leave the other piece plain. (Figs. 126 a and b.)

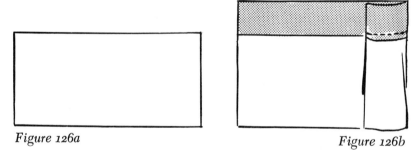

Figure 126a

Figure 126b

Attach the lining pieces to the raw edges of the welts on the wrong side of the garment. Put the enlarged piece with the facing edge against the upper welt, and sew them together through the row of stitching that is already on the welt. Join the plain lining piece to the raw edges of the lower welt on the inside.

Place the work to the left of the machine needle, with the pocket right side up. Fold back the cloth at the end of the pocket nearest the needle so that the wrong side of the work is visible. Slide the work up against the needle and sew downward on the projecting ends of the pocket parts, as well as on the lining, continuing the stitching all around the lining pieces underneath and ending on the opposite side of the pocket opening. (Fig. 127.) The shape into which the pocket lining is stitched is a matter of choice: either square or round is correct. Trim off the extra seam edges after the pocket is completed. Then press basted bindings, or welts, on the outside of the cloth and block them into proper shape. Leave them basted until the garment is finished. This will prevent them from gaping open while the rest of the garment is being worked on.

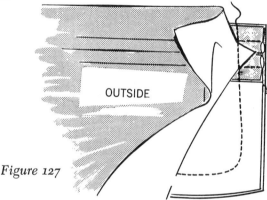

Figure 127

When the fabric used for the garment is lightweight, one of the lining pieces for the pocket can be of the same fabric as the garment while the other is of lining material. The piece cut from the garment material is then attached to the raw edges of the upper welt, and the piece cut from lining material is joined to the raw edges of the lower welt. When using heavy coatings, it is better to have the narrow facing sewed to the top of the lining piece to avoid the bulk that would be created if the whole piece were made of coating.

The one-welt or set-in well pocket

The one-welt or set-in welt pocket is another favorite because of its subtle styling. It is adaptable to every type of garment and is wearable by everyone. Unlike the bound pocket described above, it has one wide welt as the outside detail instead of the two narrow ones. It is an exceptionally nice pocket to put into garments made of fleecy or heavy-textured material because it is less bulky than other types.

Mark the placement of the pocket on the wrong side of the cloth, first with chalk and then with bright hand stitching so that the marking will show on both the right and the wrong sides of the material. The welt can be any desired width, but an inch is a very pleasing one for most materials and is popularly used on tailored items.

The welt is made from a strip of material about 1½ inches longer than the horizontal line of the goalpost, and about 3 inches wide. Fold the strip right side out and stitch it 1 inch away from the fold; then see that the remaining raw edge is an even ½ inch. Sew the welt into place *below* the horizontal line of the goalpost, going through the same line of stitching. The raw edges of the welt should be directly on the horizontal line of the symbol, and the stitching should go from one vertical line to the other. Leave the thread at least 1 inch long at the ends.

Cut pocket linings from a durable material in the color of the garment, or from the lining material that is to be used. Cut the linings as wide as the horizontally attached welt, and about 3 or 4 inches in depth, depending upon whether the pocket is to go in a coat or jacket. The coat pocket can be as deep as you wish, but jacket pocket linings must not interfere with the hem of the jacket; have the linings come to just above the jacket hem crease or higher. Add a 2-inch-wide strip of the garment fabric to the top edge of one of the pocket-lining pieces to act as a pocket facing.

Place the lining piece with the pocket facing attached to it with its right side against the right side of the garment above the horizontal line of the goalpost and stitch it into place with a ½-inch seam. The raw edges of the welt and the edge of the pocket facing meet right over the horizontal line. The stitching lines on both parts must be absolutely even with each other at the ends. (Fig. 128.)

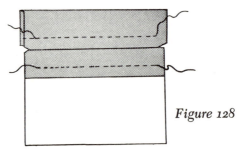

Figure 128

Before doing the cutting on the wrong side of the pocket, check to be sure that the space between the two lines of stitching is equal in width to the width of the welt from the line of stitching that is holding it in place to the fold that will be the top of the pocket detailing. When the pocket is cut through, the welt will have to fill the space between these lines of stitching. Remove the goalpost stitching carefully after the parts of the pocket have been attached and before the cutting is done.

Do the cutting on the wrong side, exactly as if it were a giant-sized buttonhole, bull's-eye and all, except start the triangle cutting about 1 inch before the end of the lines of stitching are reached. When the two ends are cut with the triangles, pull the welt through to the inside of the garment and direct it into an upright position to fit into the space provided for it. Also pull the attached lining piece through to the inside of the garment so that it hangs in a downward direction. Place the remaining plain piece of lining with its right side against the raw edges of the welt and stitch through the line of stitching that is already there. Both linings are now directed downward with the triangular tabs on top of them. Stitch the lining parts from the tab at the top of one side downward and around the whole shape, then up to the top on the opposite side, catching the tab into the line of stitching there. (Fig. 129.) Trim the outer edges of the pocket linings down to ⅜-inch width.

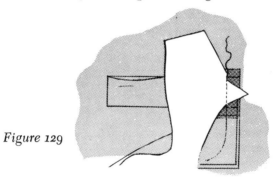

Figure 129

The flap pocket

This pocket is equally suitable for male and female clothing and is especially good for tailored coats or jackets. Make the flap first, using the pattern provided for this part. Interface the flap if the fabric used is soft and loosely woven, sewing the canvas between the outer and under part of the flap. The flap can be faced with garment fabric, or if the fabric is heavy, with lining. Construct the flap with the same precision as you would a miniature collar. Do the stitching on the canvas side, the seams staggered, and any points clipped off; if the flaps are rounded, nip the curved edges inward for greater smoothness. Then turn the flap over to the right side, baste around the outer edges, rolled over so that the groove of the seam will be on the facing side of the flap, and press well.

Mark the placement of the pocket with a goalpost in the usual way. Place the right side of the flap against the right side of the garment with the raw edges resting on the horizontal line and the flap above the line. Stitch the flap into place with ¼-inch seam. Now, make a welt from a strip of the garment fabric, either cross-weave or length-wise; fold it right side out and stitch it ½ inch away from the fold. Trim away the seam edge to ¼-inch width. Place the welt against the raw edges of the flap, below the horizontal line of the goalpost and sew with ¼-inch seam from post to post going through the first stitching. The length of the welt should be extended ¾ inch beyond the flap at each end of the goalpost. (Fig. 130.)

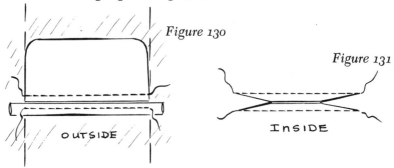

Figure 130

Figure 131

OUTSIDE

InSIDE

Cut the pocket through from the wrong side of the garment, slashing horizontally through the middle of the space between the two rows of stitching, and stopping 1 inch from each end. Continue the cutting at angles, coming right up to the end of the stitching at each row. (Fig. 131.) Then pull the welt through from the right to the wrong side of the garment; direct the flap to a downward position on the right side, and leave everything that way until the lining pieces for the pocket have been prepared.

Cut two pieces of lining the width of the welt and about 3 or 4 inches deep. A facing of garment material, 1½ inches wide, can be attached to one of these lining pieces if you wish, but it is not really necessary since the flap covers the opening of the pocket. Attach the first piece of lining to the seam edge of the flap on the wrong side of the garment. Start the stitching at the extending end of the lining piece, and then sew through the stitching that is already on the flap edge, making sure to catch in the full ¼-inch seam width at the ends of the flap, where they have an inclination to slip away if not watched. The second piece of lining is attached to the raw edges of the welt in the usual manner, sewing through the original stitching.

Place the work to the left of the machine needle with the outside of the garment up, and the flap in a downward position on the surface of the garment. Fold back the cloth at the end of the pocket closest to the needle so that the wrong side of the work is visible. Arrange the welt, the triangle, and the lining neatly in place; then sew downward over these projecting parts of the pocket, as close as possible to the clipped ends of the triangle and other projecting parts. Make sure that during all the stitching operation the flap remains in a downward position on

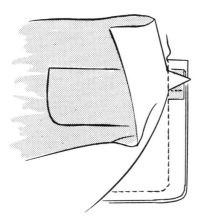

the outside of the garment, as this has a great bearing on how the flap will behave when the garment is worn. (Fig. 132.) Press the finished pocket lightly on the right side, using a press cloth to prevent marking the cloth.

A flap pocket with feature stitching

On sport coats and jackets made of camel's hair or other fleecy fabrics, the flap pocket frequently has a double row of stitching encircling the outside shape of the pocket, even though it is a set-in pocket with the lining inside the garment. The stitching is done either by hand or by machine, with the space between the rows about ½ inch or ⅜ inch apart. The flap of such a pocket is usually top stitched too, and the widths of the trim stitching match each other. Trim stitching on the flap should be done before the flap is attached to the coat.

Construct the pocket just like an ordinary flap pocket. When the pocket is completed, pin the lining against the wrong side of the garment so that it can be caught in with the feature stitching.

Draw the inner line for the feature stitching first, using chalk on the right side of the garment. Use hand sewing for guidance if chalk marking doesn't show on your garment fabric. Make this first row of stitching in a direct line with the ends of the pockets, and the outer row either ½ inch or ⅜ inch away from the first one. (Fig. 133.)

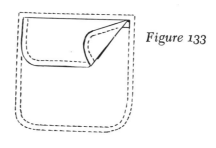

Figure 133

The shaped welt, or weskit, pocket

This is a companion pocket to the one with a flap, the welt style being used on the upper section of a sport jacket and the flapped pocket on the lower part. The shape of the welt can be varied, but the size must be comparable to the pocket marked on the pattern piece. This type of pocket is often used on girls' coats and jackets also. Quite often this shaped welt—so named because it is a unit that must be completed before it is attached—is cut wide enough to be folded over and the two ends sewn up, thus eliminating a seam at the long edge. It is similar in appearance to a flap, but somewhat narrower. When the shape of the welt is unusual or curved, the same techniques are used as when making a flap. Interfacing is used when needed for firmness. The welt should be finished, but one edge should be left open. The difference between a flap and a welt of this kind is that flaps hang downward when in their normal position, while welts stand upright on garments.

The goalpost for the placement of the pocket is marked in the usual way on the right side. Place the finished welt *below* the horizontal line of the goalpost, and sew with ¼-inch seam. Next, cut the lining wide enough to extend about an inch beyond the welt ends and about 2½ inches deep.

Sew the lining above the horizontal line with a ¼-inch seam edge, but the line of stitching on this part should be ½ inch *shorter* at each end than the stitching that appears on the welt. (Fig. 134a.) Be sure to leave the ends of the threads long enough to catch them into the next step.

Cut in the center between the two rows of stitching, on the wrong side of the cloth. One inch away from each long row of stitching, angle the cutting and bring it to the last stitch. Then do the same to the ends

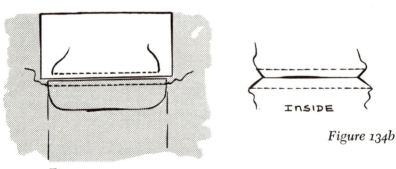

Figure 134a

Figure 134b

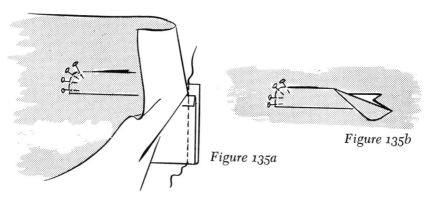

Figure 135a

Figure 135b

of the short stitching line. This will result in tabs with irregular shapes at the ends, instead of the usual even ones. (Fig. 134b.) Then pull the lining through to the wrong side of the garment, and attach another piece of lining to the raw edges of the pocket welt on the inside of the garment. On the outside, place the welt in an upright position and fold back the cloth at the end of the pocket nearest to the needle, so that the lining on the wrong side of the garment is visible. (Fig. 135a.)

The irregularly-shaped triangle tabs are *not* caught into the stitching when the vertical line of stitching is done on the edges of the pocket lining, as it usually is. These tabs remain on the surface of the garment to be caught down underneath the welt with the stitching that will hold the welt in position. (Fig. 135b.) Leaving these tabs on the right side of the garment produces a smooth surface and prevents dimples when the upright welt is sewed. If the welt is anchored by hand, it must be sewed invisibly. Machine stitching is done on the very edge of the ends of the welt, from base to top. The ends of the thread are then drawn through to the wrong side and tied.

Making patch pockets

To make good-looking patch pockets requires the same precision workmanship as is needed for any of the styles that must be built into the garment. Only then will they contribute to a handsome overall appearance. Although patch pockets are easy to make, the importance of perfect execution in construction cannot be overemphasized. Unless each step is faultlessly done, this pocket can give more of a homemade appearance than any other style. Many an amateur sewer settles for a patch pocket because she feels that she can't go wrong with it, not realizing that unless she treats it with the same respect that she does other types, the results will be disappointing.

There are a number of patch-pocket styles, but a very popular one, and the most basic in construction, is the plain one lined with lining fabric. This type of pocket is suitable for boys and girls alike, on tailored and semi-tailored things. It takes lots of punishment with no ill effects. And especially important for children's wear is the fact that patch pockets are not "outgrown" nearly as fast as the set-in types. Last year's coat with a horizontally inserted set-in pocket, for example, can look short-waisted this year, but the depth of a patch pocket does much to counteract that appearance, even though it may be equally high on the garment. It is purely optical illusion. Furthermore, patch pockets can be attached to the garment so that they can be moved down easily when necessary.

Here's the best way to make patch pockets: Cut the pocket piece about 1½ inches or 2 inches longer than what the depth of the finished pocket will be. The extra length will act as a facing at the top. Identify the fold line, where the pocket ends and facing begins, by making a ¼-inch clipping at the side edges of the pocket. Then cut the lining to the approximate depth of the pocket, or somewhat shorter, and sew it to the edge of the facing end of the cloth pocket, with a ¼-inch seam. Leave a 1-inch space unsewed in the middle of the seam. (Fig. 136a.) Now fold the pocket through the fold line, with the right sides of the fabrics together, and sew around the outer edges with regular seam allowance. If the cloth is bulky, trim the facing edge down to ¼ inch at the two ends between the lining and the top of the pocket, but allow the pocket material to remain the full width of the seam. Then clip off the corners to the stitching, to avoid bulk, both at tops and bottoms if pocket is square. (Fig. 136b.) Then turn the pocket over the right side through the small opening which was left in the center of the seam between lining and pocket fabric. Baste the pocket all around the four edges, rolling the pocket fabric slightly over the lining edge, so that no lining will show around the finished pocket. Press thoroughly on the lining side, using a press cloth to prevent the fabrics from being pushed by the iron. Hand sew the little opening in the middle of the seam before attaching the pocket.

There are many attractive ways to attach pockets. The line of stitching can be close to the outer edge or any distance away. The stitching can be done by hand or machine. It can be hand picked or saddle

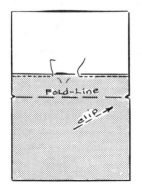

Figure 136

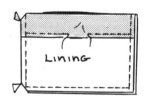

stitched. Quite often trim stitching is put on the pocket by machine after the lining has been sewed to the pocket and the pocket has been pressed, before being attached to the garment. Pin the pocket into position and hand sew around the outer edges with the bridge stitch, the one used to insert linings in coats and jackets. The edge of the pocket is lifted slightly so that the sewing can be done underneath the edge. Extra reinforcement is then given by sewing it from the wrong side. Pockets placed in this way are easily removed and lowered when the original placement has been outgrown, and no stitch marks are left, as they would be on a machine-stitched pocket.

Patch pockets on sport jackets are often stitched invisibly by hand to give the look of being sewed from the inner side of the pocket, no stitching of any sort showing on the outside. They are bridge stitched too, and also reinforced from the wrong side of the garment.

The patch pocket with separate flap

This is the pocket featured on the coat in chapter 5. The patch pocket is made exactly like the one just described. The flap is then constructed exactly like the one used for the set-in flap pocket. When both units are complete, place them in the following manner:

Mark a goalpost. Place the flap above the symbol, with the raw edges on the horizontal line, and sew into place ¼ inch away from the seam edge. (Fig. 137a.) If the fabric edges are bulky, cut off the top edge of the flap right to the stitching, and trim the rest of the edge down to ⅛-inch width. Then fold the flap downward and press. Place

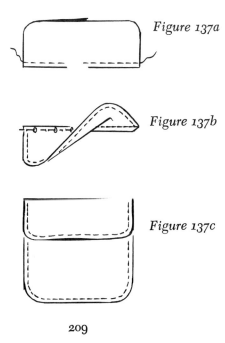

Figure 137a

Figure 137b

Figure 137c

a row of pins horizontally across the top, about ¼ inch down from the upper part of the flap, covering up the remaining raw edges of the flap; then hand sew the underside of the flap to the garment with the bridge stitch, so that the raw edges will remain permanently concealed. (Fig. 137b.)

Now place the patch pocket underneath the flap, just as close as it can go, in a direct line with the flap on both edges. Pin it into place and sew it to the garment in any desired manner, either by hand or machine. (Fig. 137c.)

Side pockets for pants

To insert pockets into side seams of trousers, first fit the pants to the person so that proper fitting is assured before the pockets are put in. Sew the side seams together as fitted, then press the seams open. Now rip open the seams from the waistline down to the depth that you expect to make the pockets. The pressed fold will greatly aid in retaining shape and keep the sides of the pants smooth and trim in appearance.

Cut two pieces of kidney-shaped pocket linings out of strong cotton for each pocket. On one of the pockets, sew a strip of pants material, 1½ inches wide. Superimpose this piece of cloth on the lining piece, not joining it as an extension as was done on other pockets. Sew the faced lining piece to the side seam of the pants back, with right sides of the fabrics facing each other. (Fig. 138a.) The plain piece of lining

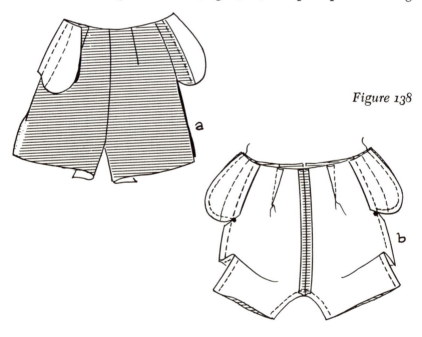

Figure 138

is joined to the sides of the pants fronts, using the creases made by the pressing as guidelines for sewing both lining pieces to their respective sides, so that the shape and fit of the pants is not altered in any way. Next, sew the sides of the back and front of the pants together, including the outer edges of the pockets. (Fig. 138b.) Attach a waistband to the pants, directing the inside of the pockets toward the center front of the pants and catching the upper parts of the pockets into the stitching of the waistband. Finish the rest of the band just as you would when attaching a waistband to a skirt.

The seam pocket

When garments are designed with vertical panels, like front and side fronts, for example, pockets are often inserted into the seams. Extensions are usually allowed on the seams in the area where the pockets go, and these extended parts eventually become the facings to which the pocket linings will be attached. If the person is shorter than average, you should hold the pattern against the person's shoulders to see whether or not the pockets need to be raised. If they do, when cutting the panels raise the extensions to a more suitable location. You can do this merely by drawing the extensions higher up on the seam, using chalk, but be careful not to raise the extensions too much.

If the individual is taller than average, the pocket extensions may have to be lowered to where the reach of the hands would be right. Make pocket linings from the material used for the garment lining, unless it is too delicate, in which case substitute a more durable material in the color of the outer fabric.

Attach the lining pieces to each of the extensions of the panels first, then pin the garment parts together for stitching. When joining the garment pieces, carry the stitching continuously around the pocket linings (Fig. 139a) and clip the seam of the side panel after the stitching so that the seam can be properly pressed above and below the pockets. Spread the seam edges apart in pressing, but press the pockets in a forward direction. Hand stitch the lining seams securely to the canvas interfacings without going through to the outside material. After the facing is attached and pressed to the inside of the fronts, tack it into its permanent position, making sure not to sew through the layers of the pocket linings. Put your hand inside the pocket when tacking these edges to be sure to keep the lining pieces separated. (Fig. 139b.)

These seam pockets are just as effective in other garments as they are in jackets and coats, and are often featured in dresses and skirts. When the pockets are not wide enough to come together in the center underneath the outside layers of the garment, it is necessary to attach a strip of lining material to each pocket lining so they can be held together and prevented from sagging over the stomach and causing

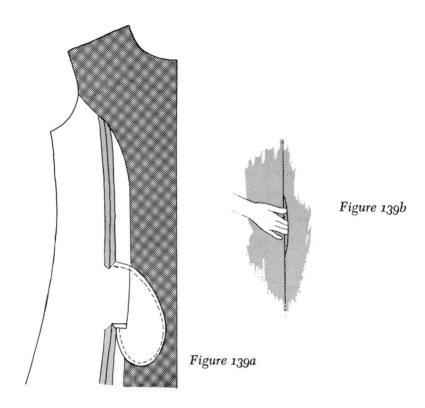

Figure 139b

Figure 139a

bulk. The strip which holds the pockets together should be about 3 inches wide and located midway between the top and bottom of the pockets. Hand stitching can be used to attach the strip in place.

11
Fashion Detailing

What is a welt seam?

Welt seams enhance the appearance of coats made of fleecy fabrics as well as those made from heavy tweeds. Even if the pattern calls for plain seams, you can improvise welt seams without disturbing the lines or size of the garment.

Cut the garment as you would for plain seaming. Sew the seam first with the right sides of the fabrics together. Then trim off one of the seam edges to ¼-inch width, but leave the other one full width. Do the trimming before you do any pressing. Then, working on the inside of the garment, press the full-width seam edge down to cover up the narrow edge. Press with a light touch to avoid marking the fabric. Turn the work over to the right side, and make a row of stitching ½ inch away from the groove of the seam line, catching the edge of the wide seam into the stitching on the underside. (Fig. 140.) Machine

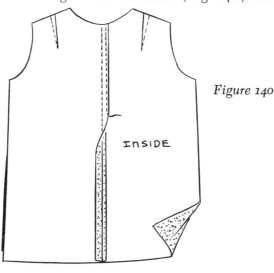

Figure 140

INSIDE

213

stitching should be about 12 stitches to the inch and no more. Too-close stitching on heavy fabrics is not flexible, and eventually pulls up and causes puckering.

If you are using solid-colored material for the garment, you can substitute hand sewing for the machine stitching on the welt seams to give the garment a rich look. There are two ways of hand finishing such seams: saddle stitching (which is an in-and-out stitching in which both the "in" and the "out" stitches are about ¼ inch in length), or hand picking. The latter is done with backstitches. Both of these finishes are popular, but hand picking holds seams in place more securely than saddle stitching.

Hand picking

After you have prepared and pressed the seams in their proper direction, the wide edge over the narrow, bring the thread through to the surface of the garment, ½ inch away from the groove of the seam, starting at either the top or bottom. With the thread on the right side of the garment, take a ¼-inch backstitch and bring the thread and needle back to the surface of the work ½ inch to the left of the starting point. Your next stitch will be ¼ inch to the right of where the needle just came out, quite close to the stitch already completed. Draw the thread up just enough to cause the surface of the fabric to dimple a little without pulling too much. The surface should dent in only where the stitching is. The rest should remain flat. Use single strands of button-hole twist or embroidery cotton of similar thickness, either in self-color or a slightly darker shade. (Fig. 141.)

Figure 141

OUTSIDE

214

Shoulders should also be welt-seamed. Although there is no hard-and-fast rule about which direction to aim the wider edge of the seam at the center back, the shoulders should be done in the following way: Trim off the edges of the garment fronts on the inside of the garment after the first stitching line has been made; then direct the back edges of the shoulders over the narrowed edges, and sew ½ inch from the groove of the seam, on the right side of the cloth, either by hand or machine, catching the wide edge of the back shoulders into the stitching.

If the sleeves have a center seam running down from the shoulders to the bottom, they should be welt-seamed too. Cut off the seam edges of the fronts so that the back seams of the sleeves can be directed forward and then sewn exactly like the shoulders, to match each other when the sleeves are inserted into the armholes. The underarm seam of the sleeve should be sewed with a plain seam and the edges pressed apart, but the garment side seams should be welt trimmed, the front edge cut off and the back edge directed over it to be sewed from the outside.

Insert sleeves into the armholes in the usual way, but at the place where the notches are matched in the front and back, clip the seam inward directly to the stitching line. The seams are then allowed to remain in their upright direction in the undersection of the armhole, but the top edges are welted, and the *armhole edge* cut off to ¼ inch from clipping to clipping. Then pin the sleeve edge over the narrow edges on the outside of the garment. The welt seam is done on the outside of the garment, by starting directly against the groove about ½ inch and then turning to sew in a line parallel to the groove around the upper edge of the armhole. Continue sewing to the opposite clipped area; then turn and sew toward the groove of the seam, and box the stitching line at both ends. (Fig. 142.)

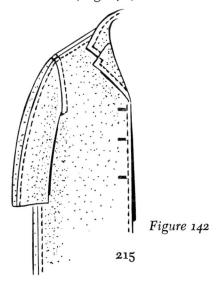

Figure 142

The collar and front edges of the garment should also be trim stitched to match the welt seams. If the stitching has not already been done on the collar, you may do it now. Start the stitching at the neckline seam at one end of the collar, and sew around the outer edges on the right side of the garment, ½ inch away from the edge. Draw the ends of the threads through to the underside of the collar, tie, and trim off closely.

When the garment has turned-over lapels and stitching is featured on the fronts, do the sewing in three separate operations that will look like one. Here's how to do it: From the top buttonhole and button, proceeding to the bottom and going right through the finished hem, sew on the *outside* of the garment about ½ inch away from the outer edge. Then start to sew upward from the button and buttonhole area but on the *inside* of the garment, overlapping the stitching line ¼ inch for reinforcement. Proceed to the point of the lapel and turn a nice neat corner, sewing toward the collar area, keeping the same distance from the edge here as on the fronts. When the collar ends have been reached, turn another corner and sew upward to the groove of the neckline seam, ending the stitching there. Transfer the threads to the underside of the collar and cut them off closely. A knot is not necessary. When the garment features buttons and buttonholes that go *right* up to the top of lapels, the sewing should be done on the right side of the garment only.

If the rest of the seams were hand picked, finish the front and collar in the same way. Hand sewing gives the appearance of going through the complete thickness of the garment, but it doesn't. Only part of the garment front is sewed through. If you want the inside of the garment fronts to look the same as the outside, you will have to sew twice—once on the outside and once on the inside, without coming to the opposite surface in either case.

Saddle stitching

A seam is made the same way whether it is to be saddle stitched or hand picked. There is a similarity in the appearance of the stitch whichever finish is used. Hand picking leaves the cloth dimpled where the stitches are, whereas saddle stitching doesn't. Both are very effective, although saddle stitching is used more for casual wear—such as summer dresses, blouses, and other indoor wearing apparel—while hand picking is most often used on coats and suit jackets.

Although one row of saddle stitching can be very effective, two or more rows are even more so. Embroidery floss or buttonhole twist can be used for this work, either in self-color, or a harmonizing or contrasting one. Woolen yarns also make effective saddle stitching for some articles, if you don't use too heavy a strand. The stitches are usually ¼ inch long, both when they are being made "in" and "out," although they can be varied, with a longer stitch on the surface of the garment and a shorter one inside. (Figs. 143a and b.) shows both ways. Experiment a little to find the stitch length and type of floss or yarn you prefer.

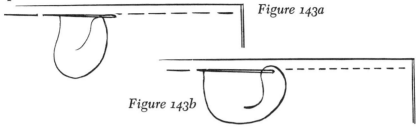

Figure 143a

Figure 143b

Trim stitching edges on tailored things

When machine stitching is featured on edges of collars, cuffs, flaps, and other parts of a tailored garment, it can be done in the process of construction while the parts are still separate units. The trim-stitched parts are then applied to the garment. When the trim stitching is done by hand, like hand picking or saddle stitching, the work can be done after the whole garment has been completed.

To stitch around the lapels and fronts of a jacket or coat styled with lapels that spread over the chest, the way a sport jacket would, for example, the stitching is done in a few steps, although the finished results look as if this trimming was done all in one operation. Do it this way: From the top buttonhole down to the bottom of the front, or to the end of the curve, if it is a cutaway front, do the machine trim stitching on the outside of the garment, leaving long threads at each end and at top and bottom too.

Now go back to the starting point of the machine stitching at the buttonhole area, turning the work over so that you will be sewing on the *facing* part of the garment. Start sewing upward, overlapping a couple of stitches that are already there, and proceed up to the point of the lapel. Then turn and stitch toward the collar. End the stitching line so it will look like the stitching on a ready-made garment of the type you are making. Copy the way it has been done there and you can't go wrong. (Fig. 144.)

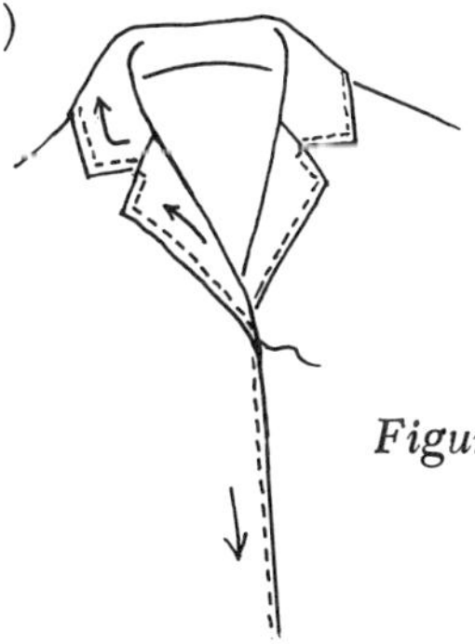

Figure 144

217

The trim stitching is repeated in the same order on the other front of the garment. Pull the long threads through the eye of a hand-sewing needle, then through to the inside of the layers. Bring the needle out to the surface about 2 or 3 inches away and cut the threads off close to the surface of the cloth so that they slip down under and disappear.

Top stitching is done piecemeal instead of in one continuous operation because the stitching looks better on the top side than on the underside, so it is the better-looking side that will be showing. The pressing on these edges is also done in the manner of the stitching, always pressing the part of the garment that will be underneath so no press marks are made on the parts that show.

On garments styled to be worn buttoned up to the neck, as well as opened, the top stitching is done on the outside of the fronts as carefully as possible to produce the best appearance on both sides of the garment, since part of the upper facing will show when the collar is worn open.

Trim stitching polyesters

The only way to flatten the seams and edges of many garments made from some synthetic materials is by stitching them flat. Regular pressing should not be skipped, however, during the construction of the garment, as it is important to direct seams so they are caught into the next joining step in the right way.

If the seams do not flatten as much as they do in other materials, they are expected to look slightly unpressed and dented inward. Press them as much as possible along the way. Only the outer edges need to be flattened by top stitching so that they do not puff after the regular press job has been done. Wherever there are layers to hold together, as in collars, cuffs, lapels, and fronts, they should be topped with trim stitching.

Although many people like to make this top stitching outstanding by using fancy silk threads, it is not really necessary. The regular thread used for general stitching does a nice neat job, as long as the lines of stitching are straight and the same distance away from the edges on all the parts of the garment that are being detailed with top stitching.

The superimposed decorative collar

One of the most effective ways of adding a smart touch to a garment is to superimpose a top collar of another material on the collar that is already there. It is often made of velvet, velveteen, or some other elegant material that will complement the garment fabric. Cut this top collar on the true bias weave of the decorative material and apply it by invisible hand stitching, the bridge stitch, after the garment is finished, so it does not affect the regular construction of the neckline. Fold the

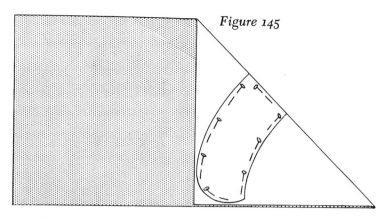

Figure 145

trimming fabric on the bias, and cut it exactly the size of the original collar, using the garment collar pattern even though it is going to be reduced in size later on. (Fig. 145.) Leave the neck edge as is, but trim away the ⅜-inch seam allowance on the other three edges. Now run a line of machine stitching around all four edges, ⅜ inch in from the edge. This stitching will control the collar edges and keep them from stretching out of shape. It is especially important if the edges are curved, because such edges are so very flexible.

Turn the outer edges of the collar under through the line of stitching and hand baste flat on all edges. While basting, roll the collar edges a little to bring the machine stitching just underneath the collar. If the neck edge of the collar is curved, you may have to clip inward on the edge to make the material fall right. (Fig. 146a.) If the neck edge is straight, it is not necessary to do any clipping. However, if the material is heavy, corners must be carefully folded and some of the seam edge cut away to avoid bulk. (Fig. 146b.)

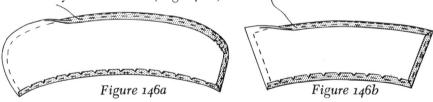

Figure 146a   Figure 146b

Arrange the top collar on the garment collar, starting at the center of the neckline and working outward toward each end. Because ⅜ inch was trimmed from the outer edges of the top collar, there will be a cloth border ⅜ inch wide surrounding the outer edges of the top collar, but the neck edge of the top collar will fit right up against the seam line that holds the original collar in place. Insert the pins as shown in Fig. 147. Hand sew the top collar with the bridge stitch, keeping the stitches easy, lest they pull and cause puckers. Remove the basting stitches and press lightly on the under-collar side. If the top collar is of velvet or velveteen use a dry iron, since steam would flatten the nap.

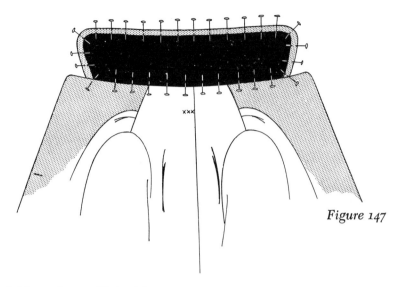

Figure 147

Finishing edges with braid

When fancy braid, of the type that is already folded over through the middle, is used on the edges of garments, it is necessary to first dispose of the usual ⅝-inch seam allowance. For example, in making a garment that has a facing on the inside of the front and neckline, the layers of the garment parts are placed with *wrong* sides together and stitched with the ⅝-inch seam allowance. Then trim the seam off right up to the stitching, and apply the braid. The first edge of the braid may be stitched on by machine and the other finished by hand, catching the hand stitches to those done by machine, and doing it as invisibly as possible. The braid can be machine stitched to the outside or the inside of the garment, and the hand stitches can also be done on either side. Just be sure they are invisible. (Fig. 148.)

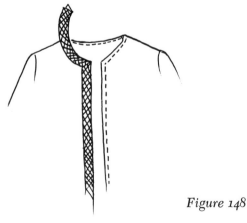

Figure 148

Applying braid when collar and lapels are featured

Again, it is important that the seam allowance be removed and the braid be sewed by machine on the first side and by hand on the reverse. Turn the ends of the braid in at the start and finish of the trimmed areas. Put the braid on in three strips, one for the collar edges, plus enough to turn in at each end, and one separate strip for each front. (Fig. 149.) Put the braid on after the hem has been turned up so that the braid can be sewed through all the layers of the garment, hem and all.

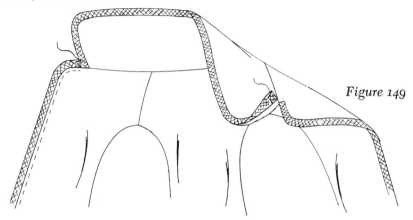

Figure 149

Using bias strips for trim instead of braid

Bias-cut strips of material can be applied in the same way as the braid to the collar and front edges of a tailored garment. Stitch the first edge on with the right sides together against the outside of the garment parts, the distance from the edge depending upon how wide a trim is desired. Tuck the second edge in neatly and hand stitch it invisibly, catching the hand stitching to the machine stitches. The width of the bias-cut strips depends upon the width of trim desired. A little experimenting with scraps of the garment cloth and the bias stripping is advisable so that you can judge the appearance of the job as well as the width of the strips to be used.

The ⅝-inch seam allowance is removed from the edges that will be finished with these bias trimmings, just as is done when using braid.

Applying scallops

Scalloping the edges of garment parts makes interesting detail. If scalloping appears on your pattern design, transfer the scallops from the pattern pieces to the wrong side of the facings of the garment parts, like the under collars, or to the under side of facings of fronts, or bottoms, using a sharp hard lead pencil and some carbon paper placed directly underneath the pattern pieces. Then stitch through the tracing carefully, making sure that the needle is left in the work where the low points between the scallops are. Lift up the presser foot so that the work can be easily pivoted to form the right shape at that point. If the points between the scallops are too sharp, there will be puckers on the right side when the scallops are turned over. The points must be shaped exactly like the tracings, with wide V-shaped lines instead of spearheads.

Trim the seams to ¼-inch width and clip straight down into the pointed seam to the line of stitching, without cutting the stitches. (Fig. 150.) Turn the scallops right side out and baste into shape for pressing. When basting be sure to mold the seams around each scallop into curves with your fingers; otherwise they will be uneven and pointed here and there.

Figure 150

Scallops can be applied to any edge you wish, whether the pattern features them or not. They can be drawn onto collarless necklines, the edges of collars and cuffs, or down the fronts and along the bottoms of all kinds of wearing apparel.

Make yourself a scalloping guide from a strip of paper folded back and forth accordion fashion. (Fig. 151a.) The folds of the guide should be the width you wish the scallops to be. (Fig. 151b.) Cut the folded guide into an arc and it is ready to use. Place it on the part of the garment you wish to scallop and draw the shapes of the scallops lightly with pencil. Then sew through the pencil lines. (Fig. 151c.)

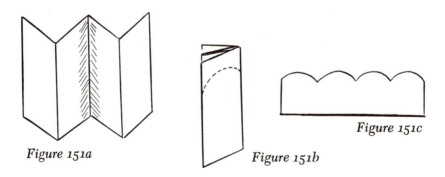

Figure 151a

Figure 151b

Figure 151c

The many uses of bias-cut stripping

Regardless of the shape in which bias stripping is going to be used as a trimming feature, be it on straight, diagonal, or curved edge, the stripping itself must be cut on the *true* bias weave. Otherwise it will not conform correctly to the shape to which it is applied.

What you should do is fold the cloth into a triangle with the cross-weave of the fabric over the straight edge of the selvage, just as if you were folding a dinner napkin into a triangle. This will produce a true bias fold. Cut through the fold and use the cut edges as guides by which to cut the binding strips. (Fig. 152a.)

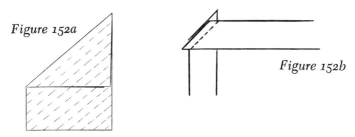

Figure 152a

Figure 152b

Quite often, when a long edge is being finished with bias stripping, it is necessary to sew several pieces of binding together to make it long enough. To do this, place the right sides of the materials facing each other and allow the pointed ends of the bias strips to extend out on each side of the widths, just as in Fig. 152b. Then sew the strips together, starting and ending your line of stitching in the little "valley" produced when the strips are placed together properly.

Bound neckline

There is no set rule as to how wide a binding should be used for trimming. When part of the bias strip is going to show on the right side of the garment as a styling detail, the width should suit the personal taste. A very popular width of bias trim allows ¼ inch to show on the right side of a garment. To make it, cut the flat bias strip about 2 inches wide and fold it right side out with the raw edges even. Before applying the binding, cut away the ⅝-inch seam allowance from around the neckline so that the bound finish will make the neck end up the same size it would be had the usual facing been applied to it instead of this type of detailing. If the seam allowance is not removed, the neck ends up too small.

Start by putting the raw edges of the binding against the right side of the neckline at the garment opening, allowing the bias strip to project ⅝ inch past the opening. Then sew it on with a ¼-inch or ½-inch seam. As you sew, hold the binding slightly stretched, but don't stretch the neck. This makes the bias go on smoothly and unless it is applied in this way, the bias trimming is very apt to pucker when finished. Then the neckline ends up too loose. When the stitching has been finished, trim the seam edges just enough to even them up, but don't narrow them down any more than necessary or the outside finish will not be the width you planned.

Turn the folded edge of the bias strip over to the inside of the neckline, but keep the raw edges upright so that the bias strip will wrap around them to form a roll on the outside of the garment. (Fig. 153.)

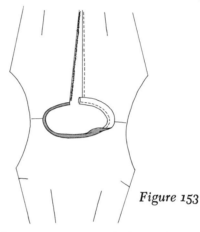

Figure 153

To finish this binding, you must work from the right side of the garment, sewing into the groove of the seam directly below the binding. It is of utmost importance to see that the raw edges are constantly wrapped in the bias strip during the stitching because if they slip away and become directed downward, the roll that forms the trim around the neck will be distorted. The raw edges that are wrapped, rather than the bias stripping, produces the rounded finish on the outside and give it a corded look. Use your left thumb to push the raw edges into the proper direction and the thumb and forefinger of the right hand to hold the work in position during the stitching. When the raw edges are caught into the stitching in the proper position, and the stitching is done right in the groove of the seam, this last stitching will not show on the outside of the garment after the neckline has been pressed on the inside. The bias will flatten down just enough to lap down over the stitches and hide them. (Fig. 154.)

You can finish sleeveless armholes in the same way. This method eliminates the necessity of putting an extra shaped facing around them, since the binding does the complete job of facing and adding firmness. The binding is done after the sides of the bodice have been joined. Start the binding at the underarm, with a narrow edge turned in.

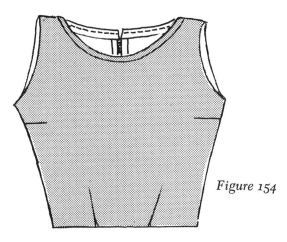

Figure 154

Even if you desire bias finish wider than ¼ inch, you should cut the binding as for ¼-inch width. Apply the binding in the same manner, but do the stitching farther in from the edge. Then hand sew the folded edge of the binding to the inside of the neckline; attach this edge either to the stitching that is visible on the inside, or to the fabric above the stitching if the folded edge doesn't quite reach the stitching. It is important to keep the outer width uniform all around the neckline. For heavy textures use the bias single instead of double fold.

For added trim interest, apply binding to the outer edges of collars and cuffs. Put the collar together with the interfacing between the upper- and under-collar pieces and with the raw edges of all parts on the outside of the collar. Sew through all the layers ⅜ inch away from the edge; then cut the edges off ¼ inch from the stitching line. Cut the bias strip that will be used for trimming to about 2½ inches wide and fold it lengthwise. Then sew it to the outside of the upper collar about ¼ inch away from the edge, making sure that the first line of stitching that holds the layers together does not show. Fold the strip over to the underside of the collar and the stitch on the right side through the groove of the seam line. The stitching won't show when the collar is finished and pressed. (Fig. 155.)

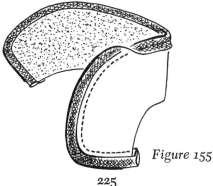

Figure 155

Attaching collars with bias strip

Bias strips are used instead of shaped facings to finish necklines when the collar on a garment will always be worn closed. This is also a very good way to treat the neckline when the material used is sheer and facings would show through. The bias finish doesn't show at all, since the collar hides it. Cut the bias strip about 2 inches wide and fold it lengthwise or, if the cloth is too heavy, use the bias strip single. Pin the raw edges to those of the collar and neckline and stitch them together. (Fig. 156.) Trim the seam down to ¼-inch width; turn the bias to the inside of the garment, and attach the fold into position either by hand or by machine. If the bias strip has been used single, tuck the raw edge of the strip and finish neatly by hand.

Figure 156

Trimmings made from "spaghetti" cording

Decorative cordings made from garment fabrics give the finished product a very smart and professional touch. From cloth cordings you can make loops for closings. The cording can be used as trim around a neckline or as an edging around a collar and other edges. The cording is very simple to make. Just cut strips of different widths on the true bias weave of the material and stitch them into tubular shapes. For short lengths of cording you can use up some of your scraps. You can even use short pieces to make long cordings by sewing the pieces together. When pressed flat, the seams will never show. For a slim type of cording cut the bias strip about 1¼ inches wide. Fold the material with right sides together lengthwise and stitch ¼ inch away from the folded edge. Stretch the strip to its utmost during the stitching so that the stitching line will have flexibility. Otherwise the thread

226

will break from the strain put upon the flexible bias weave of the cloth in turning the cording over to the right side. At one end of the stitching, flare out the seams so that the tubing will be widened out in the shape of a cone. This will make it easy to turn the cording outward.

A bobby pin is a very good gadget for turning bias tubing to the right side. Poke it through a generous portion of the wide-stitched end and slide it into position so that its open end is headed toward the inside of the tube. Continue to slide until it comes out at the opposite end, bringing the finished cording with it. (Figs. 157a and b.) The raw edges of the bias strip were left untrimmed to act as fillers, giving the finished cording a round, firm look; the cording will be about ¼ inch thick.

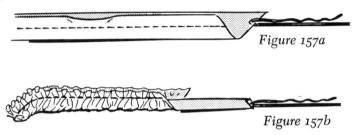

Figure 157a

Figure 157b

When a heavier cording is desired, cut the bias strip the same width as for the narrower, 1¼ inches wide, but sew farther away from the fold. Leave the raw edges untrimmed, and turn the strip right side out with the bobby pin. Additional roundness is obtained by pulling several strands of wool or nylon yarn through the tubing with the bobby pin. The number of strands depends upon the thickness of the yarn used. Make sure to use yarn that is no darker in color than the fabric used for the tubing, as dark yarns will show through and make the cording look soiled. If the cording is made of a washable fabric, use nylon yarn to avoid shrinkage problems. Also, either be sure that the yarn is colorfast or use white.

When cordings are made from extra heavy fabrics, it is necessary to cut off some of the raw edges after stitching. The heavier and harder the fabric texture, the less seam edge you can pull through the tubing without a struggle when turning it right side out. Trim off a little of the edge at a time, testing to see if it will come through. If the cording is too soft, or if it flattens out when formed into a loop, pull some yarn into it to give it firmness. Coating fabrics and velveteens may have to be treated this way.

How to make cloth loops

Although it is not necessary to select the buttons before the loops are made, it is important that you have an idea of their general size. Make a few practice loops before you do the real ones, just to see to what length they will have to be cut. Cording loops are flexible, and the buttons to go with them will not be hard to find, since the loops will expand a little. Covered buttons and tiny ball-shaped pearl or metal ones go well with loops, especially on princess-style coats and dresses for little girls.

Cut the bias cording into short even pieces, the lengths depending upon the size of loops desired. Place the first loop ⅜ inch away from the top edge of the article (let us assume that this is a neck closing), leaving enough edge for a seam at the top. Place the loops on the right side of the fabric, on the right-hand side of the opening. Form the cording into a small arc, the ends separated just enough to fit the approximate diameter of the button you'll be using. Cording has a visible seam, and the seamed side should be placed facing upward when the loops are pinned to the garment closing so that this side of the loop will be on the inside of the garment when finished. Each end of the loop is placed at the edge of the opening and pinned into place, with pins inserted horizontally. (Fig. 158.). Place the loops one against the other with no space between them. Only the arcs will have open spaces in them. When all the loops have been pinned into place, stitch them ⅛ inch away from the edges of both loops and garment opening. If you make a deeper seam, the bottom of the opening will gap.

Now place the back facing with right sides together on the garment, and pin it into position over the loops. Stitch on the garment side, sewing through the same stitching that holds the loops in place. When stitching at the bottom of the opening, shape the line of stitching to resemble a pointed U or a rounded V about ¼ inch below the opening, so that the seam can be clipped right to the stitching without danger of fraying. Then turn the facing to the inside of the garment and press. It is not necessary to tack this facing by hand, as it will stay in place when pressed well. (Fig. 159.)

Figure 158   *Figure 159*

Loop-trimmed neckline

Outer edges of collars can be very effectively trimmed with bias cording made from either contrasting or self-material. For example, if a child's dress has a white piqué or linen collar, it can be enhanced with loops of the garment material, be it plaid, check, print, or solid color. Just arrange short lengths of evenly cut cording around the edge of the upper collar, on the right side of the cloth, in any design you wish. Pin the ends of the cording just as you did on the opening. It is a good idea to arrange the cording trim from the front ends and work toward the center back so that the fronts match exactly. Slight alterations can then be made at the center back to make the loops come out even, by crowding or spreading them a little. (Fig. 160.) Stitch ⅜ inch from the edge. Place the under collar and interfacing with right sides together against the upper collar, pin and sew, sewing on the upper-collar side so that the line of stitching can be put through that which holds the loops in place. Turn the collar over to the right side, baste the outer edge, and press well on a Turkish towel so that the loops remain round and shapely. (Fig. 161.)

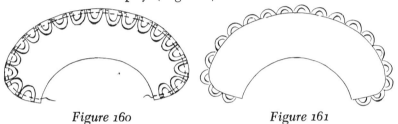

Figure 160   Figure 161

You can use bias cording to outline the neck of a collarless party dress. Cut the neckline wider and deeper than the regulation close-fitting type. Hold the pattern of the dress bodice up to your model and determine just how wide and deep the neckline should be; then sketch the new neckline on the pattern piece, adding extra, of course, for seam allowance. Cut the neckline accordingly. Then cut two sets of loops, one long set and one slightly shorter. Arrange the longer loops in arcs around the neckline, pinning them to the right side of the neck, starting at the centers of back and front and working toward the shoulders, keeping the seamed side of the cording up so that it will not show when the garment is worn. The loops should touch each other as each forms its arc. Sew these in place first; then arrange the shorter pieces in smaller arcs inside the large ones, pinning them into place and running a row of machine stitching through the first row. (Fig. 162.)

Figure 162   Figure 163

Next pin the inside facing to the outside of the bodice neckline, right sides together, and sew through the stitching lines that hold the cording in place. Trim seam to ¼ inch, and turn facing to inside of garment. Press from the wrong side on a bath towel to keep the cording round. A very nice scalloped effect is created with this treatment. (Fig. 163.)

Here is another interesting and attractive version of the corded neck trimming: Cut two sets of loops, one set slightly longer than the other, as before. Sew both sets of loops to the edge of the neckline as you did before but with the seamed side of the cording down against the garment this time. Cut a bias strip 2 inches wide, fold it through the center right side out, and place the raw edges against those of the cording and neckline on the outside of the garment. Stretch the bias strip slightly as you sew it into place with a ½-inch seam. Trim the seam down to ¼-inch width and turn the folded edge to the inside, allowing a roll of ¼-inch width to remain on the outside of the neck. Sew the folded edge inside of the garment by hand, catching the stitches to the machine ones that hold the cordings in place. (Fig. 164.) This last operation is similar to the one used on the plain bound neckline. A single row of arcs can also be used if a less elaborate trim is preferred.

Figure 164

Making and applying welt cording.

The covering for this type of cording is made from strips of bias cut material 2 inches wide, and joinings can be made quite inconspicuously. Wrap the bias strip around cable cording of the desired thickness. Most notion counters carry cording in a few thicknesses. It is usually made of white cotton and sold by the yard. After wrapping the cloth around the cording, use the cording foot to run a line of machine stitching as close as possible to the cording, the material facing right side out. This will resemble welting that is usually sold in drapery departments for inserting in the seams of slipcovers or fancy pillows. (Fig. 165a.)

When there is to be welt cording around the waist, the garment is constructed with the steps in a slightly different order from that used when the bodice and skirt are joined only by a plain seam. The bodice of the garment is completed first, fitted and sewed at the sides, the

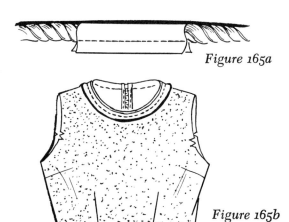

Figure 165a

Figure 165b

zipper seam left open. The skirt is also completed, with an opening where the zipper will be. (Necklines may also be trimmed with this type of cording.)

Place the welt cording on the right side of the bodice, with the raw edges directed downward and the stitching line of the cording on the chalked-in waistline. Sew the cording to the bodice with the cording foot. (Fig. 165b.) (Without this special foot, you couldn't sew close enough to the cording to do a good job.) Then pin and stitch the skirt, with the right sides of the fabric together, sewing through the same stitching that holds the cording in place.

When inserting a zipper in a garment with welt cording around the neckline or waist, it is advisable to remove some of the cording from the opened ends of the bias casing to avoid bulk: when the opening is folded over to cover the zipper, only one layer of cording will remain in the welt. The part of the welting that is turned under is empty.

Welt cording can be made of contrasting or harmonizing colors or from one of the colors of a printed design. Welting is very effective when used to outline collars, as well as on the fronts of button-down-the-front garments. Blazers are enhanced when the outer edges of fronts and collars are outlined with welting white on navy, red on gray, or perhaps a combination of your child's school colors.

Fake cording

A very easy and effective way to achieve the appearance of a corded waistline without the extra work involved, and minus the bulk, is to finish the dress completely first, hemming and all. Then make the spaghetti cording and bridge stitch it right over the seam that joins the

231

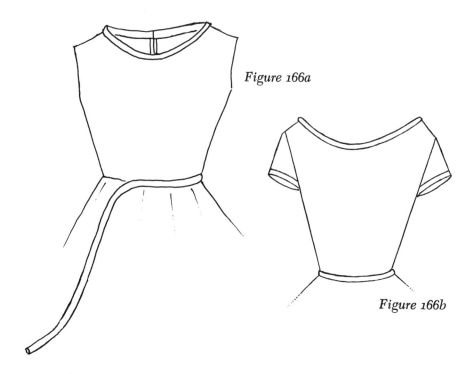

Figure 166a

Figure 166b

bodice and skirt together. Place the seamed part of the cording against the seam at the waist and this will give exactly the same effect as if the cording had been inserted. (Fig. 166a.) You can go a step further, if you want to, by hand stitching some of the cording to the neck, sleeveless armholes, or to bottoms of sleeves. You'll be pleased with the results. (Fig. 166b.)

A few belt ideas

The tailored belt

Different kinds of belt kits are sold at the notion counters of department and fabric stores, including all the essentials for making good-looking tailored belts for your home-sewn apparel. The belts come in a variety of widths and the instructions are easy to follow. Buckles in different shapes to go with the belts and adhesives needed to cover the buckles neatly with fabric are included. The kits are inexpensive. For such belts the cloth may be used either on the width or length weave, whichever is most suitable for the material being used. For example, stripes look best when they run horizontally on a belt, and so does corduroy or any fabric that has lines running through it.

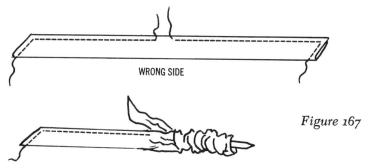

WRONG SIDE

Figure 167

The tie belt

The tie belt is usually cut from the length of the cloth so that it can be made long enough without piecing. When planning to make such a belt, reserve a strip of the material for it alongside of one of the selvage edges of the material before pinning the pattern to the garment for the rest of the parts.

Fold the material wrong side out and stitch all around, except for a short opening in the long edge right in the center, about 1½ inches long. (Fig. 167a.) Tuck a small amount of one of the belt ends inward to form a little pocket; then insert the eraser end of a pencil into the pocket and push through to the opening. When the right side of the belt comes to the opening, pull that end out and shake out the pencil. (Fig. 167b.) Treat the opposite end of the belt in the same way. After the belt has been pressed flat finish the opening with bridge stitching.

The bias cut sash

Wide sashes look best when they are cut on the bias weave of the cloth so that they crush softly around the waist. They usually have to be pieced to make them long enough, and the piecing should be done on the straight-of-the-goods edges so that they run diagonally when the sash is worn and the piecing will not show. Plan the piecing seams so they come in the part of the sash that will wrap around the waist rather than in the parts of the sash that will fall loosely below the waist. The sash can be made of either single material or double. When it is made of a single layer, the fabric should be reversible so that both sides of the sash look the same in the parts that will fall free from the waist and where both sides will show. The outer edges of this sash are rolled and the tiniest possible hem is done by hand, the kind of finish you so often see on fine silk scarves and those made of chiffon. Run a line of machine stitching ¼ inch in from the edge through the single layer and then, with moistened finger and thumb, roll the edge into a tight little hem until the raw edges disappear inside. Hand sew through the roll, then take a tiny stitch into the cloth. Hide the knot at the starting point inside of the roll. (Fig. 168.)

The bias sash is often made from double fabric, cut wide enough to form into the width desired. It is them folded over and stitched around all raw edges like the belt made from the straight weave of cloth. When the sash is turned over to the right side, the seamed edges are basted together so they can be pressed without twisting. Press the edges lightly to avoid producing sharp creases. Soft edges will look nicer.

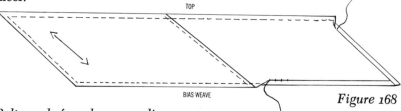

Figure 168

Belts made from heavy cording

Make a heavy cording by cutting the material about 1½ inches wide and stitching it ¼ inch in from the raw edges wrong side out. Stretch the bias strip when sewing it to give the stitches some "play" so they won't break when the belt is tied. Turn the tubing right side out with a bobby pin and then insert several strands of knitting yarn through the tube to make it round, but don't overstuff it or it will lose its suppleness. You can then tuck in the raw ends and sew them together, or pull out just a little of the yarn at the ends and tie knots in the cording. You can also decorate the ends with tassels or other decorative objects.

Belts made from thin cordings

Smaller cordings can be used for belts by either braiding them together or using them for macramé. You can also put a few thin cordings side by side and bridge stitch them together so they look corrugated in the body of the belt. Then let the ends fall separately so they will form into multiple hangings from the waistline down after being tied around the waist. (Fig. 169.)

Figure 169

The buttoned-together corded belt

Still another type of belt is made from medium-thick cording stuffed just lightly with yarns, and long enough so the cording can be doubled over to form a loop in the middle. The two cordings are then caught together invisibly by hand, leaving the loop part open so a fancy button can fit through. The button itself can be made from cording. (Fig. 170.)

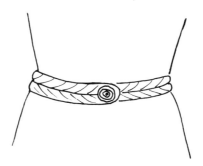

Figure 170

In Conclusion

Today's mothers, grandmothers, and aunts have many demands upon their time, and sewing is often set aside as something to be done someday in the future when the pressure is not so great.

The aim here has been to point out to the modern, busy woman how she can best utilize her sewing time to produce beautiful wearing apparel in the least amount of time with the least amount of effort. We hope this approach will enable her to obtain top value for the time spent at her sewing machine, as well as pride and satisfaction in the results.

The making of beautiful clothing is an art. Many women possess this talent without even realizing it, because they've never had the time or opportunity to discover it. Once you *do* discover it, you'll find it to be a great blessing. This book was written to help you uncover your talents, and to cultivate your interest in making lovely, worthwhile sewing projects.

Index

A-line dress
    girl's, 154, 160
    outgrown, camouflaging turned-over
        hemline, 172–173
Accessories, from outgrown garments,
    176–178, 179
"Ageless" styles, 34
Animal fibers, fabrics made from, 25,
    109. *See also* Woolens
Armholes
    adjustments in cutting, 42
    finishing
        bias-cut binding, 71
        corded, 232
        in dress with lining, 65
        in dress with underlining, 71, 181
        in flip-lined jumper, 80, 81, 82
        pile fabrics, 182
        sleeveless garment, 62, 159, 177,
            224–225
    insertion of sleeves, 59–60, 124–126
    welt seamed, in coat, 215

Ball fringe, as trim, 177
Basting
    avoiding unnecessary, 45
    collar, 52
    pocket placement, 45
Belts, 232–234
Bias strips, 221, 223–231
    armhole facing, 71
    cording, 223–231, 234
    finishing neck and armholes, 71, 159,
        223–226
    piecing of, 223
    trim using, 221–222, 223–231

Blazers, 145–147
    welt cording for, 231
Blistered fabrics, 181
Blouses, 163, 177
    cuffs, 170
    See also Shirts
Blousing, *see* Bodice (bloused)
Bodice
    fitting, 71–73
        bloused, 77–78
        empire, 79
        formfitted, 77
        in girl's dress, 159–160
        long, 79–80
    length, adjustment of, 16, 69, 78,
        154–155
    with set-in band, 173
Bolero, from outgrown garment, 179
Bonded fabrics, 188–189
Bonding net, for hems, 176, 178
Boys, sewing for
    coats, 102, 112
    pattern sizes, 22, 162
    sport shirts, 162
Braid
    to camouflage let-out hemline, 172–
        173
    as edging, 220–221
    to trim fake-fur coat, 192
Bridge stitch
    corded waistline, 231
    cording belt, 234
    linings, 138–139, 146
    pockets, 209
    superimposed collar, 218–219

Brother-and-sister clothes, 14
Buckles, covered, 232
Bust, measurement of, 16
Buttonhole pocket, 199–201
Buttonholes, 112–113
  bound, 193–198
  coats and jackets, 143, 147
  keyhole, 113
  machine-made, 32, 113, 148–149, 193
  marking, 107, 147–148, 170, 195
  placement, 147–149
  reinforcement, 113, 195, 197
Buttons
  corded loops for, 227–228
  sewing on, 149

Camel's-hair cloth, 25, 27
  coats, hand-sewn trim on, 116, 149, 205
Cardigan, from outgrown garment, 179
Cashmere cloth, 25
Catch stitch, 95, 101
Chalk for marking, 30
  to adjust pattern size, 39, 42, 69
  along cutting lines, 43–44
  darts, 44–45
  hemline, 63
  inside of garment, 56, 82, 85
  waistline, 72–73, 75, 78, 85
Checks, see Plaids
Chest measurement
  girls, 16
  men and boys, 17
Chiffon, 180–181
Children, clothes for
  fabrics, 23–24
  pattern sizes, 20–23
  ready-made, advantages of, 12–13, 14
  Sunday clothes, 14–15
Chubby children
  pattern sizes, 21
  styles, 154
Coatings
  cording from, 227
  fleecy, extra yardage required, 27
  pattern layout, 36
  synthetic, 103
Coats, 102–134
  buttonholes, 112–113
  children's, fabrics for, 23
  choice of style, 102–103

collar, 113–116
  attachment of, 116–120
    seam edges, trimming of, 114–115
  cutting fabric, 106–107
  fitting, 121–122, 125–126, 129
  interfacing, 110–112
  lapels, 120–121
  linings, 134–145
  outgrown, remodeling of, 178–179
  pattern layout, 104–106
  pockets, 199, 205, 206, 211
  pressing, 109–110
  trim stitching, 116, 217–218
  underlining, 103–104
  welt seaming, 213
Collarless styles
  neckline adjustments, 56–57
  neckline finishes
    bias cording, 229–230
    for girl's dress, 159
    for pile-surfaced material, 182
    scalloped edge, 222
Collars
  adjustment of size, 57–58
  bias-cut trim, 225
  braid trim, 221
  coat
    attachment, 116–118, 119–121
    fabrics for children's, 23
    stitching, to match welt seam, 216
  dress, 52, 159, 226
  loop trim, 229
  scalloped trim, 222
  shirt, 163–166
  superimposed decorative, 218–219
  tailored, 113–121
    attachment, 116–118, 119–121
    trimming of edge, 114–115
  trim stitched, 217, 218
  triple-layered, for sheer fabrics, 158
Colors, choice of, 33–34, 153
Cording, 226–232
  belts, 234
  button loops, 227–228
  button made from, 234
  neckline trim, 228–230
  turning to right side, 227, 234
  welt, 230–231
Corduroy, 25, 26, 182
  belts, 232
  children's leggings, 23
  hem finish, 175
Cotton fabrics
  for evening dresses, 66

Cotton fabrics (*cont.*)
napped, 25
pattern layout, 36–37
plaid, reblocking of, 183
shrinking, 29
widths, 26
Cross-stitching, 138, 139
Cuffs
bias-cut trim, 225
machine-stitched trim, 116
on outgrown sleeves, 179
scalloped edge, 222
shirt or blouse, 170
trim stitched, 217, 218
triple-layered, for sheer fabrics, 158, 180
Cutting the material, 37–38, 43–44
bonded fabrics, 188
coats, 106–107
fake fur, 191
leather, 189

Darts
adjustment of, 56
pants, 90–91
vertical, in side panels, 40–41
marking, 44–45
pressing, 12, 47, 70, 109
sewing, 45, 46, 69
silk fabrics, 180
splitting, 70, 108–109
underlining, 69–70
wrap-around skirt, 90
Double-breasted styles
placement of buttons, 149
for thin girls, 34
Dresses
adjustment of pattern size, 38–40, 42–43, 68–69, 78, 154–155
assembling, 40–41, 45–49, 52–54, 59
collars, 52, 57–59
attachment, 53–54, 59, 226
cutting, 41, 43, 69
evening, 66–76
fitting, 54–56, 71–73, 74–75, 77, 160
laying pattern, 37
lining, 64–65, 77
little girls', 151–161
choice of style and fabric, 151–154
loop trim, 228–229
marking inside for stitching, 56
outgrown, garments made from, 177–178, 179
sleeves, insertion of, 59–62, 159

underlining, 66–67, 69, 180, 182–183
See also Armholes; Bodice; Collars; Cutting; Facings; Hems; Jumper; Necklines; Sleeves; Waistline; Zipper
Drip-dry fabrics
interfacing, 52
reblocking of, 183
with non-drip-dry fabric, 161

Elastic casing at waist
knit pants, 95, 188
skirt or shorts, 177, 178, 188
Embroidery stitches
on collar, 157
with machine shirring, 157
Empire bodice, altering pattern for, 79
Evening dresses, 66–76
fabrics, 66, 180, 181
underlining, 68–70
workmanship required, 66

Fabrics
animal fibers, 25, 109
bonded, 188–189
for children's clothes, 23–26, 152, 153
drip-dry, 52, 161, 183
evening dresses, 66, 68
fake fur, 191–192
knit, 185–188
leftover, 161
lining, 134, 136
metallic, 181
printed, 182
quilted surface, 181
rayon, 26, 134, 136
right and wrong side, 45
silk, 26, 180–181
stretch, 31, 80, 185
underlining, 67, 68
velvet, 27, 182–183, 218
yardage, and width, 26–28
See also Cotton; Nap; Plaids; Polyester; Synthetic; Velveteen; Woolens
Facings
armhole, 62, 181
coat, attachment of, 117–118, 119–120
fabrics with nap, 182
flap pocket, 204
neck, 53, 54, 181
adjustment, 57

Facings (*cont.*)
  dress with underlining, 70–71
  girl's dress, 159
  shirt, 164
Fads, teen-age, 13–14
Fake fur
  coat, 191–192
  lining, 136, 144
Fake leather, 190–191
Fitting, 15
  altering pattern size, 38–40
  coats, 121–122
  dresses, 54–56, 71–73, 74–75, 77,
    160–161
  flip-lined jumper, 82
  pants, 91–93
  shoulders, importance in, 15, 18–19,
    35, 38
Flannel
  cotton, for interlining, 135
  for leggings, 23
Flap pockets, 203–205
Flaps
  marking placement, 45, 54
  patch pocket with, 209–210
  pocket, interfacing of, 111, 203
  trim stitched, 217
Flat-felled seams, 163, 166–167, 169–
  170
Flip lining, jumper with, 80–82
Fly-front closing, 93–94
Fraying, prevention of
  in armhole facings, 62
  in bound buttonholes, 193, 194, 198
  in metallic fabrics, 181
  with underlining, 67
French cuffs, 170
Fringe
  on girl's dress, 173
  on midriff top, 177
Fullness
  in bloused bodice, 77–78
  in hem of flared coat, 132–133
  See also "Magic stitching"; Shirring;
    Skirts (gathered, pleated); Smock-
    ing

Girls, clothing for
  coats, 102, 112, 132
  dresses, 33–34, 38, 66, 151–161
  pattern sizes, 22
  teen-age, 33–34
Grosgrain ribbon, on skirt without
  waistband, 89

Gusset, in kimono sleeve, 41

Hand picking, 214, 216
Hand sewing
  flap pocket, 205
  seam pocket, 212
  welt seams, 214
  zipper, 51
Hemline crease
  fabrics that shed or disguise, 23, 24
  ways to camouflage, 172–173
Hems and hemming
  allowance, 16–17, 63, 76
  catch stitch, 95, 101
  coats, 130–134
  finishing
    bonding net, 176
    dresses, 63
    jumper, 82
    knit fabrics, 175, 187
    linings, 65
    sheer materials, 158
    underlined evening dress, 76
  fullness, in flared garment, 132–133
  leather garments, 189
  lengthened garments, 171–172, 173–
    175
  marking, 62–63, 160–161
  "mice teeth" stitch, 63–64, 139–140,
    147
  pants, 95
  pleated skirt, 100–101
  pressing, 63, 64, 82, 101, 132
  rolled, on bias sash, 233
  width of hem, 63, 76
"Hidden areas," and size adjustment,
  20, 38–39, 56
  skirts and pants, 83–84
Hip measurement
  girls and women, 16, 83, 97
  men and boys, 17
  for skirt, 85
Hooks and eyes
  fake-fur coats, 192
  skirt band, 88
  skirt without band, 89

Interfacing
  collar, 52, 163–164, 165, 166
  cuffs, 170
  cutting, 111
  fabrics, 110–111
  fake-fur coats, 192
  hem on coats and jackets, 133

Interfacing (*cont.*)
  knit materials, 186
  neckline, flip-lined jumper, 80
  pocket area, 199, 206
  pocket flaps, 203
  prints, 182
Interlining, 135–136

Jackets, 102, 145–149
  boys', 22
  collar and facings, 119–121
  hem interfacing, 133–134
  length added to, 17
  linings, 146, 147
    zipped-in, 142–145
  made from outgrown coats, 178
  sleeves, insertion of, 146
  woman's, 83
  See also Lapels
Jumper
  flip-lined, 80–82
  outgrown, skirt made from, 179
Junior Miss patterns, 22

Kimono sleeve
  altering pattern, 41
  shoulder shapers for, 128–129
Knit fabrics, 185–188
  hem, 175, 187
  pants and skirts, 92, 94–95
  polyester, 29
  special patterns for, 187–188
  thread for, 31
  widths and yardage requirements, 28

Lace, 180
  as hem finish, 63, 76, 82, 187
  knits, 187
Lamé, 181
Lapels, 117, 120
  braid trim, 221
  machine stitched, 217
    to match welt seam, 216
  trim stitched, 217–218
Larger women, patterns for, 19–20
Leather, 189–190
  fake, 190–191
Leftover fabrics, uses for, 161
Leggings, fabrics for, 23
Length
  added, 42
  adjustment of, in pants, 91–93
  measurement of
    coats, 129

underlined evening dress, 75
  See also Bodice
Linings
  attachment, 138–139, 141–142, 146
  bonded fabrics, 188–189
  coats, 130, 134–135
  cutting and assembling, 64–65
  dresses, 64–65
  fabrics, 134
  flip, for jumper, 80–82
  jacket, 146
  knit fabrics, 186
  pants, 92
  patch pocket, 208
  skirts, 89–90
  set-in pocket, 200, 201, 202, 204, 206
  underlined evening dress, 77
  zipped-in, 142–145, 146
  See also Interlining; Underlining
Long-torso bodice, altering, 79–80
Long-waisted figure, adjustment of pattern for, 154
Loops
  button closing, 227–228
  corded belt with, 234
  neckline finish, 228–230

Machine stitching, as trim, 116, 217–219
Macramé, cording used for, 234
"Magic stitching"
  armhole, 59, 61, 124–125, 159, 181
  bloused bodice, 78–79
  gathered skirt, 95–96
Marking, inside garment, 56, 82, 85
  See also Buttonholes; Darts; Hems; Pleats; Pockets; Waistline
Measurements, 16–17, 68
Men, sewing for, 16
  pattern sizes, 17
  sport shirts, 162
Midriff top, from outgrown dress, 177–178
Millium linings, 136–137
Muslin, for test pattern, 189, 190-191

Nap, fabrics with, 24–26, 182–183
  fake fur, 191
  pattern layout, 104, 105–106
  suede, 189
  suede cloth, 191
Neck size, measurement, 17
Neckband, 165–166

Necklines
  collarless, adjustments for, 56–57
  facings, 53, 71, 181
  finishing
    bias-cut binding, 71, 223–224, 225
    cording, 229–230, 231, 232
    dress, 159
    flip-lined jumper, 80–81
    underlined dress, 71, 181
  fitting, 18, 19, 20, 38
  trimming, 52, 228–229
  See also Collars
Needles, sewing machine
  ball-point, 185, 186
  for sewing leather, 190
Notches, clipping of, 44
  in cap of sleeve, 59

Off-grain fabrics
  bonded, 188
  woven, reblocking of, 183
One-way fabrics
  laying pattern on, 38, 104
  plaid, 184
  yardage allowance, 27
One-welt pocket, 201–203
Outgrown clothes, ways to salvage,
  171–179
Overblouse, from outgrown dress, 177
Overhandling, effects of, 45
  armhole seams, 61–62

Panne velvet, 182
Pants
  altering pattern, 90–91
  fitting, 91–93
  fly-front closing, 94
  pattern sizes, 83
  pull-on, 94–95
  side pocket, 210–211
Patch pockets, 207–210
Patterns
  altering size, 35–36, 38–39, 42–43,
    68–69, 79
  choice of, 33–35
    for plaids and checks, 183
    for printed fabrics, 182
  guide sheets, 104
  layout, 36–38, 184
    coat linings, 135
    fabrics with nap, 104, 105–106
  lengthening, 42

shirts and blouses, 162–163
  shortening, 43
  sizes, how to select, 15, 18–19, 35, 38
  skirts, pants and shorts, 83
Petite children, pattern sizes for, 21
Piecing
  bias-cut sash, 233
  bias stripping, 223
  skirt waistband, 86
Pile fabrics, 24–26, 182–183
  as coat linings, 136
  fake fur, 191
Pinking, 43
  armhole finish
    bulky fabrics, 62
    lined dresses, 65
  hem finish
    pleated skirt, 101
    knit fabrics, 187
  neck facing, 53
    dress with underlining, 71
  shears, 43
Pinning
  bodice, 71–72, 73
  coat seams, 108
  collar, 52
  during fitting, 55–56
  hemline, 62, 63
  neck facing, 53
  of pattern to fabric, 37, 104
  side seams, 59, 75, 82
  skirts, 84
    pleated, 98–99
    wrap-around, 90
  sleeve into armhole, 59–60
Plaids, 23–24, 153, 162
  choice of style, 24
  extra yardage, 27
  matching, 183–184, 188
  reblocking, 183
Play clothing, ready-made, 14
Pleats
  in coat lining, 135
  marking, 98–99
  pressed, 96–97
  unpressed, 96
Plump girls, styles for, 34
Pockets
  bound, 199–201
  flap, 203–205
  marking and placement, 45, 107,
    123–124, 209, 211
  moving location, 102–103

Pockets (*cont.*)
  patch, 207–209
  seam, 211–212
  set-in, 199–207
  side, for pants, 210–211
  welt, 201–203, 206–207
Polyester materials
  directions for shrinking, 29
  thread for, 31, 186
  trim stitching of, 218–219
Press cloths, 29, 88, 109, 205
Pressing
  armholes, 61–62, 126
  collar, 116
  darts, 12, 47, 70, 109
  hemline, 63, 64, 82, 101, 132
  importance of, 47
  jacket, 150
  sleeves, 124
  synthetic fabrics, 110
  waistline seam, 75
  woolens, 108–109
Press-on material, to reinforce button-
    holes, 113
Princess style, 37–65, 154, 190
  assembling, 160
  button loops for, 228
  outgrown, tunic made from, 177
Printed fabrics, 182
Pull-on pants, 94–95

Quilted-surface fabrics, 181

Raglan sleeves, 128–129
Rayon
  fabric widths, 26
  for lining, 134, 136
Ready-made clothes, advantages of, 12–
    13, 14
Remnants, 23
Rippling in armhole seams, how to cor-
    rect, 61

Saddle stitching, 216–217
  patch pocket, 208–209
  welt seam, 214
Sashes, 157
  bias cut, 152, 233–234
Scalloped trim, 221–222
Scissors, 29–30
  pinking shears, 43
Seam allowance, 43
Seam guide, on sewing machine, 46–47
Seam pocket, 211–212

Seam tape, uses of
  coat hem, 130
  dress hem, 175–176
  jacket lining, 149
  skirt waistband, 88
  waistline stay, 75
Seams
  armhole, 59–61
  flat-felled, 163, 166–167, 169–170
  hand picked, 214, 216
  jacket, binding of, 146–147
  neckline, 53–54
  pressing of, 47, 52, 108
  shoulder, 44, 52, 70, 71
    welt, on coat, 215
  side, 56, 59, 74, 160
    shirt, 169–170
    skirt, 84, 85
  stitching, 45–47
  trimming, 12
    collar, 114–115
    neckline, 54
  vertical, 45–47
  waistline, 75
  welt, 45, 110, 189, 213–216
Sewing equipment, 29–30
Sewing machine, 29, 30, 31
  cording foot, 231
  needles
    ball-point, 185
    insertion of, 31
  seam guide, 45–46
  sewing over pins, 45
  thread-breaking, causes of, 31
  zipper foot, 70
  See also Zigzag stitching
Shaped welt pocket, 206–207
Sheer materials, 180–181
  triple-layered hem, 158
Shirring, 155–157
Shirts, 162–170
  boys', 22
  collar, 163–165
  cuffs, 170
  girls' and women's, 163
  measurement for, 17
  neckband, 165–166
  patterns, 162
  sleeves
    inserting, 166–167
    openings, 167–169
Short-waisted figure, pattern adjust-
    ment for, 155

Shorts, 93–94
  made from outgrown skirt, 178
  pocket, 199
Shoulder-blade area, adjustment of pattern to widen, 42
Shoulder pads, for sport jacket, 146
Shoulder shapers
  kimono and raglan sleeves, 128–129
  set-in sleeves, 126–127, 146
Shoulders
  coat, adjustment in width of, 125–126
  importance of fitting, 15, 18–19, 35, 38, 106
Shrinking, directions for, 28–29
Side panels, and pattern alteration, 39, 40–41
Silk
  fabric widths, 26
  underlining, 180
Skins, see Leather
Skirts
  bonded fabrics, 188–189
  fitting, 84–85
  gathered, 95–96, 177–178
  length, 16–17, 68
    adjustment of, 68, 69
  made from outgrown garments, 179
  pattern size, 83
  pleated, 96–101
  waistband, 86–88
  without waistband, 88–89
  wrap-around, 90
Ski clothes, stretch fabrics for, 185
Slacks, see Pants
Sleep-wear, ready-made, 12–13
Sleeveless styles
  conversion of outgrown garment to, 177
  finishing, 62, 159, 224–225
Sleeves
  coat, 124–128
    interfacing bottom of, 134
    lining, 140–141, 145
  dress, insertion of, 59–62, 159
  elbow darts, 47
  kimono, 41
  length, measurement of, 17
  lengthening, 42, 162
    outgrown, 178–179
  lining fabrics, 136
  openings, 167–169
    continuous-lap, 167–168
    faced, 168
    tailored placket, 168–169
  pressing, 124, 179

  raglan, 128–129
  seams, 59
  set-in, 126–127
  sheer fabrics, 180–181
  shirt, insertion of, 166–167
  two-piece, 124–125
  welt seaming, 215
  width, adjustment of, 43, 61
  See also Armholes
Smocking
  hand, 155
    imitation of, 157
  machine, 32, 155
Sport jackets, 145–148
  flap pocket, 205
Sport shirts, 162
  boys', pattern sizes, 22
Stab stitching, 111–112
  tailored coat, 114, 132
Steam iron, 47
  for coat seams, 109
  inadequate for shrinking woolens, 29
  See also Pressing
Stitches
  bridge, 138–139
  catch, 95, 101
  cross, 138, 139
  hand picking, 214, 216
  hemming, 63–64, 131–132, 139–140, 146, 209, 218, 219, 231
  "mice teeth," 63–64, 139–140, 147
  saddle, 208–209, 214, 216–217
  shank, 137
  stab, 111–112, 114, 132
  See also "Magic stitching"
Stitching
  fake leather, 190
  flap pocket, 205
  hand
    fake fur, 191–192
    hemming, 63–64
  knit fabrics, 186
  leather, 189, 190
  machine, as trim, 116, 217–218
  marking inside of garment for, 56
  over pins, 45
  pleats, 99–100
  pockets, 204–205, 208–209
  turned-over hem, 175
  See also Zigzag stitching
"Straight of the goods," 37–38, 104–105
Stretch fabrics, 185
  interfacing for neckline, 80
  special thread and needles, 31

244

Striped fabrics
  belts, 232
  for chubby girls, 154
  for thin girls, 34, 153, 154
  skirt waistband, 86
Styles, choice of, 33–35
"Styling areas"
  in fitting, 56, 72
  and pattern size, 20, 39
Sub-teen pattern sizes, 22
Suede, 189, 190
  imitation, 190, 191
Synthetic fabrics
  children's clothing, 26
  coats, 103
  dresses, 151
  fabric widths, 26
  as interfacing, 80, 163
  as interlining, 135
  knits, 185
  pressing, 110
  special thread and needles for, 31
  trim stitching of, 218

Tacking
  armhole facings, 62
  neck facings, 54
Taffeta
  for evening dresses, 66
  as facing, 182
Tailor's canvas, 110
Tall children
  pattern sizes for, 21
  styles suited to, 153
  yardages, 27
Teen-agers, clothing for, 13–14
  pattern size, 19, 22
Test patterns, 189, 190–191
Thin girls, styles suited to, 34, 153
Thin neck, adjustment to fit
  collar, 58–59
  collarless neckline, 57
Thread, choice of, 31
  for fake leather, 190
  for leather, 189
  for polyester, 31, 186
  for stretch fabrics, 184
Tie belt, 233
Tiny women
  adapting patterns for, 19
  fitting, 54–55
Toddler sizes, 21–22
Top stitching, 218
Topper, made from outgrown coat, 178
Trim stitching, 217–218

Trimmings
  bias-cut, 221–226
  braid, 172–173, 192, 220–221
  corded, 226–231
  to camouflage hemline, 172
  fringe, 173, 177
  scalloped, 221–222
Trousers
  length, measurement of, 17
  pattern size, boys', 22
  women's, see Pants
Tucks, horizontal, in bodice, 155
Tunic, made from outgrown dress, 177
Tweeds, for children's coats and suits,
  23, 106
Twill, for leggings, 23
Twins, sewing for, 14

Underlining, 67–68, 69–70
  coats, 103–104
  delicate fabrics, 180, 187
  metallic fabrics, 181
  printed fabrics, 182
  velvets, 182–183

Velvet, 182–183
  decorative collar, 218
  extra yardage required, 27
Velveteen, 25, 26, 182
  for children's leggings, 23
  cording, 227
  decorative collar, 218
Vest, made from outgrown garment,
  179
Vicuna cloth, 25

Waistband
  attachment, 86–87, 96
  grosgrain ribbon, on skirt without, 89
Waist length, see Bodice
Waistline
  adjustment in pattern, 69
  corded, 230–232
  finishing, 75, 179, 188
  fitting, 74–75
  marking, 71–72
    bloused bodice, 77–78
    pants, 92
    skirt, 85
  measurement, 16, 17
Wedding dresses, 77
Welt cording, 230–231
Welt pocket, 201–203, 206–207
Welt seaming, 110, 213–216

Welt seaming (*cont.*)
    in leather, 189
    marking placement, 45
Welts
    buttonhole pocket, 199, 200–201
    flap pocket, 203–204
    one-welt pocket, 201, 202, 203
Weskit pocket, 206
Woolens
    fabric width, 26
    as interlining, 135
    napped, pattern layout, 25, 104
    pleated skirts, 97
    pressing, 109
    shrinking, 28–29
Wrap-around skirt, 90
Wrinkling, in fitting process, 56, 74

Yardage requirements, 26–28
    extra, how to determine, 26–28, 106
    leather and, 189–190
    lining, 134
    plaids, 184
    pleated skirt, 97
    underlining, 68

Zigzag stitching
    blind hemming with, 176
    buttonholes, marking of, 113
    fancy, 157
    finishing lined garments, 65
    as hem finish, 175
Zipped-in linings, 142–145, 146
Zippers
    center back, 48–50, 160
        flip-lined jumper, 81–82
        underlined dress, 70, 74
    fly-front closing, 94
    hand stitched, 50–51
    invisible, 51, 70, 82
    in leather garments, 189
    neck facings and, 54
    polyester, 29, 51
    skirt, 86
        gathered, 95
        lined, 90–91
        pleated, 100
    shorts, 178
    shrinking, 29
    welt cording and, 231
    See also Zipped-in linings